# Foundations of
# Christian Worship

# FOUNDATIONS OF CHRISTIAN WORSHIP

*Susan J. White*

Westminster John Knox Press
LOUISVILLE • LONDON

*Book design by Sharon Adams*
*Cover design by Pam Poll Graphic Design*

*First U.S. edition published in 2006*
Published by Westminster John Knox Press
Louisville, Kentucky

This book is printed on acid-free paper that meets the American National Standards Institute Z39.48 standard. ♾

PRINTED IN THE UNITED STATES OF AMERICA

06 07 08 09 10 11 12 13 14 15—10 9 8 7 6 5 4 3 2 1

Library of Congress Cataloging-in-Publication Data is on file at the Library of Congress, Washington, D.C.

ISBN-13: 978-0-664-22924-5
ISBN-10: 0-664-22924-7

For
William George Storey
and
Makhosazana Nzimande,
laying the groundwork
for a more just and tolerant world

# Contents

# Preface and Acknowledgments: "Going to Church"

If you were to ask a random sample of ordinary people the question "What do Christians do?," most of them, even if they know nothing at all about the beliefs or the ethical demands of Christianity, would say: "Christians go to church!" Although it takes a variety of different forms and has a wealth of different meanings, going to church for worship remains one of the most identifiable features of Christianity. For many Christians, going to church provides them with their primary experience of the Scriptures, of praying, of praising God, and of the company of other believers. For others, of course, gathering for worship on Sundays and holy days and on occasions of family joy and sadness is but one thread in a richer tapestry of Christian living which would be described as "worshipful." In either case, going to church for worship can be such a natural part of our experience of faith that we rarely stop to think about it at all.

This volume is an attempt to provide a structure for thinking seriously about worship as a part of Christian faith and experience, and for addressing the questions What is Christian worship? and Why do Christians worship as they do? In order to accomplish this we will look at forms of prayer and structures of time, at the place of music and the arts, at biblical norms and contemporary issues of authority, ecumenism, and interfaith relations. We will look at how certain elements of our worship came into being, and we will see why some of these elements eventually became extinct.

But while the various components and settings of Christian worship are the immediate topic of our study, the deeper object is actually to learn something about the church, and to ask the question, What can we know about the

Christian church by looking at the ways in which it gathers (and has gathered in other times and other places) for prayer? It is said that the essential rhythm of the Christian life is a movement between gathering and scattering, between coming together to make the body of Christ visible and tangible and moving out into the world as individual Christians to live out the call of Christ in service and witness. These two essential movements of the church inform and uphold one another, and to tell the full story of what the church is and what it can be, we must tell the story not only of its doctrine and its social action, but the story of public worship as well.

The first thing we notice when we begin to look at the story of Christian worship is that all Christians do not worship in the same way. It may seem too obvious to mention, but this simple observation will ground all of our explorations into the question Why do Christians worship as they do? We will begin by examining the various ways in which Christians, past and present, understand what it means to worship, and what models they use to explain and interpret the activity of Christian public prayer. Then we will search out the foundations of the study of worship, foundations which rest on the Bible, on theology, on the dynamics of our human existence and of our Christian history. Marcel Breuer, the great German architect, used to say of his church buildings that "God dwells in the details," and we will turn next to the details of our worship, the various elements out of which it is formed. Because the component parts of Christian worship are intimately related to one another, each adding its meaning to the texture of the whole, decisions made in the small things of worship can make significant differences in the overall experience. We shall see how the choices made by various groups in the structuring of these essential building blocks of worship begin to explain the differences we observe among them.

The story of the church's worship, like the story of the church itself, is a human story. And the next sections of the book will look at the ways in which worship intersects with the changing lives of Christians at various points, the ways in which worship serves to nourish individual and corporate faithfulness, to offer comfort, to celebrate joy, to express gratitude and love. We will ask what it means that the church initiates new members through baptism, gathers to eat and drink around the Communion Table, prays for those joining themselves in marriage, mourns with the bereaved, and comes together regularly for acts of thanksgiving and praise to God. We will also look at what it means to be a Christian at the beginning of a new millennium, and what special challenges this situation poses for our traditional forms of worship. Religious pluralism, rapid social change, globalization, and the search for a contemporary spirituality are also chapters in the story of the Christian church at prayer.

The story of the church's worship, however, is not the story of "worship in the abstract." When we try to imagine the thing called "worship," our minds inevitably take us to very specific places and times in our Christian experience, a particular baptism or wedding, a certain preaching service or celebration of the Lord's Supper. And although on the whole we will have to speak about general categories in this book, we must also keep in mind that for the Christian people worship is not experienced in terms of general categories. Rather they experience services of worship as real, concrete examples of the Christian church at prayer in given situations. Therefore, the last chapter of this volume is composed of a series of "case studies" which will give students of Christian worship and other study groups the opportunity to put what they have learned to the test in hypothetical pastoral situations.

And finally, many of the readers of this book will be making decisions about the shaping of worship in the congregations which they serve. A number of appendices to the main text of this volume are designed to help in the planning and evaluation of services: checklists, prayer-writing exercises, and texts for theological analysis. Through the centuries Christians have used many terms to talk about their worship; some of these are very familiar—words like "baptism," "sermon," and "hymn." Others are part of a more technical vocabulary used by students of worship—part of the "jargon" of worship studies—and it is useful for those who wish to gain a working knowledge of Christian worship to know these terms. Therefore, there is a glossary at the end of this volume which contains most of the definitions used in the academic study of worship.

In the writing of this book, I have accumulated a number of debts, personal and professional. I am particularly thankful for the buoyant good cheer of my husband, Kenneth Cracknell, and for his unflagging support and good counsel during the time this book was being written. Katherine Godby gave a number of hours of her thoughtful attention to the text; to her and to my students in the Cambridge Theological Federation and Brite Divinity School (who served as "human guinea pigs" for much of this material) I offer my sincere appreciation. Both those who have taught me about worship and those who have studied worship with me have contributed a wealth of insights to the writing of this book. As a tribute to all of them I dedicate this book to two particular people: an emeritus professor of liturgical history (and now a bookseller) from the United States and a student of theology from South Africa. I hope that they will accept it as a sign of my love and gratitude.

S. J. W.
Fort Worth, Texas
December 1996

# Preface to the American Edition

I am very grateful to Westminster John Knox Press for encouraging an American edition of this book, which was originally published for the use of seminary students, ministers, and local preachers in the United Kingdom. After teaching in England for many years, I moved to the United States in 1995 to teach at Brite Divinity School, Texas Christian University. In that intentionally and emphatically ecumenical situation, rooted in the deep ecumenical spirit of the school's founding denomination, the Christian Church (Disciples of Christ), it was not uncommon to have twenty or more different ecclesial traditions—from Roman Catholics to Unitarian-Universalists—represented in the basic course on Christian worship which I taught each year. Many of the challenges of that situation are reflected in the changes made to the original edition of this book. Here I have tried to take account of the current diversity of worship practices, the latest generation of official service materials, and the cultural, intellectual, and practical challenges that mark the North American situation in the first part of the twenty-first century. My thanks go, as always, to my students, and especially to those students preparing for ordained ministry. Their pertinent questions and sharp insights have pushed me to think about this material in new ways and to appreciate, again and again, the joys and difficulties of worship planning and leadership in Christian congregations.

S. J. W.
Fort Worth, Texas
June 2005

# 1

# The Foundations of the Study of Christian Worship

What does it mean to study Christian worship? How do we go about it? And, more importantly: where do we begin? In many ways, beginning the study of something new is not unlike beginning to build a house, and just as in house building, the first task is to lay the foundations, so that whatever gets added on top will be solid and well-supported. So we will begin here by determining what kind of foundations undergird the study of Christian worship. In this case there are four, and they might be called the "cornerstones" of the study of worship.

First, because worship is a religious phenomenon, we start by thinking about it from a theological perspective. What part does our worship play in the totality of our relationship with God? How does our own theology color our understanding of what it means to worship? Then, because we are studying Christian worship, we must look to the foundational documents and experiences of Christianity (the Bible and the events recorded in the Bible), and to an understanding of the journey that Christianity has taken since its beginnings (Christian history). And finally, because worship is a human activity, the student of worship will also have to be a student of human beings, how they think, feel, and behave as individuals and as groups. Because of this, the study of worship is also related to what are usually referred to as the human sciences: anthropology, sociology, and psychology. All of these together—theology, Bible, history, and the human sciences—form the foundation stones on which the study of Christian worship rests, and we will look at them in turn.

# WORSHIP AS AN ASPECT OF CHRISTIAN THEOLOGY

The study of Christian worship is partly a study of how Christians worship. But before we can address questions of how we worship, a more basic question needs to be asked: Where does worship fit in the larger pattern of Christian life and thought? Or, to put it in another way, What is our theology of worship? Christians through the centuries have answered this question in different ways, and have used different models, different theological approaches, to help them understand what happens in worship. Here we will discuss six basic theological models that Christians, past and present, have used to explain what Christian worship is.

## Worship as Service to God

Many Christian communities have understood public worship as a service to God, a duty that God's human children perform in grateful obedience to the One who is the source of their life and their salvation. Indeed, the English word "worship" itself (from the Middle English "weorth-scipe") carries with it this sense of ascribing to God the honor and worth which is due by right. And when we say that we are attending a worship "service," this same idea is being expressed; that we are undertaking common worship as a way of serving Almighty God.

In many of our traditions, we pray that God will accept our worship as a "sacrifice of praise and thanksgiving," and this language of sacrifice is yet another way of talking about worship as a service to God. The Torah bears witness to the belief that God had established a system of sacrifices (the offering up of animals, birds, and fruits of the harvest) which would be an effective sign of Israel's devotion and obedience, and a way of maintaining the covenant relationship between God the Provider and humanity. And today when we speak of our ordinary worship as a "sacrifice," we are suggesting that it functions in a similar way, as a sign that we offer to God all that we have and all that we are: heart and mind and possessions, body, and soul. In our hymns and our prayers, in our preaching and in our creeds and affirmations, we discharge the debt we owe to God for all the blessings bestowed upon us.

But this theology of worship raises a number of questions. Why does God need anything from the creatures made in God's own image? Is it not the height of presumption to suggest that we frail human beings have anything at all to offer God? This was precisely the difficulty that the great sixteenth-century reformer Martin Luther (1483–1546) had with worship as he knew it in the late Middle Ages: that by seeing worship as duty and service Christians had gradually come to interpret their common prayer as a human "work" which appeased God and earned the worshiper merit.[1] Do we not come to God in worship with empty hands, and is not any sort of language of "offering" or "sacrifice" a denial of the absolute sovereignty and self-sufficiency of God? John Wesley (1703–1791) and his brother Charles Wesley (1708–1788), the founders of the Methodist family of churches, recognized this difficulty, and many of the hymns they wrote and translated for the Methodist people address it directly. One such hymn asks the question:

> What shall we offer our good Lord,
>     Poor nothings! for his boundless grace?
> Fain would we his great name record
>     And worthily set for his praise.

But for the Wesleys, and for many of their spiritual descendants, the answer was straightforward. We have nothing to offer to God except that which God has given us first: our lives, our talents, our ability to know and to praise God.

> Great object of our growing love,
>     To whom our more than all we owe,
> Open the fountain from above,
>     And let it our full souls o'erflow.[2]

And it is this overflowing of God's blessing that allows us to return to God in worship that which God has already given to us.

## Worship as the Mirror of Heaven

For many Christians, worship that takes place in church is an attempt to duplicate, to recapitulate, the worship of God that takes place eternally in heaven. Although this theology of worship is particularly associated with the Orthodox and Eastern Rite traditions,[3] one can see strains of it in many other groups as well, and especially among Christians suffering under oppression. This model of Christian worship rests on the idea that ceaseless praise of God is the ultimate human destiny, the activity for which all humans were created, and that in giving ourselves over to worship here on earth, we are preparing ourselves for our eternal vocation.

When we enter into Christian worship, we enter into a different dimension of time and space, a cosmic dimension, where we can gradually attune ourselves with the ceaseless praises of the heavenly hosts. In the chants, the prayers, the hymns, and in the glory of the physical surroundings, we are taken out of ordinary space and ordinary time (this is why, for example, no clocks are allowed in Orthodox churches). We step into a "heavenly geography." But worship in this kind of model is not a way of avoiding the harsh realities of the world as it is; it is rather a way of participating in God's redemption of the world, by revealing the true meaning of time and space in God's eternal purposes. If we enter into worship fully, desiring only to praise God with all our heart and mind and strength, then we will understand that time and space are not for us to use, selfishly and wantonly, but for God alone to use for the good of the world. This is what is meant when we say that worship has an "eschatological" dimension, because it points forward to the time when "God will be all in all."

You can see this idea at work in the hymn called the Sanctus, which many Christians say or sing as a part of their celebrations of the Lord's Supper. In its most usual version it says:

> And so, with angels and archangels and all the company of heaven, we laud and magnify your holy name, ever more praising you and singing:
>
> Holy, holy, holy Lord, God of power and might, heaven and earth are full of your glory, Hosanna in the highest.

This hymn takes as its inspiration the vision of the final consummation of all things in the book of Revelation. For those who hold this view of public prayer, worship gives us a foretaste of the great banquet in heaven at which all creation will join in the praises of its Maker and Redeemer. Keeping the Christian year is another way of ensuring that our lives as worshipers on earth are in tune with heaven. A good example of this theology at work is found in the Christmas hymn "Songs of Praise the Angels Sang," which first speaks of the rejoicing in heaven that occasioned the birth of Jesus, and then goes on to say:

> Saints below, with heart and voice,
> Still in songs of praise rejoice,
> Learning here by faith and love,
> Songs of praise to sing above. [4]

Those who view their worship on earth as mirroring the worship of heaven often interpret the various parts of the service and the worship space symbolically, or mystically. (This is especially true in the Orthodox traditions of Christian worship.) The altar represents, for example, the throne of Almighty God, the choir is the angelic chorus of seraphim and cherubim, the ceiling of the church building is the vault of heaven, the candles represent the light of the risen Christ, and so forth. These images are not simply designed to remind us of deeper realities, but are true epiphanies, or revelations of God. They draw us into a worshipful relationship with the things that they symbolize.

Many critics of this theology of worship argue that since we have no idea at all what the worship of heaven entails, to try to dramatize it on earth is a futile exercise at best; at worst it is audacious and prideful. It may indeed be the case that there are some hints in the book of Revelation about the worship of heaven, but that is a vision of the end times, and not a blueprint for our Christian worship in the present. Critics also say that to enter into an otherworldly or mystical realm in worship is simply a way of anaesthetizing the Christian conscience, and that such essential Christian undertakings as mission, evangelism, and social action are rooted in the deep recognition of world as it is, not in a dream of heaven as it might be.

But there is a real sense in this theology of worship that in fixing our eyes on God's future, we may obtain a vision that can move us toward saintliness. If worship can provide us with a vision of the world as God intends it to be, it can sustain and uphold us in the human struggle, as well as in the work for justice and peace on the earth. In the period of apartheid in South Africa, for example, worship in the township churches served to set oppressed people down in another world, reminding them that God had an alternative vision for the earth and sustaining them in the midst of their suffering. This theology of worship reminds us that our true home is the "new heaven and the new earth" that God will establish, and that to worship rightly is to catch a glimpse of our true identity as citizens of heaven.

## Worship as Affirmation

If the previous theology of worship was focused on the end times, the theology of worship we will look at now is fixed on the interim, on the meantime. Many Christians are convinced that the primary purpose of Christian worship is to affirm, inspire, and support believers in the Christian vocation. To be a true disciple of Jesus Christ is difficult, if undertaken seriously and with dedication. It sets Christians against "the world, the flesh, and the devil" and puts them in situations of sustained risk. Like the Jesus they follow, they may be misunderstood, insulted, betrayed, or even murdered for their faith in God. But in Christian worship, we touch again and again the ground of our belief, and in so doing we are enabled to renew the struggle against the forces of darkness that prevail around us. Worship, in this view, is an oasis of peace and refreshment.

The essential function of Christian worship, then, is to reinforce the Christian ethic, to convince beleaguered Christians that God is fighting with them, and to provide a forum for sharing testimonies of the victories already won for God. In this way, it can inspire us to new heights of service and witness. Very often the Psalms are a significant part of the worship that rests on this theology, since in many of the Psalms the writer speaks of being "assaulted on all sides" by enemies, and begs to be vindicated by God in the presence of the wicked. A good example is Psalm 56, which begins:

> Be gracious to me, O God, for people trample on me;
>    all day long foes oppress me;
> my enemies trample on me all day long,
>    for many fight against me.
>
> O Most High, when I am afraid,
>    I put my trust in you.
> In God, whose word I praise,
>    in God I trust; I am not afraid;
>    what can flesh do to me?

Worship in this model is primarily intended for the "insiders," for those committed Christians who feel keenly the assaults of the world as they attempt to live out the various forms of Christian discipleship. Because they are "insiders," worshipers are familiar with the images and the stories of hope from the Scriptures and from the Christian tradition. These images and stories can be employed in the various media of Christian worship: preaching, prayer, and song. In this way, our sense of the dependability of God is deepened, and we know that we can call upon God to answer us in time of need or trouble. Much of the church music that comes out of situations of oppression and injustice reflects this theme. Look, for example, at this African American spiritual, which was written during the period of slavery:

> Swing low, Sweet Chariot,
> Comin' for to carry me home.
>
> I looked to heaven and what did I see,
> Comin' for to carry me home,
> A band of angels comin' after me,
> Comin' for to carry me home.

Critics of this view of Christian worship say that while affirmation is a necessary ingredient in Christian worship, it can run the risk of glorifying the status quo. Human beings, even faithful Christian believers, have many things about them that need challenging and setting right. Christian worship that persistently gives the message that God's primary concern is to make our own lives comfortable and safe fails to take into account the inevitability of suffering. Our sensitivity to the human condition will surely atrophy if we come to believe that God is always going to intervene in situations of injustice, and God's reconciling mission will be accomplished whether or not we ever act courageously and decisively. They also argue that this view tends to turn worship into a spiritual ghetto, as a haven for the broken and bruised, a "life-boat without anyone strong enough to row."

But those who speak of worship as primarily an experience of affirmation say that it is only by receiving from God, only by seeing our worship as a time for humble, patient, and expectant waiting for God's healing and life-giving power, can we act in the world with any sense of conviction and strength. It is through an acknowledgment of our radical dependence that we are lifted up and empowered.

## Worship as Communion

Many other Christians believe that in their common worship they are making their relationship with God and with the Christian community a visible, audible, and tangible reality. In this theology, worship is a way of forming and sustaining essential relationships (both divine and human), and for this reason the word "communion" is often used to describe what happens in Christian worship. The English word communion translates the Greek word *koinōnia,* which in the New Testament means "fellowship," or "sharing," or "participation." It is used in descriptions of worship in the earliest Christian communities, which met to devote themselves to "the apostles' teaching and fellowship ( *koinōnia*), to the breaking of bread and to the prayers" (Acts 2:42).[5] Like those who work from the model of worship as service, those who see worship as communion would affirm that part of their relationship with God indeed involves our responsive self-offering to the God who created and sustains us. They are aware, however, that their experience of God is also one of receiving the gifts of God, and that that experience needs visible and tangible expression as well. But in this theology of worship our common prayer is not only a "vertical" movement between Christian believers and God; it is also a "horizontal" movement between and among the members of the Christian community. Both fellowship with God and fellowship with other Christians are necessary components of Christian worship.

Many would use the analogy of the incarnation to describe and explicate their experience of worship. In the incarnation the fullness of human responsiveness to God and the fullness of God's self-revelation met in the person of Jesus of Nazareth, and became "embodied." In a similar way, our human response and God's self-giving to us become "embodied" in Christian worship; they take shape and form. So, in this model, speaking to God is balanced with listening to God; offering to God is balanced with receiving from God, and giving and receiving from our fellow Christians is also a significant feature. This model implies that worship is not simply something we do with our brains, but with our whole selves. We were created by God with bodies and desires, as well as minds, and all of these must come into play when God and human beings enter freely into loving communion with one another in worship.

Any love relationship seeks self-expression, and the love relationship between God and human beings is no different. In worship, according to this way of thinking:

> I come with joy to meet my Lord,
>     Forgiven, loved, and free!
> In awe and wonder to recall,
>     His life laid down for me.
>
> I come with Christians far and near,
>     To find, as all are fed,
> The new community of love
>     In Christ's communion bread.[6]

In this view, all material things are potential revelations of God's love to those who see with the eyes of faith, and, conversely, faithful people can use all material things to express their love and gratitude to God. This understanding of the inherent holiness of the created order is carried over into Christian worship, and worship in this model is usually rich in visual, audible, tangible, and even olfactory elements. The fellowship of Christian believers is equally a visible sign of God's love, and so the formation and maintenance of communities of faith is also highlighted.

Critics of this theology of worship say that although we are indeed called into communion with God, this communion is wholly dependent upon God's initiative, and they argue that there is a danger here of suggesting an equality between the partners in the divine-human relationship. Others would wish to be more reticent about the degree to which the transitory material creation can communicate eternal truths. Ideas and ideals, they say, are the highest form of Christian revelation, and the things of this world are susceptible to misuse and misinterpretation. There is also the danger here of idolatry, of the material things themselves becoming the object of worship instead of the God who has created them.

But there is in this model the overwhelming sense that we were created for relationship with God, and to express that relationship in every way possible is both God's deepest desire and our highest human calling. God does not want our servile obedience, but wants us to use our God-given freedom to become full partners in the creation and re-creation of the world. In worship that creative partnership is honored, strengthened, and given true and joyful expression.

## Worship as Proclamation

In many strands of Christian thought, the true Christian vocation is to announce the good news of God in Christ, to declare the gospel of the workings of God in and for the world. Those who think of worship primarily as proclamation wish to highlight the idea that worship is the principal place where Christians gather together to make their public affirmation and witness. In worship, like-minded Christians meet together to say who and what they are and, in so doing, to reinforce their own Christian identity. Indeed, the proclamation of Christ, crucified and risen (the Christian kerygma) is the power that creates the worshiping community itself. As the First Letter of Peter says, "You are a chosen race, a royal priesthood, a holy nation, God's own people, in order that you may proclaim the mighty acts of him who called you out of darkness into his marvelous light" (1 Pet. 2:9).

Christians "declare the mighty acts of God" in different ways in their worship: in the use of creeds and affirmations of faith, acclamations, and in preaching and testimony. In addition, of course, many of our best-loved hymns are used to make the event of worship a kerygmatic event:

> A mighty fortress is our God,
> a bulwark never failing;
> our helper he amid the flood
> of mortal ills prevailing.
> For still our ancient foe
> doth seek to work us woe;
> his craft and power are great,
> and armed with cruel hate,
> on earth is not his equal.
>
> Did we in our own strength confide,
> our striving would be losing,
> were not the right man on our side,
> the man of God's own choosing.
> Dost ask who that may be?
> Christ Jesus, it is he;
> Lord Sabaoth, his name,
> from age to age the same,
> and he must win the battle. [7]

This hymn does one thing and does it well. It tells the story of the victory of Christ over sin and death, and it tells that story with conviction. This is the proper work of the Christian people, to express fully and firmly their Christian faith so that the world might believe. Indeed, the word "liturgy," which is a common synonym for public worship, comes from this idea of worship as a "public work." It originates in two Greek words, *laós*, meaning people, and *ergon* meaning work. In the New Testament *leitourgia* is used to describe the general ministry of all Christians. Paul, for example, tells the church at Corinth (2 Cor. 9:11–12): "You will be enriched in every way for your great generosity, which will produce thanksgiving to God through us; for the rendering of this ministry (*leitourgias*) not only supplies the needs of the saints but also overflows with many thanksgivings to God." This implies that the "liturgy" is a ministry of the whole congregation, and further that it is a ministry not only of thanksgiving and praise, but of service to the community as well. Unlike the previous model, Christian worship is not something that is done for the benefit of the worshipers themselves, but done by the worshipers for the sake of others.

There are those who would say, however, that Christians need more from their worship than an opportunity for proclamation, even when that proclamation is conjoined with service. Christians need comfort in times of trouble and reassurance in times of anxiety. They need to listen to God as well as to speak of God. They need a place to express their doubts and fears as well as their confidence and trust, and a place to join with other Christians to ask God for answers to their prayers. Other critics say that if our worship is seen primarily as proclamation we are simply "preaching to the converted." Those in need of hearing the healing and reconciling word of God proclaimed are not in our churches, but in our backstreets and office buildings and schools, and it is there that proclamation belongs.

But those who hold to the proclamation model of worship argue that the power of remembering what God has done and retelling it in the gathered community goes beyond mere self-congratulation. It is a ritual of remembering without which the community of faith is threatened with extinction: in this model "to forget is to die." To support this idea, they look back to the worship of the Jewish synagogue, which became in times of exile and distress the primary place for the remembering and recitation of God's mighty acts in history. Day after day the people gathered to recite the Benedictions of God:

> Blessed is the Lord our God, Ruler of the universe,
>     who has given us a Torah of truth,
>     implanting within us eternal life.
> Blessed is the Lord, the Giver of Torah.[8]

And so they went on: "Blessed is God for this," and "Blessed is God for that," until the story of God's deeds is told, and so continues to be told to the present day. In this way the community has survived to tell the story to future generations. There is a very real conviction undergirding this theology of worship that the power of remembering what God has done and proclaiming it publicly in Christian worship is the only thing that will keep Christianity alive through the twenty-first century.

There is a variation on this theology of worship as proclamation that became particularly important to the evangelical revivals from the eighteenth century onwards. Many of those who have sought to address unchurched people and those who have never heard the Christian message believe that worship should be understood as a primary evangelistic tool, the principal "adver-tisement" for the Christian life. Worship in this view provides an experience of foundational teaching and invites first steps toward commitment appropri-ate for the seeker, and must therefore be highly engaging and easy to under-stand. Again, those who resist this notion about worship argue that worship should never be simply a means to an end, but rather always an end in itself, and that the kind of "dumbing down" that is necessary to accommodate the needs of those on the margins of Christian believing leaves little to satisfy the more faithful and dedicated worshipers.[9]

## Worship as the Arena of Transcendence

Many Christians would say that all of the previous models suffer from a com-mon defect: they make Christian worship seem much too safe and predictable. To enter the presence of the living God in worship, they argue, is a highly dan-gerous enterprise, in which the awesome holiness, majesty, and power of God may at any time break into our experience and transform us. "Come no closer," God says to Moses (Exod. 3:5), "Remove the sandals from your feet, for the place on which you are standing is holy ground," and many Christians are con-vinced that same power with which God created the world may at any moment be unleashed again. And just as Moses "hid his face, for he was afraid to look at God" (v. 6), so too should we come into the presence of God with a sense of reverence, awe, and expectation.

Certainly one key word in this view is "transcendence," with worship seen as the arena within which our encounter with the transcendent God takes place. This emphasis on divine transcendence leads to an equal emphasis on the activity of the Holy Spirit, who acts as the mediator between the "wholly-otherness" of God and the "this-world-ness" of humanity. In one sense, of course, the most appropriate response to the encounter with the living God is silence:

> Earth from afar has heard thy fame,
> And babes have learned to lisp thy name;
>    But O the glories of thy mind
>    Leave all our soaring thoughts behind.
>
> God is in heaven, we dwell below;
> Be short our tunes, our words be few;
>    A sacred reverence checks our songs,
>    And praise sits silent on our tongues.[10]

The typical Quaker meeting is an example of this sort of silent waiting upon God's transforming revelation. It operates on the conviction that any set forms of prayer or ritual action will distract the worshiper from a total attentiveness to the workings of God, and obstruct the human-divine encounter. And so members of the Society of Friends (Quakers) gather every Lord's Day to keep a holy silence, as they wait expectantly for the Spirit to move within the community. For the Quakers, the community's principal responsibility in worship is to set up the conditions that will facilitate this encounter between God and humanity.

For other Christians who think of worship as the arena for encounter with God, waiting in silence is not the only way of encouraging our receptivity. Prayer, singing, and preaching can all be ways of opening the heart and mind of the believer to the presence of God. In many of the earliest services of worship for which we have evidence (from the second and third centuries), calling upon the Holy Spirit to come into the gathering was an important component, and this "invocation" of the Spirit is still a significant feature of our worship. At the ordination of ministers, many Christian communities sing a hymn that was first sung in the ninth century:

> Come Holy Ghost, our souls inspire,
> And lighten with celestial fire;
>   Thou the anointing Spirit art,
>   Who dost thy sevenfold gifts impart.[11]

There is also a concentration here on the signs by which we can be assured that our encounter with God has taken place: the gifts of the Holy Spirit. Various communities of faith emphasize different gifts of the Spirit: some will value speaking in tongues (Acts 10:45–46),[12] and the interpretation of tongues (1 Cor. 14:13); others look for the gifts of healing and prophesy, for uncontrollable physical movements such as falling, shouting, laughing, and dancing, and even on occasion the power to handle deadly serpents and to drink poisons (Mark 16:18) without coming to harm. But in every case, these gifts of the Spirit are testimonies of a face-to-face encounter with the living God.

The building of the Christian community is also emphasized in this model. "Since you are eager for spiritual gifts," says the apostle Paul to the church at Corinth, "strive to excel in them for building up the church" (1 Cor. 14:12). This can be the most intensely democratic way of looking at worship, since all members of the Christian community have an equal opportunity to encounter God in worship, and have access to the gifts of the Holy Spirit.

Critics of this theology of worship would argue that its strengths are also its weaknesses: that spontaneity can result in chaos, radical democracy can lead to lack of discipline, and independence can promote an unhealthy individualism. They would ask the same question of a Christian community working from this theology of worship that Paul asked of the church at Corinth: "If you say a blessing with the spirit, how can anyone in the position of an outsider say the 'Amen' to your thanksgiving, since the outsider does not know what you are saying?" (1 Cor. 14:16). Is there not a danger here of isolation from the needs and demands of the world as people bask in their own spiritual experiences? Critics also warn that in opening worship to the spontaneous we may lose touch with the rich treasury of prayers, hymns, creeds, and acclamations which have arisen during the first twenty centuries of Christian history, and miss the important lessons which Christians throughout the ages have to teach us about the liturgical "diet" which is most healthy for the well-nourished Christian. They also say that the good news of Jesus Christ is that "the kingdom of God has come near to you" (Luke 10:9), and that to understand worship as an experience of intimacy with a nurturing God is more in line with the New Testament witness than to view it as the experience of a capricious and potent deity.

But the power of this theology of worship is that it refuses to "domesticate" the holiness of God, and affirms the necessity of an experience of that holiness for the Christian life. The religious (or "mystical") experience is not simply a "high" for the spiritual elite, but should be the quest of all Christians who are seeking to be "perfect . . . as your Heavenly Father is perfect" (Matt. 5:48). To see Christian worship as the potential meeting place between human beings and the God who is "wholly other," between creature and Creator, is one way of keeping before us the necessity of reaching toward the transforming power which is the *mysterium tremendum* (overwhelming mystery) of God. And quite often that transforming power leads to heroic Christian acts directed at overturning the "principalities and powers" which defy the will of God. The unrelenting quest for world peace undertaken by the Society of Friends, for example, derives its essential energy from a form of worship in which the Spirit (what Quaker theologian Robert Barclay called "the pure breathings of God which is Inner Light") was available to all.

These, then, are six principal ways in which Christians have understood what it is they are doing when they gather for worship. Other minor thematic threads have also been woven into the fabric of the Christian theology of worship: worship as religious entertainment, worship as a fence against outsiders, worship as psychological support. But none of these rises to the status of a significant theology of worship. Of course, the models we have discussed here are not mutually exclusive. Each affirms something basic and necessary to our understanding of Christian common prayer. Worship is at the same time service and affirmation and proclamation; it is a place to encounter transcendence and it is a place to renew and celebrate our communion with God. If we collapse the tension between and among these images, we become narrow and myopic in our vision of what Christian worship can be. But the various Christian worship traditions can often be identified by their emphasis on one particular theological approach to worship over the others. As individual Christians we also may find that one or the other of these approaches to Christian worship is a more natural part of our theological approach. But all of them declare the necessity of seeing worship as part of the shared world which God graciously sets up with us, and of taking worship seriously as an essential part of the Christian life and calling.

## THEOLOGY FROM WORSHIP

The relationship between worship and theology does not go only one way. While it is important to understand that there are theologies *of* worship, it is equally important to understand that there are theologies *from* worship. Early Christian theologians routinely used the forms of worship they knew as the raw material for the formation of their theological understandings. The liturgy becomes a primary source for arguments about every facet of Christian doctrine: the nature of God, the church, the sacraments, the human person, and sin. "We pray in this way and this proves that the church believes . . ." is the kind of statement commonly found in the theological writing of the most significant Christian authors.

At the same time it is also important to remember that for many people worship is the primary context for the development of their own theology. The theology implicit in the hymns and prayers, the theology that is proclaimed and preached gives worshipers "food for thought" as they form their Christian worldview. This is why the decisions made by worship leaders about the details of services are so crucial, since these details are the carriers of contemporary "orthodoxy." Unfortunately, orthodoxy is often understood as a word that refers to thinking the right things about the Christian faith. However, "orthodoxy" came originally from the Greek words *orthos* (meaning "correct" or "true") and *doxa* (meaning "praise" or "prayer"). And so orthodoxy stressed not so much the importance of thinking aright, but of praying aright.

Therefore it is always important for participants in Christian worship to ask themselves, "What is this service really saying? What is it saying about God, about redemption, about the Christian life, sin, death, and so forth?" and "What am I saying when I pray these prayers and sing these hymns and make these affirmations?" There is an old Latin saying from the fifth century which is often abbreviated "*Lex credendi, lex statuat supplicandi*": "The law of believing stands on the law of praying." In other words what we pray and what we believe are mutually interdependent, and praying is not only a way of expressing, but also a way of forming our Christian beliefs.

# THE BIBLICAL FOUNDATIONS
# OF THE STUDY OF WORSHIP

What does it mean to say that we ground our study of Christian worship on the Bible? To the extent that the material in the Old and New Testaments is the foundation of all Christian living and believing, we may mean only that the Bible is therefore necessarily the foundation of the study of worship as well. It may mean that there is useful information in the Bible about how worship was conducted in Christian and Jewish antiquity, or that it provides necessary proof-texts for our contemporary worship practice. None of these can be denied, but there is more to say about the biblical foundations of Christian worship than this. The Bible underpins both Christian worship and the study of Christian worship in several different and complex ways.

First, it is the Word of God, read and preached and received, that calls the Christian community together to worship. Whenever the public proclamation of God's loving purposes calls forth praise, bonds the fellowship of believers into the body of Christ, opens the Christian heart, and releases sacrificial self-offering, true worship is born. This image of the people of God gathered around God's word is at the heart of the study of Christian worship, because without the Bible there would be no Christian worship.

Ironically, biblical scholars also tell us that without Christian worship there would be no Bible either, that the Bible itself is, in a very real sense, the product of the early church's common prayer. Stories of the life and ministry of Jesus and the labors of the early apostles, letters of instruction and spiritual counsel, and visionary descriptions of the final consummation of all things were circulated among the earliest Christian communities and read in common worship so that all could hear and respond. Those writings which were identified by the gathered church as being authentic to its experience of the risen Christ were regularized and codified as the Gospels, the Epistles, the book of Acts, and Revelation. This deep interrelationship between our worship and the Scriptures continues today. As the Bible is read in worship week in and week out, it is reborn as the living Word of God for the community of Christian believers. Worship is the place where the Bible comes alive, and comes alive in us. Although at various times in the history of Christian worship the connection between Bible and worship became strained or obscured, to study the worship of the Christian church without grounding it on a biblical foundation is to risk the collapse of our work.

Indeed, the quest to return Christian worship to its biblical roots when it has gone astray has been the direct cause of various "reformations" in the history of the church. Time after time the church has sensed that it has lost its way, that the biblical foundations of its worship had slipped and needed to be restored to a proper alignment. As we saw above, if the quest to make worship more "biblical" is an attempt to reduplicate the worship of the earliest Christians it is probably doomed to failure. At the simplest level, we lack sufficient information about this layer of worship history for this sort of effort to succeed. If, on the other hand, it is a quest to restore biblical images to the center of the Christian liturgical imagination, it is the cause of true reformation.

The Bible itself confronts our worship in a number of ways. First it raises question of true and false worship. What are our idols? Where do we put our trust? It also speaks to us about the relationship between our worship in church and the quality of our life in the world. In a sense, the voice of God speaking through the prophet Amos still speaks to the Christian church today: "I hate, I despise your festivals, and I take no delight in your solemn assemblies. . . . Take away from me the noise of your songs; I will not listen to the melody of your harps. But let justice roll down like waters, and righteousness like an ever-flowing stream" (Amos 5:21, 23–24). Unless the community is seeking to be a just community within itself and also seeking justice for all people, then the worship of God in church is to no avail.

Although the Bible does not prescribe any particular form of Christian worship, it does suggest to us what the broad outlines of our common prayer will be. Thanksgiving to God and repentance, prayerful concern for the needs of others and acknowledgment of our own needs, the breaking of bread and the baptism of new Christians, songs of praise and adoration, reciting the mighty acts of God: all of these can be said to be "biblical" forms of worship. In addition, the biblical images woven in and through our worship become occasions for setting alight the Christian imagination, and thus for beginning to envision new ways of being human. The Old Testament scholar Walter Brueggemann describes the process this way:

> The action of meeting begins—music, word, prayer, theater. At its center, the minister reads (or has read) these very old words, remote, archaic, something of a threat, something of yearning. In the listening, one hears another world proposed. It is an odd world of "no male or female," of condemned harlots and welcomed women, of sheep and goats judged, of wheat and tares tolerated, of heavy commandments and free grace, of food given only for work, and widows and orphans valued in their nonproductivity. If one listens long and hard, what emerges is a different world.[13]

To say that our study of worship should be founded on the Bible is to make a statement about the centrality of the Bible in the quest for the understanding of all the various forms our Christian faith and believing takes. But the complex issues within biblical interpretation, exegesis, and theology make it a difficult document to use when we study worship. As we have seen, the New Testament contains no systematic exposition of what true Christian worship should be. Nor does it give us a list of which worship practices prescribed in the Old Testament are to be retained and which are to be abandoned. There are indeed fragments of hymns and creeds and prayers, the scholars tell us, but nothing like a "service sheet" or even a good description of ordinary worship practices among the earliest Christians. So although we have inherited the Bible as the source of the living tradition of the church, it is impossible to turn it into a worship textbook.

The Bible does, however, set up for us certain broader goals for contemporary students of worship to keep in mind. In each case these goals can be seen as pairs of opposites, and maintaining a balance between the two polarities in each case is the work of the Christian church in every age. Whenever the tension between them is consistently collapsed in favor of one side or the other our worship goes astray. The following is a list of nine pairs of opposites, each of which the Bible lifts up as a value for worship. (The pairs of opposites are highlighted and the biblical text that follows each pair is a suggestion for reading and reflection):

- Is our worship to be an occasion for *comfort* or for *prophecy*; are we to rejoice in where we are or focus on where we ought to be? (Matt. 5:23–25; Acts 2:44–47)
- Is our worship about our *present* life or our *future* state? Is it to confirm who we are now or to draw us forward toward who we are meant to be in the future? (1 Cor. 16:1–4; Luke 22:14–19)
- Is our worship to be a source of *individual* communion with God, or is it to be a *corporate* act of the whole gathered church? (Matt. 6:5–7; 1 Cor. 11:27–34)
- Is our worship to be about *order and stability*; or is it to be about *flexibility and creativity*? (1 Cor. 10:23–33 and 11:14–18)
- Is our worship *outwardly expressive* of our faith or a way of *exploring the interiority* of our faith? Are we to be active or receptive in our worship? (John 4:22–25; Acts 19:1–13; Rom. 12:1–2)
- Is our worship to be *inclusive* of varieties in faith and believing, or *exclusive*, for the sub-set of "true believers"? (Luke 9:1–7; Acts 10:44–48)
- Is our worship an event of the *material world* or of the *spiritual world*? Is it a celebration of creation or redemption? (Luke 21:14–27; John 4:21–26)
- Is our worship an act of the *emotions* or the *mind* or the *body*? Is it affective, cognitive or behavioral? (Luke 24:13–35; Rom. 8:5–8)
- Does our worship reflect our *relationship to authority* or is it a *celebration of our freedom* in Christ? (Matthew 12:1–8; Rom. 8:1–5)

These certainly do not exhaust the questions the Bible addresses to our worship. But they do give us some idea of the kinds of issues we need to keep in mind when we say that our study of Christian worship is "founded" on a biblical base.

## THE HISTORICAL FOUNDATIONS
## OF CHRISTIAN WORSHIP

There are deep and intimate connections between our worship and our history. At the simplest level, like all aspects of Christian life and thought, worship has a history, and the study of this history can illuminate the way the Christian church has perceived and expressed itself in various times and places. Unfortunately, much of this history is lost to us. We do indeed have innumerable documents, the texts of prayers and sermons, service books and hymnals from ages past. But Christian worship is not a text or a book. It is an event of the Christian people at prayer, and that event is not easily captured. Liturgical texts can sometimes tell us what was said or sung in worship, but they cannot tell us what the experience of worship was like for the ordinary worshiper. In addition, this documentary history of worship has most often been told from the perspective of those in power: bishops and clergy, theologians and royalty. So the history that we are able to decipher is generally biased and does not provide the full picture. As we move on in our own study of Christian worship, aspects of that history will be drawn on to explain why worship looks the way it does in the present. But always we must understand that we are only getting one part of the story of worship as it changed through the centuries.

But there is a more important historical foundation for the study of Christian worship, because our worship itself is an expression of a certain wider history: that is, the history of our redemption. This is as true for us as it was for our Jewish and Christian forbears. We can see this in the Jewish celebration of the Passover. When faithful Jews in any age gather for Passover, they enter into a form of worship that springs directly out of the history of God's dealings with Israel. The Passover meal (the Seder) is a way of recalling and giving thanks for the exodus from Egypt, and for the redemption from slavery and oppression it represents. God acted decisively in history, and therefore the pious Jew comes again and again to praise and to thank God in worship. In the same way, our Christian worship springs directly out of Christian history. God acted at a particular historical moment to redeem us in Christ Jesus, and therefore we gather to pray and sing and make our offerings. Or, as the First Letter to the Corinthians puts it: "For our paschal lamb, Christ, has been sacrificed. Therefore let us celebrate the festival" (1 Cor. 5:7–8a).

However, there are two separate kinds of history that undergird our Christian worship. There is, as we have said above, the large-scale history of what

God has done for us all in Christ's life, death, resurrection, and ascension. But there is also the more local history of what God has done in our own lives and in the life of our community. We worship God as an acknowledgment of both of these kinds of Christian history, and in our worship these two histories engage in a creative dialogue with one another, out of which new life and faith emerge. Charles Wesley, who expressed his Methodist theology in over 9,000 hymns, felt keenly this meeting of the large-scale and small-scale histories of redemption, and wrote about it in one of his most famous verses:

> He left his Father's throne above—
>     So free, so infinite his grace—
> Emptied himself of all but love,
>     And bled for Adam's helpless race.
> 'Tis mercy all, immense and free;
> For, O my God, it found out me![14]

Changes in worship through the centuries can be seen as the result of the creative interaction, the dialogue, between these two elements: the "macro-history" of God's salvation of the whole of humankind and the "micro-history" of God's dealing with us in the here and now. This is what it means when we say that worship not only arises out of history, but that it also has a history.

For the student of worship, a working knowledge of the history of how Christians have worshiped in the past has three distinct functions. First, the study of history will relativize our contemporary practice. "The past is a foreign country," the saying goes, "they do things differently there." The study of the past tells us that Christian worship, like other aspects of Christian life, changes over time, and that it was not the same in the past as it is today. This helps us to put the present into perspective and to avoid the pitfall of making the sort of worship we are most familiar with into an idol, saying, "In this form of Christian worship and in no other can one find God." If we know, for example, that unfermented Communion wine was only introduced in the late-1870s, and was not at all a part of the agenda of most of our Protestant forebears, then variations in Communion practice do not seem quite so shocking. There are few eternal verities in Christian worship.[15]

The second reason for students of Christian worship to know about the past is that it helps to explain the present. There have been many decisions taken about worship in the past that still impinge on today's worship, and many historical "accidents" that have become enshrined in our contemporary common prayer and its environment. Sometimes later generations, having forgotten the original reason something was said or done, have offered quite a different interpretation. One example will suffice. Various explanations are generally given for the presence in most churches of a fence around the Communion

Table (called either the "altar rail" or, more properly, the "Communion rail"). It is said that this barrier was originally designed to mark out a holy space around the Lord's Table, and to allow parishioners to kneel reverently while receiving the Communion bread and wine. But the original purpose goes back to the late Middle Ages, when churches functioned not only as places for worship, but also as public meeting places, centers for local commerce and social interaction. One significant problem, however, was the presence in churches of dogs, who found the gathering a profitable place to scavenge for food. Without suitable barriers, it was likely that the Communion bread would become dog food, and fences with closely set upright posts were put in place in response. Gradually, the problem of canine infestation declined, but the fences remained. As the memory of their original purpose faded, successive generations of worshipers sought more pious explanations for the presence of Communion rails, and those explanations have largely survived to the present day. To suggest that an important feature of our contemporary church architecture is the result of unwelcome invasions of medieval dogs may be distressing to some. But without a knowledge of history we are likely to continue perpetrating sentimental and inaccurate information. Everything that happens in Christian worship has a history, and to learn that history not only equips us for intelligent participation, but also connects us with the faith of our Christian forbears.

Finally, a study of the history of Christian worship enables new possibilities for the present. It is said that we cannot know what the church can do until we know what the church has done. The story of the Christian past tells us that the possibilities for speaking about God, for imaging Christ's work of redemption, for affirming our belief, for expressing our devotion and our joy are much wider than we know. In the story of Christian worship we have the story of the way faithful people through the ages have employed a vast array of words and actions to praise God in worship, and that treasury of words and actions is ours to plunder. This is not to say that everything from the Christian past is appropriate for today's worship. Serious theological and historical judgments have to be made in each case. It is to say, however, that being captive to the present can be just as much a problem for Christian worshipers as being captive to the past.

Like many other historians, historians of worship put their data into various periods or eras of worship history. Putting history into periods is not without significant problems. It is always only by hindsight that we begin to see in the various stretches of human history particular patterns and characteristics which seem to be distinctive. (In other words, people living in the year 1200 had no idea that they were living in the "Middle Ages.") To put the history of worship into periods is to give it a manageable shape, and to allow us to understand the relationship between the texture of worship and the more general texture of the period. But we must not be misled into thinking that periodization is anything more than a tool that human beings use to understand the disparate details of their own historical experience.

Historians of worship usually divide their subject into five distinct periods: apostolic (the period during which the New Testament writings were being compiled), patristic (usually from about 200 to 700), the Middle Ages (this is the most difficult period to delimit, but is usually set between 700 and 1500), Reformation and post-Reformation (from 1500 to 1800, more or less) and the modern period (from 1800 to the present).

The documentary sources for the study of worship vary according to the particular period that is being investigated. For some periods we have manuscripts of prayers and stage directions ("rubrics") for the celebration of worship, but for others we may have only fragments of hymns or prayers. These bits of information are combined with such things as descriptions of services, church legislation ("canon law"), and polemical tracts and sermons, to give us some understanding of how worship was conducted at a given time. Overall, each period has its own problems in gathering and analyzing evidence. The New Testament writers, for example, did not intend to answer our contemporary questions about the way the earliest Christians worshiped, and they leave us with only the most fleeting glimpses of what was taking place. The authors of the Epistles, Gospels, and the book of Acts simply presumed that their audience had an intimate, working knowledge of what took place in their worship, and that no systematic explication was necessary. (This means that whenever the cry goes up from the Christian people, "Why can we not worship as they did in the New Testament?", the response must always be: "Because we know so little about what they did!"). The early history of Christian worship, certainly up to about the year 1000, is like a giant jigsaw puzzle for which we have only a few pieces. We have sufficient pieces to discern the broad outlines of the picture, but so many of the fine details are missing that we can make only intelligent guesses about the picture as a whole.

Until very recently one kind of evidence has been seriously neglected by students of Christian worship. This is first-person writing and testimony about the experience of Christian worship. As we said earlier, although official liturgical texts are informative about the kinds of things said and done by worship leaders, they tell us very little if anything about the ways in which ordinary worshipers participated in worship and interpreted their worship practice. In order to get at this, scholars of worship have begun to turn to evidence from diaries, letters, court testimony, and journals, both published and unpublished. Although first-person narratives such as these give us evidence from a fairly narrow demographic stratum (those who could write and had the leisure to write), it does give a very real and lively sense of the reality of worship "on the ground," and has yielded several surprises. Elements of Christian worship that may be highly significant for clergy are revealed to hold little significance for the laity (and vice versa), and pronouncements on the essentials of doctrine may not penetrate the religious imaginations of worshipers as deeply as those in authority might have wished. These kinds of evidence have as many interpretive difficulties as other types of source material, but they are beginning to be placed into creative dialogue with official rites, texts, and theological treatises that have been the primary sources of more traditional worship histories.[16]

To say that history is one of the foundations of the study of worship is to say that we are people with a past, and that our past has in many cases determined the shape of the present. It is also to say that the witness of faithful Christian people, in various ages and circumstances, struggling to find appropriate ways to worship the God who sustains them, must be taken seriously as a part of the armory of the contemporary church. Soon enough, of course, our own worship will have become a part of that historic chain of faithfulness, studied for evidence of the ways in which the human encounter with God was celebrated in public prayer at the beginning of the third millennium.

## THE HUMAN SCIENCES AND THE STUDY OF CHRISTIAN WORSHIP

As we all know, the activity we call "worship" is not confined to Christian believers and Christian communities; members of every religious community across the globe participate in various rites and ceremonies that they would categorize as worship. Over the past seventy-five years or so, many of those working in what we broadly refer to as the human sciences (that is, sociologists, psychologists, anthropologists, ethnographers, and sociolinguists) have been looking very seriously at worship as an aspect of human behavior. They investigate the wide diversity of forms of worship and try to ascertain what functions and characteristics they share. How can those who attend a Quaker Meeting, a Hindu funeral, a tribal puberty rite in Brazil, or a Methodist Covenant Service all be convinced that they are "worshiping"?

Human scientists are particularly interested in worship as a human phenomenon because they believe, provisionally at least, that worship may be one of the very few human cultural universals. That is, that the human species, all across its geographical range, across all social and cultural boundaries, and for all its known history (possibly over three million years) seems to engage in this behavior in one form or another. For the human scientists, the scientific study of worship adds one more piece to the puzzle of what it means to be a human being. And of course for Christians these insights are important as well, because the study of worship as a human phenomenon raises the question of theological anthropology. What does the design of the human being as a "worshiping animal" say about the God who created it?

We have learned a number of important things from the human scientists. One of the most important is the value and function of the foundational story or myth to our Christian worship. Unfortunately, in ordinary discourse the word "myth" has taken on a negative connotation: It is thought of as a story that is misleading, or not factually true. (For example, "It's only a myth that boys are brighter than girls.") But in the human sciences it has a technical meaning, which emphasizes not the facts of the story, but its function for those who tell it. Myths attempt to speak about the deepest human realities, but in the form of narrative, metaphor, and imagery rather than in analytical or scientific language.

All worship, say the human scientists, is rooted in a particular myth, a story that expresses the values and ideals of the community that claims it. This story binds the community together and is retold and re-presented in various ways in worship; it is sung, recited, reenacted, and woven into prayer and praise. At the annual Passover Seder the story of the liberation of the Hebrew people is told and dramatized. In the tribal rites of the aboriginal people of Australia the story of the ancient days, when all things came into being through the dreams of the animal ancestors, is recalled. And every time Muslims gather for common prayer they remember the story of God's revelation to Muhammad. What is fundamentally important in every case is not the historical reliability of the particular story but rather its truthfulness in the deeper sense. These stories are "true" because they talk truthfully about the most basic values, hopes, and aspirations of a particular community, about its origins and its destiny. They are "true" in a way that allows people within that community to recognize themselves and to find their identity. So when people in the human sciences talk about "the Christian myth" they are not implying that the Gospels are fallacious or historically inaccurate. They are saying, rather, that the story of the life, death, and resurrection of Jesus functions as a source of meaning, purpose, and identity for the Christian community.

This retelling of the Christian "myth" can happen in a number of ways in our worship. Most basically, of course, it occurs when the Bible is read in church, when the great stories of the Old and New Testaments are retold in order to remind us of who we are as a Christian people under God. It also happens each time the Lord's Supper is celebrated, recalling the promises of Jesus to be with his people always. But there are also denominational and local myths that are important as well. Methodists may tell the story of John Wesley's escape from the fire at Epworth, and thereby reinforce the sense that their destiny as a Methodist people was in God's hands from the beginning. We may tell the stories of how our local church came into being, and how it has grown in good times and in bad, and in so doing we reinvigorate our sense of community belonging. Whenever we tell the stories of who we are, our sense of our own identity as individual worshipers and as a worshiping community is deepened. And for this insight we have to thank the human sciences.

This concern of the human sciences with the formation and self-expression of true communities has led us to think about another aspect of our Christian worship. When the human scientists ask, "What is it that binds worshiping communities together?" the retelling of the community's story or myth is only part of the answer. The other part has to do with the function of symbols within the community. Again, the word "symbol" has also taken on a negative meaning, used to describe something that is empty of meaning ("His gift of flowers was only a symbolic gesture"). But a symbol for the human scientists is a more neutral term, referring to a mode of human communication that uses actions, objects, and gestures to convey meaning. A symbol, in other words, embodies meaning.

Words are very good media for the communication of ideas and concepts, for the sharing of knowledge and information. But they are less successful at conveying the more experiential and affective aspects of our lives, for expressing such things as love, loyalty, sadness, trust, power, anger, and hope. These intangible features of our experience are more fully, adequately, and easily communicated by symbols, by which we express our deepest ideals and feelings. There are hundreds of daily examples of this. International protocol rests on a complex language of symbols. Who has been sent to a certain state funeral to represent the government? Who is seated next to whom at a parliamentary dinner? What sort of gift was given to the President of Somewhere to the Prime Minister of Somewhere-else? And in our own families as well we see the importance of symbols by which we express our affection, fidelity, and concern: the preparation of a special birthday meal, the provision of a cup of coffee each morning, the giving of an engagement ring. These symbols are not just visual aids. They are a part of the essential structure of relationships, allowing human communities (large and small) to express complex emotions for which words are often inadequate.

And the Christian community operates in very much the same way as other forms of human community. It too uses symbols to express its deepest bonds and emotions, to express the experience of Jesus Christ alive in its midst, the gratitude for what God has done, and the love of Christ that permeates the gathering. But things can go dramatically wrong with the Christian use of symbols, and misplaced or dysfunctional symbolism has been the cause of several reformations in the history of Christian worship.

Symbols can become dysfunctional in a number of ways. A symbol is designed to point beyond itself to a deeper reality, to be a vehicle for the experience of God and a means of expressing our faith, hope, and love. When any symbol fails to do this, when it points only to itself and not to the intangible reality it signifies, it has lost its power. At various times in the church's history, certain symbols ceased to be an aid to worship and became instead occasions for idolatry. On those occasions "puritan movements" stepped in to remind the church of the true object of its worship. In the First Letter to the Corinthians, Paul reminds us that while everything is lawful, not everything is useful for the building up of the body of Christ (1 Cor. 10:23). This is certainly true in the case of religious symbolism.

At the same time, those in the field of neurobiology have been working hard to understand the reciprocal interaction between worship and the human brain. Is there a particular neural pathway that comes into play when prayer in common is experienced as an encounter with transcendence? What is the interplay of the various senses—cognitive, affective, olfactory, tactile—that are employed in worship, and is sensitivity to these things hardwired into our human anatomy? These kinds of questions, many of which intersect with issues arising within the discipline of psychology, are beginning to form a new and exciting field of inquiry for those who seek to understand the underlying biological mechanisms that are in play when people worship.

But as useful as these insights from the human sciences have been to students of Christian worship, thinking about our worship as an aspect of human behavior, as a "human phenomenon," can be difficult. When we recognize that Christian worship has a great deal in common with the worship of other religious people, questions are raised about the uniqueness of Christianity and Christian common prayer. If Sikhs and Hindus and Jews all gather around their sacred scriptures and tell the story of their ultimate transformation, what does that say about the validity of our own proclamation and preaching? If the capacity and drive to worship is hardwired into the human anatomy, then what further criteria do we use to say that any one particular form of worship is more acceptable than another? If tribal people sing hymns and share bread in a sacred meal, what implications has this for our own celebrations? Simply to divide the various manifestations of the human impulse to seek out the Eternal in prayer and praise into categories of "true" and "false" worship is overly simplistic, and deeper thought is required of students of Christian worship.

Nevertheless, we must be willing to see the human sciences as one of the cornerstones of our study of worship. We come to worship as human beings, as living organisms. We come with human personalities and desires, and physical, mental, and psychological capacities. We come with the human need to be in relationship with others of our species, and the human drive to express ourselves. The more we can learn about the constraints and possibilities of our humanity, the better we are able to understand our worship of the God who created us human.

These, then, are the cornerstones of our study of Christian worship: the Bible, theology, history, and the human sciences. The complete foundation, though, consists of a wide variety of different aspects of the Christian life. Indeed, everything that feeds the historical imagination, everything that nourishes the Christian heart, everything that opens the eyes to symbolism and imagery, everything that fuels pastoral insight and creativity, is necessary, because it is on these things that our common worship is built.

But there are warnings here as well for the study of worship. When the great dean of St. Paul's Cathedral, William Ralph Inge, was asked if he studied the church's liturgy, he replied that he did not. "Neither," he said, "do I collect postage stamps." Although this is usually interpreted as evidence of a wholly dismissive attitude toward the study of Christian worship, it is much more a profound statement about the deep significance of worship within the life of the church. Just as the most important thing about postage stamps is not their shape, color, or size, but what they do, this is also the most important thing about Christian worship. Worship is not simply another object for study, but a living, breathing event of grace for the Christian people. Unless we keep this in mind, the study of our worship, however well-founded, will be lifeless.

# 2

# The Components of
# Christian Worship

Now that we have laid the foundations for our study, the next task is to ask the question What are the fundamental building blocks of Christian worship? What are its essential components? Certainly, like other complex systems, Christian worship is more than simply the sum of its constituent parts. It is an integrated experience, an event, and we can easily diminish our understanding of worship by reducing it to nothing but a collection of bits and pieces to be analyzed. But at the same time, there are a number of essential features which are common to all the various forms of Christian worship, and which can be said to make up its overall pattern and texture. To return to our comparison between the study of worship and building a house, we may experience the house as a totality, but it is the details—the size of the windows, the height of the ceilings, the color of the walls—which work together to shape our overall experience of the house. In this chapter we will try to identify the various components of Christian worship, and to discover what each contributes to our total experience of worshiping.

## PRAYER

To say that prayer is a component of Christian worship is almost a tautology. Indeed, many people define worship itself as "the church at prayer," as the prayerful conversation or discourse between the Christian community and the God who has called it into being. The content of this discourse has a great deal of variety about it: Christians and their God will have quite different things to

27

say to one another on the occasion of a baptism, for example, than on the occasion of a civil disaster. The prayers of our Christian worship also come from a wide variety of sources and from many layers of Christian history. Some are as old as the church itself; some are being said for the first time on a given occasion. And many fall somewhere in between, having been claimed for contemporary Christians from the great treasury of prayer which is the church's inheritance. This balance between old and new in prayer is one of the great strengths of the Christian liturgy.

But whatever its content, whatever its age and pedigree, prayer, like other types of conversation, is characterized by certain essential structures, by differences in its various forms and functions. As it happens, there are relatively few kinds of prayer structures, and these structures have remained quite stable throughout Christian history. A close look at each of these genres (forms) of prayer can tell us a great deal about the community of faith and about its relationship to God in worship. It can also help us to understand how "prayers" as distinct entities relate to "prayer" as an approach to the Christian life as a whole.

## Praise or Adoration

Praise is perhaps the most spontaneous form of Christian prayer. The experience of God's holiness, mercy, and goodness calls forth from the worshiping congregation the simple declaration of love. The book of Revelation describes such a prayer when it says: "Then I heard what seemed to be the voice of a great multitude, like the sound of many waters and like the sound of mighty thunderpeals, crying out, 'Hallelujah! For the Lord our God the Almighty reigns, Let us rejoice and exult and give him the glory . . .' " (Rev. 19:6–7a).

Our praise of God arises out of the recognition of our creaturely dependence on God who is the Creator of all things, the Alpha and Omega; it is a sort of holy "Wow!" at the glimpse we have been given of God's majesty and power. In discovering who God is, we are driven to our knees in worship. Therefore, the prayer of adoration is generally deemed to be the most appropriate beginning for any service of Christian worship. It calls the congregation to come before God saying: "We are here because we love you. We love you because you are the kind of God you are."

In most cases, the prayer of praise consists of a description of our own feelings of adoration and the ways in which we will honor God in our worship. Psalms 149 and 150 are good examples of this type of prayer. Both begin and end with the simple acclamation "Praise the Lord," but in between are exuberant descriptions of the various forms our praise will take:

Praise him with trumpet sound;
   praise him with lute and harp!
Praise him with tambourine and dance;
   praise him with strings and pipe!
Praise him with clanging cymbals;
   praise him with loud clashing cymbals!
Let everything that breathes praise the LORD!
               (Ps. 150:3–5)

The prayer of adoration is not the time for anxiety or for expressing our feelings of inadequacy in the presence of God's majesty, nor to focus on our own needs and desires. It is rather the time to turn our entire attention to the God who has called us to worship, and to state clearly, simply, and unambiguously who that God is.

While prayers of praise and adoration certainly serve to set the tone for the beginning of a service of worship, such prayers can come at other points in the liturgy as well. In most American churches, the famous final verse from a hymn by Thomas Ken (1637–1711) is used when offerings of money are brought to the front:

Praise God from whom all blessings flow,
Praise God all creatures here below.
Praise God above all heavenly hosts.
Praise Father, Son, and Holy Ghost.[1]

This kind of short hymn of praise, usually to the Trinity, is called a doxology, from the Greek word *doxologia* meaning "words of praise." We find other forms of the doxology used to conclude the recitation of the psalms ("Glory be to the Father, and to the Son, and to the Holy Spirit. As it was in the beginning, is now, and ever shall be, world without end. Amen."), and in the ancient hymn called the Gloria in Excelsis, also called the "Greater Doxology." From the sixth century onwards, this hymn fulfilled the function of praising God at the beginning of the Sunday eucharistic service, and is still found as the centerpiece of the opening section of contemporary services of Holy Communion.

Glory to God in the Highest,
And peace to God's people on earth.

Lord God, heavenly King,
Almighty God and Father,
We worship you, we give you thanks,
We praise you for your glory.

Lord Jesus Christ, only Son of the Father,
Lord God, Lamb of God,
You take away the sin of the world:
Have mercy on us;
You are seated at the right hand of the Father:
Receive our prayer.

For you alone are the Holy One,
You alone are the Lord,
You alone are the Most High,
Jesus Christ, with the Holy Spirit,
In the glory of God the Father. Amen. Amen.

We have already looked at the ancient hymn of praise called the Sanctus,[2] which in many churches forms part of the Communion prayer and which speaks of the congregation echoing the eternal praises of heaven. The so-called "Praise psalms" (Ps. 147–150) can also be used as prayer responses to the Scripture readings or to the sermon. And to return our thoughts again to the simple adoration of God before the service ends and we return to our daily lives can also be appropriate.

At various times in the course of our Christian lives one or another of the many facets of God's being may be at the forefront of our consciousness, and so the content of the prayers of adoration and praise can change depending on the season or occasion. In the season around Christmas we might praise God for being vulnerable to the limitations of our humanity. At Easter we speak of God's power over sin and death, and at a wedding we praise the God of love. Biblical themes that will be highlighted later in the service can be drawn into this prayer, so that the congregation is not bombarded with a vast array of images of God, but can concentrate on one or two.

## Thanksgiving

If the prayer of adoration is focused on who God is, then the prayer of thanksgiving is focused on what God does, has done, and is doing for the community of faith and in the world. To find the roots of thanksgiving as a form of liturgical prayer, we must look deep into Christianity's Jewish past. Many times in this volume we will refer to the worship patterns of pre-Christian Judaism, since these make up the soil out of which Christian worship grew. Jesus was a worshiping Jew. He went to the synagogue on the Sabbath (Luke 4:16–30), prayed at the temple on holy days (Matt. 21:23–27), and celebrated festival meals in the home (Luke 22:7–23). After Jesus' death, Christian communities, Jew and Gentile alike, took over a number of Jewish forms of prayer wholesale, and adapted and modified others. In addition, there are certain features of the overall mentality, or spirituality, with which Christians approach their common prayer that are inherited from their Jewish liturgical "parent."

This parentage is very obvious when we look at prayers of thanksgiving. For the pious Jew, God has always been known in and through concrete historical acts in the life and history of the community of faith. God is deserving of thanks for intervening on the community's behalf to redeem it, to lead it back from iniquity and into covenant with God, to bless it with peace and prosperity. The "Song of Moses" (Exod. 15:1–18), for example, is an extended prayer of thanksgiving. Having been brought safely out of Egypt, Moses thanks God by reciting the mighty acts of God by which the people have been redeemed.

> I will sing to the Lord, for he has triumphed gloriously;
>     horse and rider he has thrown into the sea.
> The Lord is my strength and my might,
>     and he has become my salvation . . .
>                                         (Exod. 15:1–2)

To thank God, then, always begins with remembering what God has done, not in the abstract, but in specific, historical terms. For Israel, all of history, every historical event, becomes a theophany, a manifestation of God and of God's love. This sense of giving thanks for what God has done carries directly over into Christian thanksgiving prayers, even though the content has been changed somewhat to encompass the historical events most significant to Christian believers.

The primary historical event for which Christians give thanks to God is the life, death, and resurrection of Jesus Christ. This becomes the lens through which all other events are seen and interpreted. At the same time, thanksgiving to God for creation, the abundance of the earth, the blessings of the old covenant, the power of prophecy, for the community of the church, the gift of family and friends, and the innumerable blessings of daily life; all of these also find a place in Christian thanksgiving. But the lynchpin of it all is the Christ event.

Usually, the point in the worship service at which prayers of thanksgiving fall most naturally is after the reading and proclamation of the Word of God. To have been confronted with the works of God proclaimed in the Old and New Testaments, and to have heard in the sermon what that means in real terms for Christian community and the world, we turn to God in response. The words of the great thanksgiving hymn "Now thank we all our God" give us some idea of the shape of such prayers:

> Now thank we all our God,
>     With hearts and hands and voices,
> Whom wondrous things hath done,

> In whom the world rejoices;
> Who from our mothers' arms
>     Hath blessed us on our way
> With countless gifts of love,
>     And still is ours today.[3]

This way of thanking God by remembering what God has done will have different emphases for different occasions in the worship life of Christians. At a wedding, for example, we might thank God for the ways in which married love reflects God's care for the world; at an ordination, it is appropriate to thank God for the gifts bestowed on persons for ministry; at a funeral we thank God for a particular life, lived in the promise of the resurrection hope. Of course the paradigmatic thanksgiving prayer of this type is the central prayer at the Lord's Supper, which in many traditions is called the "Great Thanksgiving."

## Petition

It is precisely because of the confidence with which we can say in our prayers of thanksgiving: "O God, you have done great things for us!" that the Christian community can say with equal confidence: "Come now and do for us once again what you have done in the past" in the prayers of petition. In remembering and reciting the saving deeds of God, we are brought face-to-face with the knowledge of our radical dependence upon God. With that realization comes the recognition that in the depths of our pain and despair and fear there is only one source of help: to the God who loves us and who has intervened on our behalf over and over again. At the heart of Christian petition (or supplication), then, is the overwhelming sense of the trustworthiness of God.

The pages of the New Testament are littered with affirmations about the responsiveness of God to our prayers of supplication:

> Is there anyone among you who, if your child asks for bread, will give a stone? Or if the child asks for a fish, will give a snake? If you then, who are evil, know how to give good gifts to your children, how much more will your Father in heaven give good things to those who ask him! (Matt. 7:9–11)

And in the pattern for prayer that Jesus taught his disciples, God is asked to "give us this day our daily bread."

Because they rest on our confidence in the reliability of God, the prayer of supplication or petition has tended to follow a typical pattern. It begins by recalling the ways in which God has answered our prayers in the past, the concrete manifestations of God's goodness, and then it moves on to ask God to act on this occasion with the same power and mercy we have experienced before. This prayer pattern has very ancient roots, and is the traditional form of Jewish blessings, at meals and on other occasions.

The collect (called in some traditions the "Opening Prayer") is a particular form of petitionary prayer, which expresses our supplication to God in the context of a specific occasion. In liturgical books from the sixth century onward, each day of the Church Year and each special occasion (a wedding, funeral, or baptism, for example) had its own collect. The collect was originally said by the presiding minister at the beginning of the service on behalf of all the people, in order to "collect" their prayers together into one, but today these prayers are often said in unison.

This is a collect for the Day of Pentecost:

> Almighty and ever-living God,
> you fulfilled the promise of Easter
> by sending your Holy Spirit
> and opening the way of eternal life
> to every race and nation.
> Keep us in the unity of your Spirit,
> that every tongue may tell of your glory;
> through Jesus Christ our Lord,
> who is alive and reigns
> with you and the Holy Spirit,
> one God, now and for ever. Amen.

Like other collects, this prayer follows a specific pattern. The collect is usually trinitarian in its overall form: it addresses God the Father, through the Son in the power of the Holy Spirit. In this case, the Pentecost themes of the promised sending of the Spirit and the availability of the gospel to all people are given shape by the traditional collect format.

A collect usually begins with an "ascription," the naming of God in a certain way that highlights particular attributes ("Almighty and ever-living God"). Next the prayer moves on to an acknowledgment of what God has done for us ("you fulfilled the promise of Easter by sending your Holy Spirit and opening the way of eternal life to every race and nation"). Then it petitions God to act in a similar way again, here and now ("Keep us in the unity of your Spirit") in order that some particular goal may be reached ("that every tongue may tell of your glory"). Traditionally, the collect ends with a Trinitarian doxology ("through Jesus Christ our Lord, who is alive and reigns with you and the Holy Spirit, one God, now and for ever. Amen"). Although not all collects contain every one of these elements, they all follow a similar trajectory. More importantly, as prayers within the general category of supplication, they all rest on the reliability of God's promises and God's action in history on our behalf.

## Confession

"Confession is good for the soul," the old saying goes. Once we have acknowledged who God is and what God has done, it is inevitable that we will turn our
thoughts to the distance that exists between the goodness of God and our own
worthiness to receive it. It is not that we need to grovel before we can worship
with any real sense of devotion. It is rather that as we worship we gain a sense
of the ways in which we have fallen short of God's intention for us, as individuals and as a church. The existence of sin and the need to confess it before God
and before one another is a basic reality of the Christian life, a reality that is
expressed in the worship service as prayers of confession. "Remember then
from what you have fallen," the readers of the book of Revelation (v. 2:5) are
reminded, "repent, and do the work you did at first." This is the cycle of contrition and restoration that Christians repeat over and over again until death.

There is some debate about precisely where in the service the prayer of confession belongs. Some would argue that it must be placed close to the beginning of the service, that as soon as we have been confronted with who God is
we must turn to the ways in which we have offended God's holiness and justice. Others add that we need to "clear the decks" by confessing our sins before
our worship will be acceptable to God. But to put the prayers of confession
near the beginning of the service runs the risk that they will be vague and
abstract, since until we are addressed by the word of God, proclaimed and
preached, we do not yet know the concrete things we have to confess. For this
reason, many services are planned so that the prayer of confession is placed
after the sermon. There is also the difficulty that if the prayer of confession
occurs near the beginning of the service it sends the subtle message that we
are focusing our attention on ourselves and our unworthiness, rather than on
God and God's goodness.

Wherever it is placed, and however explicit it details our fault, the prayer
of confession has a typical shape and function. Often it begins very much like
the prayer of petition, declaring who God is, what God has done for us, what
God intends for the world. In the light of this, we are moved to acknowledge
the things we have, in the words of the sixteenth-century Book of Common
Prayer, "done and left undone, through ignorance, through weakness, through
our own deliberate fault." In a service of corporate worship, the subject pronoun of this confession should always be in the first person plural (we), signal-
ing that as a community we are bonded together by a "baptism of repentance
for the forgiveness of sins" (Luke 3:3). We bear responsibility for one another,
we confess to one another as well as to God, we need each other in order to
grow toward holiness (Eph. 4:1–6).

Sometimes the prayers of confession follow a responsive pattern, in which a short statement of confession is made, followed by a repeated verse such as the ancient "Lord, have mercy. Christ, have mercy. Lord, have mercy" (called the *Kyrie eleison*). The petition for God's mercy becomes an integral part of the prayer of confession.

> We confess to you, O God, all our past unfaithfulness;
> the pride, hypocrisy and impatience of our lives,
> our self-indulgent appetites and ways,
> and our exploitation of other people.

> Lord, have mercy.
> Christ, have mercy.
> Lord, have mercy.

> We confess our obsession with worldly goods and comforts,
> and our envy of those more fortunate than ourselves.

> Lord, have mercy.
> Christ, have mercy,
> Lord, have mercy.[4]

Confession, whether made in public worship or in private meditation, is always set within the promise of God to forgive sins, a promise embodied in the life, death, and resurrection of Jesus Christ. That is why an essential counterpart to the prayer of confession is a declaration of pardon or assurance of God's persistent willingness to forgive. This can be something as simple as, "This is the good news: Your sins are forgiven," or a more complex form of assurance which picks up on motifs from the lessons or the theme of the day. This declaration of forgiveness is sometimes called an "absolution," especially in traditions in which the role of the ordained ministry is closely linked with Jesus' commission to the disciples, "Receive the Holy Spirit. If you forgive the sins of any, they are forgiven them; if you retain the sins of any, they are retained" (John 20:22–23). But the witness of Christian history is that the ministry of forgiveness and reconciliation is one in which all Christians can claim authority. Together we have heard the gospel of God's generosity and mercy, and together we are responsible for telling one another again and again that that promise remains true despite fault and failing.

There are certain contemporary problems with prayers of confession. In the modern West, the concept of sin has all too often been reduced to sexual or financial indiscretion, and the deeper questions about the true nature of human sinfulness often are left unaddressed. Many feel that in the absence of specific, identifiable acts of wickedness, there is little to confess; others claim that our lives are so thoroughly conditioned by guilt and shame that conventional forms of confession and forgiveness are inadequate. Those who have thought about the historic role of women in the church suggest that much of the sinfulness spoken of in traditional forms of confession (generally devised by men) does not apply to the situation of women's sin, that for men and women sinfulness takes quite different forms. The classical Christian confessions of anger, the misuse of power, aggressiveness, and lust need to be replaced (at least on occasion) by confessions that acknowledge such things as complicity with our own oppression, willingness to let others define the nature and purpose of our vocation, and passivity. In any case, those who wish to argue that the church has outgrown the need for acts of confession of sin may wish to ponder whether the church should abdicate the responsibility for dealing with human shame and guilt within a theological framework to mental health professionals, the authors of popular self-help books, and TV talk-show hosts.

## Intercession

If petition is prayer for our own needs, intercession is prayer for the needs of others, for all in trouble, sickness, or want, and for situations of conflict and distress. In 1 Timothy, Paul urges the Christian community that "supplications, prayers, intercessions, and thanksgivings be made for everyone . . ." (1 Tim. 2:1). Prayer for others in the context of Christian worship, as on all other occasions, is rooted in the Christian virtue of compassion, of suffering with others, and out of our Christian compassion we strive to pray for the needs of others with the same intensity that we pray for our own needs. Our plea to God to act in situations of human suffering is also rooted in the confidence that God's ultimate will for all the world is that it will be healed, redeemed, freed from suffering and evil, war, death, and injustice.

Liturgical intercessions are also called the Prayers of the People, a term which communicates the sense that praying for others is at the heart of the Christian vocation. Because of its essentially communal nature, it is most appropriate for the prayers of intercession to be led by a member of the congregation, and they often take the form of a dialogue between leader and people. Sometimes the leader of the intercessions stands near the center of the congregation, rather than at the front, again emphasizing the whole congregation's common ownership of the prayer.

Often intercessory prayer is designed as a litany. As a form of prayer, the litany is very ancient, found in services of Christian worship from as far back as the mid-fourth century. The litany is a dialogue, in which the people give fixed responses to a series of biddings (also called bidding prayers) said by the leader. Although litanies can vary in their content, the litany form is seen to be most appropriate for intercession, since it highlights that God's workings in the world are always a kind of cooperative dialogue between divine action and human action, divine will and human will. The responses themselves can vary, but most are cries to God to listen and to act:

> **Leader:** Heal and comfort all who suffer
> **Congregation:** Lord, hear our prayer.

or

> **Leader:** Keep in safety all whose work is dangerous.
> **Congregation:** Lord, mercifully hear us.

Intercession is, quite simply, the Christian community's prayerful response to the problem of evil. Intercessory prayer does not say that the pain of human life is simply an illusion, some form of good in disguise. Christian intercession calls evil what it really is: a deformation of the world as God intends it to be, and it asks God to make good on the promise of the gospel. But intercessory prayer does not stop there. There are certain real implications in praying for others as disciples of Jesus Christ. As disciples of Jesus Christ we have committed ourselves not only to praying for change in situations of human pain and need, but also to being agents of change in the name of Jesus Christ. Intercessory prayer, then, is more than a set of directions for God, it is our school of Christian love. It is the point at which we say "Here am I, Lord. Send me!" and it teaches us where we can expect to be sent.

## Anti-structural Prayer

Not all prayer falls easily into one of the categories above. We have already seen that in some traditions of worship there is a high premium placed on spontaneity, to the extent that each act of worship can be a wholly impromptu response to the stirrings of the Holy Spirit. In such cases, the likelihood of prayer that does not follow traditional patterns is increased, with various members of the congregation contributing as the Spirit descends upon them. The gift of speaking in tongues is most characteristic of the Pentecostal traditions of worship, although it can be found in other charismatic traditions as well.

Spontaneity has always been an element in Christian worship. In Paul's letter to the church at Corinth, he describes how the gifts of the Spirit are to be used, and not abused, in the assembly. Speaking in tongues (*glossolalia*) can be "speaking into the air" (1 Cor. 14:9b), or it can be "for building up the church"(1 Cor. 14:12); and Paul warns of the necessity of interpretation in order that the gift of tongues may not become a source of pride and division within the worshiping community. "What should I do then? I will pray with the spirit, but I will pray with the mind also; . . . Otherwise, if you say a blessing with the spirit, how can anyone in the position of an outsider say the 'Amen' . . . ?" (1 Cor. 14:15–16).

This type of prayer not only falls outside ordinary prayer structures, it often falls outside ordinary structures of human discourse, since it is the free expression of the Spirit's promptings. Glossolalia can consist of single words repeated over and over, fragments of sentences, run-on phrases that have no discernible grammar, or even other kinds of noises such as barking and crowing. When more than one person is speaking in tongues it can create the sense of a cacophony of sound within the worshiping community, but this should not be confused with chaos, since for insiders there is usually a clear and discernible pattern present. Many times this type of prayer is not only verbal but physical, and various body movements (handwaving, falling, swaying, dancing) accompany the words that are said.

The other principal type of anti-structural prayer is silence. Liturgical silence is not simply the absence of sound, but an intentional provision of space within which the Spirit of God may move. Prayerful silences are most usually associated with worship within the Society of Friends (Quakers) and the monastic religious orders. But with the popularity of forms of corporate worship as experienced at such ecumenical communities as Taizé in France, silence in worship has increasingly become a part of the ordinary worship life of Christians in more traditional congregations as well.

Silence can be a time of waiting for God to speak, or a form of wordless prayer in which the community can gather in unity. It can be meditative contemplation on the word of God, or a deep experience of God's presence for which the most natural response is silence. ("Be still, and know that I am God.") Silence can also be interspersed with more formal prayers of confession, intercession, petition, or thanksgiving, in order to allow space for the congregation to discern the will of God in the words that have been spoken. But whatever form it takes, silent prayer in the context of corporate worship, either as a programmed element or as something that is allowed to happen spontaneously, can deepen and intensify the community's experience of God and one another.

## Exhortations

Although these are not prayers in the strict sense of the word, they are an integral part of the corporate prayerfulness of the Christian community. Exhortation serves to call people to prayer, to declare and make explicit the community's intention in gathering, and to give those gathered a sense of the nature and purpose of the occasion. Usually, the exhortation is in the form of an address to the congregation by a worship leader who stands facing them. The most familiar exhortation is the one made at the beginning of the wedding service, which in its traditional form begins, "Dearly beloved, we are gathered here in the sight of God and of this company to join this man and this woman in holy matrimony." Other forms of exhortation are made as introductions to the rite of baptism:

> Sisters and brothers, baptism is a gift of God. It declares to each of us the love and grace of God. In this sacrament we celebrate the life of Christ laid down for us, the Holy Spirit poured out on us, and the living water offered to us.[5]

The "Call to Worship" is a particular form of exhortation, usually consisting of a pattern of address and response. The Call to Worship is a statement of God's presence with us, to which we reply with an affirmation of our readiness to worship God in Christ. The Call to Worship is not meant to be a petition for God's presence, an invocation of the Spirit of God, or an acknowledgment of our human frailty before God, but a simple and straightforward declaration of why we are together. It is rooted in our trust that "where two or three are gathered in my name, I am there among them" (Matt. 18:20). The Pastoral Prayer is a form of prayer dear to many congregations, but its roots do not lie very deep in Christian liturgical history. The Pastoral Prayer is most often an amalgam of many of the prayer types we have been discussing here: praise and thanks to God for mercies granted, petition for the needs of the congregation, intercession for the needs of others. All too often in practice these are jumbled together, ignoring logical sequencing and leaving the congregation to bounce from one theme to another without time to give prayerful attention to any single element before moving to another. It also fails to allow for the congregation's very real need to "own" the prayers they are invited to make, to voice their responses more substantively than with a simple "Amen" at the very end. Those who are bound to the tradition of the Pastoral Prayer might profitably reflect on the "plotting" of such a prayer, and the ways in which its theological trajectory draws hearers through the various stances before God invited by the constituent parts.

We have said that the formal object of the study of Christian worship is not particular texts or services, but the church itself, the church at prayer. What do the forms of prayer we have been discussing say about the nature and purpose of the church? The church's prayers of thanks and praise to God affirm that we are rooted in the memory of God's saving activity in history and stand in anticipation of the fulfillment of that activity in the present and future. The church which petitions God in prayer declares that the basic stance of the Christian life is one of confidence in God, and that this confidence allows us to come before God with our wants and needs. In its prayers of confession the church acknowledges the holiness and mercy of God and the reality of human sin, and whenever the church intercedes for the needs of others it claims its part in the outworking of God's will for the world. And finally, the church that is willing to allow its prayer to be guided and shaped by the Holy Spirit, and to wait in silence for the presence of God, declares its openness to being led by God to an unknown future. By looking carefully at the various ways in which the church addresses and has addressed God, we begin to lay the foundations for working out a theology of the church which is both resilient and faithful to the experience of Christian people.

## CREEDS AND AFFIRMATIONS OF FAITH

Although worship as a whole is a vital expression of the Christian faith, there is one particular element of worship that serves to concretize and focus the doctrinal standards of the church. The classic definition of a creed is "a statement of Christian belief," and indeed the word creed comes from the Latin word *credo*, meaning "I believe." The earliest affirmations of faith were short statements proclaiming the divinity of Jesus Christ, such as "Jesus is Lord." (". . . no one can say 'Jesus is Lord' except by the Holy Spirit" 1 Cor. 12:3). Other portions of biblical material are identified as rudimentary creeds, which were very probably used for the instruction of new Christians. In Peter's speech in Acts 10:34–43, the universality of God's saving work and the story of Jesus' ministry, execution, and resurrection is proclaimed, along with the church's calling to "preach to the people and to testify that he is the one ordained by God as judge of the living and the dead" (v. 42).

The creed played an essential role in the worship of the early Christian communities. When new Christians were baptized, they were asked to confess publicly their faith in Jesus Christ as Lord and Savior. Although these confessions were originally quite simple expressions of adherence to Christ, they gradually expanded to include affirmations about the incarnation and resurrection, God the Creator, the Holy Spirit, and the church as a mystical Communion of believers. By the end of the fourth century, the basic structure and content of this simple creed was complete, and ever since it has been known as the Apostles' Creed. For over 1800 years, the Apostles' Creed has been the principal affirmation of faith for those being baptized.

But with growing concern over diversity in Christian practice and theology beginning in the late third century, more elaborate creeds were devised, and were included in services of worship as ways of unmasking heretics and testing for orthodoxy. The most important of these is the affirmation of faith known as the Nicene Creed, which was outlined at the Council of Nicaea in

325 and reached its final form at the Council of Constantinople in 381. Like the Apostles' Creed, the Nicene Creed is trinitarian in its shape, with clauses affirming the divinity of God the Father, Jesus Christ, and the Holy Spirit, and assertions about the nature of the church ("one, holy, catholic") and the future consummation of all things. The politics of orthodoxy had hijacked the creed, and it soon became understood as an official codification of the beliefs of the church, rather than a joyful affirmation of an experience of saving faith. As a part of canon law, the creeds were often used not so much as vehicles for Christian worship, but as weapons in legalistic debate about who was a "true Christian" and who was not.

But by the early Middle Ages the Nicene Creed came to be a normal part of public worship, positioned after the sermon as a response of the believing church to the Word of God. The post-Reformation period saw the rise of various anti-creedal factions, who argued that all the existing creeds were works of "human composure" and therefore detracted from the unique place of Scripture in establishing doctrinal standards for the Christian church. Others who wished to remove creeds from public worship maintained that they violated the believer's freedom of conscience, and closed off the possibility of new communications of the Holy Spirit. Many of those who rejected creeds reminded their followers of the long history of the creed being used as an agent of persecution.

More recently, however, many churches have undertaken the production of new creeds, not as weapons against heresy, but as ways of nurturing the Christian faith in the contemporary context. The "Canadian Creed," the "Korean Creed," "Our Social Creed," and others written since the 1960s have found use in public worship. But there has also been a rehabilitation of the traditional creeds—the Nicene Creed and Apostles' Creed—and a return to including them as normal elements in Christian worship. On occasion some churches, such as the Christian Church (Disciples of Christ), have taken a strongly anti-creedal stance, claiming that creeds have done serious damage to the unity of the Christian faith by turning the one body into warring groups of "insiders" and "outsiders." For advocates of the liturgical use of creeds, the creed is seen as a symbol of the calling of the church to be a confessing church. They remind the church of who and what it is, helping to ensure that the church remains true to its calling.

## MUSIC

It is almost impossible to imagine worship without music, which has enriched the experience of Christian public prayer through the centuries. In many ways the history of Christian worship directly parallels the history of the music written to be performed in church. The most common forms of music in churches today are congregational hymns and sacred songs, choir anthems, psalms and other sections of Scripture (canticles) set to music for singing, and instrumental music. In some traditions of worship, various forms of chant are also important.

## Hymns

Hymnody is such a familiar part of our Christian worship that we may not take the time to ask ourselves the question: What is a hymn? Usually a hymn is defined as any form of sacred poetry that is set to music for singing (usually by a congregation) in worship. Over the centuries, hymns have been vehicles for our praying, for praising God, for expressing our thanksgiving, our lament, and our holy joy as Christians. But hymn singing is not an exclusively Christian occupation, since many other religious traditions also set their own sacred texts to music for congregational singing.

Neither is it a modem invention; references in the Old Testament provide clear evidence of the use of hymns in pre-Christian Jewish worship. The hymn known as the "Great Hallel" (Ps. 113–118) was sung on the seven mornings of the Feast of Tabernacles; participants sang the "Hosanna!" verses from Psalm 118:25 while the priests circled the altar of the whole burnt offering (called the "holocaust") waving palm branches toward the sacrifice. After this they retired from the altar at the sound of a trumpet, chanting repeatedly "Beauty be yours, O Altar!", and as evening approached there was another round of songs and hymns, and men danced with torches in their hands. (The Hallel was also sung during the slaughter of the Passover lambs at the temple.)

New Testament references to hymn singing are less common than those found in the Old Testament. But they are significant to our understanding of the worship of the earliest Christian communities. Paul exhorts the Christians in Ephesus (Eph. 5:18b–9) to "be filled with the Spirit, as you sing psalms and hymns and spiritual songs among yourselves, singing and making melody to the Lord in your hearts." In the Letter to the Colossians the Christian community is given similar encouragement, and singing is clearly viewed as a fitting way of expressing the holy joy of life in Christ. We also have some indication of what these hymns might have been, since there are several texts within the New Testament itself which biblical scholars have identified as hymns for use in worship, for example Ephesians 5:14 ("Sleeper awake! Rise from the dead and Christ will shine on you.") and 1 Timothy 3:16 ("He was revealed in flesh, vindicated in spirit, seen by angels, proclaimed among Gentiles, believed in throughout the world, taken up in glory").

Although the singing of hymns was a part of the Christian worship throughout its formative period, there was a general prohibition against singing in parts. Under the influence of Greek philosophy, any sort of fragmentation was believed to be evil and synthesis and unity to be godly. And so the greatest possible harmony was pursued as the keystone of effective Christian vocal music, the true musical expression of the community's *koinōnia*, the union of souls. The entire Christian community, singing in unison as with one voice, was an offering to God, the source of all unity. The argument for monophonic singing was supported by references in early liturgical texts and letters of spiritual counsel that spoke of the angels in heaven singing "with one voice." As the idea spread that worship on earth was meant to be the mirror of the heavenly liturgy (see pp. 3–6 above), singing in Christian worship was also ideally to be in unison. Cyril of Jerusalem (ca. 315–386) warned: "unless we sing in unison in our worship, we will never be able to join our voices with 'the voices of the angels and archangels and all the company of heaven'.")

Hymn singing was also a vital weapon in promoting the various points of view in the period of the christological and trinitarian controversies. During the great ecumenical councils of the fourth century, representatives of each side to the debate would sing out their own version of the faith in hymns, and on many occasions the noise of competing choirs grew to an intolerable level. But this trouble over orthodoxy in hymns led church leaders to insist on authorizing hymn texts for Christian worship, thus reducing the vitality of the creative process of hymn writing.

Not only the texts, but also the tunes for hymns began to come under increasing scrutiny. At first there seems to have been a wide variety of melodies for the various hymns used in Christian worship in the early centuries, and it is very likely that every Christian community had its own musical settings. But with the quest for unity—"one Empire, one religion"—which grew steadily after the reign of the Emperor Constantine (ca. 288–337), and with the rise of Rome as the power center of the Empire, things began to change. In the fifth century, Pope Celestine I (who was the bishop of Rome between 422–432) supervised the formation of a special school of singers (called a *schola cantorum*), and this choir was continued by his successors so that by the turn of the sixth century there was already a long tradition of liturgical music in Rome. Pope Gregory the Great (pope from 590–604) with his passion for organization, arranged to have all of the chants used by the *schola* codified and regularized, and he sent the members of the choir all over the empire to ensure that these chants were used everywhere without variation. In this way the so-called "Gregorian chant" came to be the standard of church music for worship, and by about the year 800 most of the local music traditions had died out altogether.

There were questions raised about what kind of persons would be allowed to sing in worship. John Chrysostom says that even though Paul had commanded women to be silent in church, they might sing the psalms. "In this singing," he says, "old men lay aside the rigor of age; downcast middle-aged men respond cheerfully, younger men sing without the peril of wantonness, and tender maidens without the fear of damage to the adornment of their chastity." It also seems to be the case that choirs of virgins were responsible for some of the singing in worship, at least in some places. But in many cases women were strictly forbidden from singing. In the middle of the fourth century, Cyril, Bishop of Jerusalem says: "The virgins should sing or read the psalms very quietly during the liturgy. They should move only their lips so that nothing is heard, for I do not permit women to speak in church." And in some other places the voices of women are not to be heard at all in church services: "They may not sing, nor take part in the responses, but they should only be silent," one Syrian bishop exhorts his congregation. Women's singing was considered by church leaders to be too "sensuous" to be included in the worship of God, and by the middle of the sixth century at least one church council put out a decree that declared: "It is not permitted for choirs of virgins to sing in church." In most cases, the voices of young boys were preferred for liturgical singing in this early period, and monasteries became educational centers where boys were trained as singers for Christian worship.

For the first seven or eight hundred years, then, hymns were generally sung to set chant melodies by choirs of men or young boys and by the male members of the congregation more generally. Gradually, part singing began to replace unison singing, with different voices taking the various parts of the text simultaneously, creating a layered effect. This is described as "polyphony." In polyphonic music, each voice part remains independent of the others, moving along at its own pace with any harmony happening only accidentally at certain points in the music. Thus, polyphony is distinguished from monophony (unison singing) on the one hand, and on the other hand from homophony (in which there is a strong melody line and a number of other lines of music sung at the same time which harmonize with it).

In the period from the tenth to the sixteenth centuries there was a flowering of all kinds of liturgical music, including hymns. Latin poets wrote for the various liturgical days and seasons, and wealthy and influential people (and especially popes, the higher clergy, and members of royal and other noble households) employed court composers who were given a free hand in writing music for the worship offered in their private chapels. Such people as William Byrd (ca. 1543–1623), Giovanni Palestrina (ca. 1525–1594), and Thomas Tallis (d. 1585) all worked for such private patrons, and this tradition of court composers continued throughout the Renaissance, resulting in a rich tradition of music for use in the church's worship.

Renaissance music, like Renaissance art and architecture, was bold, ornate, and full of dramatic devices, flourishes, pauses, and disjunctures. This is the sort of music the magisterial reformers would have heard in church in the early years of the sixteenth century, at least in the cathedrals, larger churches, and royal chapels. Now one might think that someone like Martin Luther, who was critical of so much of the Catholic worship and devotion of his day, would have had difficulties with the use of music in worship. But Luther himself was a musician, and a lover of music, and he spoke of music in worship as the "handmaid of theology," ranking the congregational hymn as second only to preaching as the best medium for the proclamation of the gospel. In the end, Luther was perhaps the single most creative force in the development of sixteenth-century hymnody, mainly because he was eager to exploit all kinds of sources for his music. Latin hymns, German drinking songs, old psalm chants: all alike became vehicles for making the Word of God come alive for the Christian congregation. At the center of this creativity were the Lutheran chorales, vernacular, four-part settings of sacred texts used in services as congregational hymns.

Others of the reformers were less convinced about the value of hymns, and many (such as John Calvin and John Knox) insisted that only psalms and a few Scripture texts were appropriate for the Christian people to sing. This negative attitude toward "hymns of human composure" carried over into the English Reformation, and so it was not until the late 1600s that hymnody became a regular feature of English worship. The pivotal figure in this shift was Isaac Watts (1674–1748) a Nonconformist minister, who was convinced that metrical hymns must be written as the human response to the Word of God, an essential element of congregational praise. His *Hymns and Spiritual Songs* (1707) became the most influential hymnal in the history of English worship. Many of his hymns are still in regular use today, including "Jesus Shall Reign Where'er the Sun," and "O God, Our Help in Ages Past."

By every reckoning, the mantle of Isaac Watts was picked up by Charles Wesley (1707–1788). Charles Wesley wrote over 9,000 hymns, and they are a primary source for our understanding not only of Methodist theology, but of Christian theology more generally. Like the Wesleys' theology, the hymns are devotional and introspective, filled with passion and immediacy, and with assurance of the saving grace of Christ for all people. Particularly significant is the collection of 166 eucharistic hymns, which signifies a recovery of the doctrine of eucharistic sacrifice largely absent from Protestant theology since the Reformation.

In the United States two streams of hymnody, the Wesleyan and the metrical psalmody of the Puritan singing masters and lay poets, combined with frontier revivalism to form a potent force for the spread of the gospel in a vast territory. As revivalism spread down the Erie Canal, following the path of the westward expansion, revivalist hymnody accompanied it, taking hold of the religious imaginations of working people throughout the country. Simple, easily memorized lyrics, often repeated over and over again, expressed trust and confidence in the saving grace of Jesus. Hymn writers and translators were also at work in more traditional Christian settings, and the lost treasures of medieval Latin hymnody and sixteenth-century German Lutheran hymnody were recovered. At the same time, the fervent pietist hymnody of immigrants from Germany and Scandinavia joined these streams to add its own vitality to the mix. Although much Victorian hymnody partook of the religious sentimentalism of the age, the best hymns of the nineteenth-century continue to be used to enable the Christian people to express their devotion in song. Contemporary hymn writers, in collaboration with composers, have taken innovative approaches to the Christian hymn, incorporating the needs, concerns and hopes of the modern world into poems of beauty and grace. In addition, hymns from around the globe have found their place in the contemporary repertoire of many congregations, allowing us to share in the Christian experience of other cultures.

In the preface to his *Collection of Hymns for the Use of the People Called Methodists*, John Wesley said that the hymnal should be "a little body of experimental and practical divinity." By this he meant that the singing of hymns both expresses and forms our theology and that the hymnal is a resource for theological reflection and spiritual development. The Protestant churches have always understood not only that hymns play an essential role in our search for a deeper relationship with God and a deeper commitment to Christian living and service, but that our corporate worship is somehow incomplete without the warmth and passion of hymn singing. It is all too easy for a congregation to become captive to a narrow range of familiar hymns, and it is part of the pastoral responsibility of the worship leader to encourage the most extensive hymn repertoire a congregation is capable of handling.

With the experience of nearly two thousand years of Christian hymn singing behind us, how are those preparing for Christian worship to make decisions about the choice of hymns? Several questions should guide the choice: Is this hymn a medium for the Word of God? Is it arranged so that it encourages congregational singing? Is it a hymn that is truly corporate in its language and intention; is it "accessible" in form and content? Is the theology of the hymn consistent with Christian faith and doctrine? What is its function in the service? (Where does it belong?) Does it further the theme and overall intention of the service? When we are serious about asking and answering these questions, the singing of hymns becomes a singularly effective vehicle for the mutual encounter between God and human beings in worship.

## Instrumental Music

We have a great deal of Old Testament evidence for the use of instruments and singing in pre-Christian Jewish worship, and the use of specific instruments for specific liturgical purposes seems to have been regarded by the people of Israel as a divine commandment. At the beginning of the tenth chapter of the book of Numbers, for example, the Lord is instructing Moses on the making of silver trumpets, and later in that chapter we find the injunction:

> You shall sound an alarm with the trumpets, so that you may be remembered before the LORD your God. . . . On the days of rejoicing, at your appointed festivals, and at the beginnings of your months, you shall blow the trumpets over your burnt offerings and over your sacrifices of well-being; they shall serve as a reminder on your behalf before the LORD your God. (Num. 10:9b–10)

Flutes seem also to have had a place in the worship of the temple, and were played by the Levites particularly at the ritual offering of the Passover lamb. The author of Chronicles (1 Chr. 24:6–7) indicates that two hundred and eighty-eight musicians were needed to accompany temple worship in the period after the exile. In all, nineteen different types of instruments are mentioned in the Old Testament, although it is likely that not all of these found use in worship. Centered as it was on the reading and exposition of the Scriptures and prayer, worship in the synagogue seems not to have included instrumental music.

Because of its essential continuity with the synagogue service, the worship of the earliest Christians probably did not include instrumental music. The only New Testament references to instruments in worship are found in the book of Revelation, and most scholars interpret these passages as symbolic rather than as descriptive of actual practice. Indeed, it seems likely that the association of instrumental music with temple sacrifice led to an outright rejection of such music in primitive Christian worship. But gradually, instrumental music began to appear in services of Christian worship, beginning in about the mid-second century.

Soon, however, even this limited use of instrumental music began to create difficulties. As Christianity began to expand and to coexist with other religious communities in the region, a problem seems to have developed when pagan and Christian music were increasingly confused with one another. In many pagan traditions, for example, instrumental music was thought to ward off disease because it frightened the particular demons responsible for illnesses. At the end of the fourth century, the great bishop of Constantinople John Chrysostom (ca. 347–407) had to warn mothers against putting little bells around their children's necks and wrists as talismans, pointing out that the protection which comes from the cross was more powerful in keeping their children from harm.

Some of these early Christian leaders found the difficulties with instrumental music in worship too severe, and counseled Christians to abandon the use of instruments and singing altogether.[6] In support of their attempt to abolish music from Christian worship, many of these writers cite Amos 5:23, in which God rebukes the Israelite community for its unjust dealings with its neighbors, saying, "Take away from me the noise of your songs; I will not listen to the melody of your harps." The force of these prohibitions escalated throughout the first four centuries, until the penalties for Christians who wished to play musical instruments were quite severe. In the canons attributed to Saint Basil (ca. 330–379) we read: "(1) If one who reads the scriptures in church learns to play the guitar, he shall confess it. (2) If he does not return to playing it he shall suffer his penance for seven weeks. If he keeps it he shall be excommunicated and put out of the church."

But there was a serious difficulty with arguments against the use of instruments in church since it was clear that in the Hebrew Bible generally, music of every kind was approved by God (and in many cases advocated by God) as a suitable form of worship. If God had sanctioned the use of instrumental music in the worship of the Jews, why was it not equally appropriate for their Christian descendants? In response to this difficulty, John Chrysostom argued that God had allowed the instrumental music in Jewish worship as "a concession to the weakness of the Jews," and with Christ it was rendered obsolete, like the blood sacrifices in the temple. Eventually, prohibitions against the liturgical use of instruments declined, and by the seventh century they had returned as a normal part of worship in the West.

The instrument which would dominate Christian worship for the next thirteen centuries made its first appearance in the beginning of the 700s and spread widely throughout Europe. Early pipe organs were simple affairs, but gradually became more elaborate, increasing their range and power and quickly earning the title "king of instruments." With a keyboard range of five octaves (augmented by another two and a half octaves in the pedals), and a wide variety of available tones and timbres, the organ creates a rich tapestry of sound both as a solo instrument and as the accompaniment for choir, solo, and congregational singing. Church music for the pipe organ is among the greatest of all musical literature.

A new wave of anxiety over the use of instrumental music in worship was inaugurated by the puritan wing of the English church in the sixteenth century, and several petitions were circulated to dismantle church organs and to ban other instruments from church. Finally, in 1644, legislation was passed instructing that church organs be demolished, and very few escaped destruction. With the restoration of the monarchy in 1660, the ban on the liturgical use of instruments was rescinded, and a great age of English organ building began. Other groups, such as the Moravians and Mennonites continue their ban on instrumental music in church, and the four-part a cappella (unaccompanied) singing of hymns adds an undeniable beauty to their worship.

At the end of the eighteenth century, the music of town bands began to be popular adjuncts to Christian worship, and various wind, brass, and percussion instruments were played from the rear galleries of churches to accompany congregational and choral singing. This trend was deprecated by many church leaders as contributing to the degradation of Christian worship, and to the general inferiority of church music in the period. But the town band was a part of a more general quest for the democratization of music in worship, which had been started by the Wesleys earlier in the century and would continue throughout the nineteenth-century evangelical revival.

As late as 1903, particular instruments were still being banned from Christian worship. In that year, a papal declaration prohibited the use of the piano in church (in favor of the harmonium), and current debate over the use of electric and electronic instruments, drum sets, and hip-hop turntables partakes of the same spirit of anxiety. The idea that some instruments are inherently more "religious" or "ethical" than others is of itself difficult to take seriously. But one must acknowledge the fact that some instruments are very closely associated with forms of secular music which express antireligious themes, and that their use in services of Christian worship may make some people uneasy. In this regard, the primary task of the worship leader is to ensure that whatever instrument or device is used, it is appropriate for the occasion and well played, while having sympathy for the feelings of members of the congregation.

There is, however, a more serious concern about the use of instruments; they can easily become the occasion for ostentation and self-indulgence in worship. The line between music as a performance and music as a vehicle for Christian worship is easily crossed, and the use of instruments in particular can be a source of unwelcome pride, both for the individual performer and the congregation as a whole. Many musicians who are deeply grateful for the gift that God has granted them, and who have given disciplined attention to the nourishment of that gift, see the offering of music in worship as a profound privilege. This is not to say that our church musicians should be taken for granted or deprived of adequate remuneration. It is to say that this sort of attitude is infectious, and the spirituality of congregations can be deepened and enriched by the presence of such people.

## The Psalms

The Psalms (from the Greek word *psalmoi*, meaning "songs") have found widespread and continuous use in Christian worship from its earliest days. Because they speak of the breadth of relationship between human beings and their God, and because they speak of it with such power and beauty, the psalms are among the best-loved elements in Christian common prayer. The collection of Psalms is divided into five sections[7]—probably in imitation of the five books of the Torah—each ending with a doxology. The Psalms were the hymnbook of Israel's temple worship from the period of the Second Temple onwards, and were used in various ways in the synagogue as well. By the time of Jesus, psalms probably served as sung responses to the readings in the synagogue, although in the earlier period they functioned as Scripture readings rather than as songs. The Psalms are the most frequently quoted passages from the Hebrew Bible in the New Testament, and various descriptions of early Christian worship in the book of Acts and elsewhere speak of the singing of "hymns and psalms and spiritual songs."

Although there were many hymns and scriptural canticles used, the singing of the Psalms soon became an indispensable element in Christian worship. Eusebius of Caesarea (260–340), says that, "the command to sing psalms in the name of the Lord is obeyed by everyone in every place." The Psalms were often interpreted allegorically, as prefiguring Christ and his passion, the church, and the struggles of the sinner against temptation, and often christological doxologies were added after the final verse. (Most often in Christian worship the singing or recitation of a psalm still concludes with this kind of doxology: "Glory be to the Father, and to the Son, and to the Holy Spirit. As it was in the beginning, is now and shall be forever. Amen.")

Beginning in the fourth century, groups of people who wished to live in a more godly way went into the desert to dedicate themselves to acts of self-denial and prayer, and at the center of their devotional life was the memorization and repetition of the psalter. In the centuries that followed, the singing of the one hundred and fifty Psalms on a daily, weekly, or monthly rotation became the invariable centerpiece of all monastic worship. But not everyone had the ability to commit the entire psalter to memory, and as this became the ideal for Christian worship more generally, some mechanism needed to be found to enable lay people to continue to participate in psalm singing. A solution to this problem was the development of antiphons, a verse or part of a verse taken from a psalm and set to a simple melody. This antiphon was repeated by the congregation at the beginning and end of the psalm itself, which was sung by a single voice (a cantor) or choir. By the eighth century, the antiphon for a given psalm changed according to the day and season of the church year, and eventually became an elaborate piece of vocal music in its own right. By the time of the Continental Reformation it had overshadowed the psalm itself in ordinary Sunday worship, and the psalter ceased to be the hymnbook of the Christian people.

Many who sought to reform the church's worship in the sixteenth century were eager to restore the psalter to its rightful place. John Calvin, Luther's younger counterpart who guided the reformation of the church in Switzerland, was acutely aware of the power of music to stir the soul and the emotions. But where Luther had been willing to use a wide range of textual sources for worship, for Calvin, the only appropriate texts for singing were the Psalms, and he set about producing metrical (versified) psalms for congregational singing. Calvin had no objection to borrowing Lutheran tunes; his only requirement was that the music mirror the majesty of the text. At this time, there was still no real distinction between secular and sacred music. Street songs, school songs, and military tunes could all be matched with sacred texts. However, like many in the early centuries of Christianity, Calvin forbade instrumental music in church, so the Psalms were sung a cappella. In 1539, the first psalter with tunes was published in Strasbourg, containing eighteen psalm settings, and music for the Song of Simeon (Luke 2:29–32), the Nicene Creed, and the Ten Commandments. In 1542 the *Genevan Psalter* was published, and it formed the basis for all the reformed psalters that followed. Many of our contemporary hymn tunes originate in this collection, the most famous of which is probably "Old Hundredth."[8]

The stirrings of reformation in England also resulted in a wealth of congregational music. In 1540 Miles Coverdale (1488–1568) had produced the first English-language version of the Psalms set to music (*Goostley Psalms and Spiritual Songs*) with fifty-one different tunes. Like his continental contemporaries, Coverdale had used a number of sources for his music, including both Gregorian chants and German chorale melodies. But this book was banned by Henry VIII because of its Lutheran influence. After Henry's death, however, the production of music for use with the new Book of Common Prayer was deemed to be essential, and in 1550 John Merbecke (d. ca. 1585) produced *The Book of Common Prayer Noted*, in which the fixed prayers of the Communion service (including the Litany) were set to chants for congregational and choral singing. Soon various composers were putting their talents into a psalter for congregations to sing, and in 1551 the most durable of these, prepared by Thomas Sternhold and John Hopkins, was published. It contained forty-four psalms set to music and was the principal songbook for English Christians for nearly one hundred and fifty years.[9] The psalm-singing tradition was transmitted to the American colonies with the Pilgrims, whose essentially Puritan theology enforced the sense that the Psalms were the only truly godly form of

Christian congregational song. Even today in some of the smaller Reformed sects, the psalter set to simple melodies remains the only form of music found in worship.

With renewed interest in monastic worship among Christians of many denominations, and the popularization of music from religious communities such as Taizé in France and Iona in Scotland, the liturgical use of the Psalms has undergone something of a revival in recent years. Many musicians and worship leaders have begun to explore different ways of singing the Psalms, to write new antiphons and creative psalm settings, and there is now a genuine seriousness about placing the Psalms at the center of worship and devotion.

## Other Forms of Liturgical Music

While hymns, psalms, and instrumental music are the main types of music for Christian worship, various other forms are also used. The choir anthem has its roots in the early Middle Ages, when religious and biblical texts began to be set for singing by trained choirs rather than by the congregation as a whole. Most of the church's greatest composers have turned their hand to the writing of choir anthems, and the anthem holds a respected place in the wider history of music. Although the choir anthem can enrich and facilitate the common prayer of the congregation, it makes serious demands on the time, energy, and skill of a choir, and is not at all a necessary part of Christian worship.

In the traditional eucharistic rite, certain texts are used invariably, week after week. These form what is called the "ordinary parts" of the service (as differentiated from the "proper" parts, which change to suit the liturgical season or occasion). In the Roman Mass, the ordinary parts are called by their Greek and Latin names: the Kyrie Eleison ("Lord, Have Mercy"), the Gloria in Excelsis ("Glory to God in the Highest"), the Credo ("I Believe In God, the Father Almighty . . ."), the Sanctus and Benedictus ("Holy, Holy, Holy" and "Blessed Is He Who Comes in the Name of the Lord"), the Agnus Dei ("Lamb of God"). These ordinary parts of the liturgy, when set to music, are called collectively the service music (or the "Mass setting"). Usually a composer writes a full "setting" including all the ordinary parts of the service, and although the most elaborate of these are intended to be sung by the choir, it is more appropriate if they are simple enough to be sung by the entire congregation.

Canticles (from the Latin word for "song") are biblical texts other than the Psalms that are set to music for singing. The canticles most commonly used in Christian worship are the Song of Mary (the "Magnificat") from Luke 1:46–55, the Song of Simeon (the "Nunc Dimittis," Luke 2:29–32), and the Song of Zechariah, Luke 1:68–79, but others have a privileged place at certain times. In the season after Easter, the so-called "Easter Anthems" (from Phil.

2:6–11 and other places in the Epistles) are appropriate as ways of voicing the community's convictions about the person and work of Christ.

Various forms of contemporary music do not fit easily into one of these categories. Meditative chants which repeat the same word or words, Christian rap, hip-hop, and praise songs, rock operas such as *Godspell* or *Joseph and the Amazing Technicolor Dreamcoat*, music which provides "texture" or "background" to an action in the service, all may find a place in Christian worship on occasion. But the witness of Christian history is that a balanced diet of congregational hymns and psalms, with a choir anthem, vocal solo, or instrumental piece as a garnish now and again, keeps the Christian community healthy and well nourished. Music can either draw members of the congregation deeper into the worship of God, or it can distract or misdirect them. Therefore choices in the area of music for use in Christian worship are among the most significant we make. Although beauty alone is not a sufficient reason for choosing a piece of liturgical music, the beauty of the right piece of music can deepen our experience of God and our understanding of what God has to say to us. As the contemporary hymn writer Fred Pratt Green says in a stanza of a recent hymn:

> How often, making music, we have found
> A new dimension in the world of sound,
> As worship moved us to a more profound
> Alleluia![10]

## TIME

According to the prophet Isaiah, God "inhabits eternity" but at the same time "dwells with those who are contrite and humble of spirit" (Isa. 57:15). Human beings do just the opposite: we inhabit time and yet have one foot in God's eternity. Time is a part of the structure of our human experience, and also a part of the environment within which Christian worship takes place, part of what gives it shape and structure. In addition, our approach to time in our worship is a way of expressing what we believe as Christians, a form of communication about our values, ideals, and theological convictions. Christian worship allows us to enter time in all its dimensions; into the historic past, the present moment, and the promised future. We read the history of God's dealings with the people of Israel and the life of Jesus, we know the present reality of God's love, and we look to the time when "God will be all in all." In our worship we are enabled to integrate all three of these "tenses" of life—past, present, and future—into a creative whole that has the power to renew and restore.

One of the ways in which this happens is in the ordering of days, weeks, and years in the liturgical calendar. Contemporary life is governed by a multiplicity of calendars: the academic calendar, the calendar which governs professional football games, financial calendars for income tax and business profit reporting, the civil calendar. Each individual calendar reflects the interests of the particular community that uses it, in this case a school community, a community of sports fans, a community of corporate stockholders, and a nation. Calendar implies community. In addition, the way we keep time is evidence of our priorities, since for better or worse, the things to which we give the greatest amount of time are the things that are most important to us.

To understand the Christian calendar, then, is to understand certain essential things about the community of Christian believers. When we worship according to a pattern of days and seasons we proclaim that we take time seriously as a locus of God's self-revelation and self-giving, we affirm that God is made known in and through human history. The Gospels themselves bear witness to this when they pay such close attention to the time in which various things took place: "At that time the festival of the Dedication took place in Jerusalem. It was winter, and Jesus was walking in the temple, in the portico of Solomon. . . ." (John 10:22–23). The Christian calendar is not an annual refresher course in Christian history, nor is it a mechanism for making some days and seasons more "holy" than others. It is rather a testimony to the Christian attitude toward the reality of time itself. As the Christian calendar heightens our consciousness of the holiness of some particular times, we begin to attend to the essential holiness of all of time.

In the New Testament, there are two Greek words used to translate the English word "time." The first is *chronos*, which is the more general term, indicating any fixed period (such as the human life span), a straight line from the past to the future. The kind of time denoted by the word *chronos* is not understood as a recurring cycle or spiral, as in many of the fertility cults of the ancient Near East, but as an arrow, pointing always toward the final judgment. It is *chronos* that Charles Wesley is describing when he writes:

> Our life is a dream,
> Our time as a stream
> Glides swiftly away,
>     And fugitive moment refuses to stay.
> The arrow is flown,
> The moment is gone;
> The millennial year
>     Rushes on to our view, and eternity's here.[11]

The second word for time is *kairos*, which denotes a decisive moment, the time at which something significant happens. Where *chronos*-time is neutral, without any particular meaning, *kairos*-time is time with a content, and the content is invariably related to salvation. In the Septuagint, the Greek translation of the Old Testament, *kairos* is the "time for everything under heaven" in Ecclesiasticus, and in the New Testament, it is the *kairos* that one must recognize in order to fulfill its demands in Romans 13:11. Jesus weeps over Jerusalem, predicting dire consequences on account of her inability to see the significance of the moment: ". . . they will not leave within you one stone upon another; because you did not recognize the time (*kairos*) of your visitation from God" (Luke 19:44b). There are thousands of *kairoi* in the life and ministry of Jesus and in the lives of the Christian people, thousands of decisive moments, full of the promise of salvation. In a sense the Christian calendar proclaims that time is not simply meaningless, but decisive for salvation; it focuses and stylizes the sense that all time is *kairos* time. Although some Biblical scholars argue against the theological significance of these two New Testament words for time,[12] the idea that God infuses our times of celebration with redemptive meaning has been an extremely important one for the understanding of Christian worship.

## The Christian Year

Like all calendars, the Christian calendar discloses Christian priorities. It is centered on two main focal points, the two central *kairos* times of the church: the birth and the death/resurrection of Jesus Christ. Just as the principal moment of salvation for the Jews was the Passover, the principal moment for the followers of Jesus was the death and resurrection of Jesus. It is no accident that the Gospels place these two events together. The Christian Passover (*pascha*), what would later be translated as "Easter" in English, is clearly the earliest Christian festival. It seems likely that from the beginning it was celebrated annually to coincide with the Jewish Passover (the 14th day of the Jewish month of Nisan), and perhaps in the earliest years following the death of Jesus it was only then that the memorial of the Last Supper was re-enacted.

The date of Easter soon became a controversial matter. Should Christians continue to keep the 14th of the Jewish month Nisan (on whatever day of the week it happened to fall) as the commemoration of Jesus' passing over from death to life, or should it always fall on a Sunday, the day of the resurrection? Although by the end of the second century most Christian churches had agreed to keep Easter on the Sunday nearest to the Passover, the debate continued, and pockets of Christians here and there continued to keep 14 Nisan until the end of the fifth century. In the early centuries Easter was a unified celebration, combining commemorations of the crucifixion, death, and resurrection of Jesus. Soon, however, Easter dissolved into separate commemorations marking the various events leading up to Jesus' death/resurrection on the days of the week preceding, and the original paschal unity fragmented into Palm Sunday, Maundy Thursday, Good Friday, Holy Saturday, and the Great Vigil of Easter.

Easter was the ordinary time for baptisms, and the time for those who had been excluded from the Christian fellowship because of serious sin to make their public confession and be re-admitted. In the weeks before Easter both these groups, the catechumens and the penitents, underwent a final period of intensive preparation, including examinations of conscience, exorcisms, fasting, and prayer. Gradually, these disciplines were adopted by all Christians in the weeks before Easter, as a way of opening themselves to the riches of Christ's resurrection. At the Council of Nicaea (325) the period of preparation and fasting before Easter was fixed at forty days (excluding Sundays), mirroring the forty days Jesus spent in the wilderness fasting and preparing for his ministry.

The fifty-day period after Easter, known as the Pentecost and ending with the feast of Pentecost, underwent a similar kind of extension and division. For the Jews, Pentecost had been the celebration of the first grain offering after the harvest, and later came to be the principal commemoration of the giving of the Law at Sinai. Pentecost, along with the Passover and the Feast of Tabernacles, was one of the three great "pilgrimage feasts," when pious Jews went to the Holy City of Jerusalem to make their sacrifice at the temple (Exod. 23:17). For Christians it came to be regarded as the birthday of the church, since it was at the feast of Pentecost that the Spirit-filled believers gathered at Jerusalem, and "began to speak in other languages, as the Spirit gave them ability." (Acts 2:4b). For almost four centuries, Pentecost and the ascension of Jesus were celebrated together. Augustine remarked of this period that:

> These great fifty days after the Lord's Resurrection form a period not of labour, but of peace and joy. That is why there is no fasting and we pray standing as a sign of resurrection. This practice is observed at the altar on all Sundays, and the "alleluia" is sung to indicate that our future occupation is to be none other than the praise of God.

The week before Easter (Holy Week) was later elaborated with ceremonies reflecting the last days of Jesus' life, including commemoration of the Last Supper and footwashing on Thursday, and the veneration of the cross on Friday with three hours of vigil (paralleling the three hours during which Jesus hung on the cross, Luke 23:44–45). Ash Wednesday was added in the eleventh century to mark the beginning of the Lenten fast, symbolized by the placing of ashes (made from burning the palms from the previous Palm Sunday) in the shape of a cross on the foreheads of members of the congregation.

This, then, forms the first "cycle" of the Christian year. Centered on the *pascha*, the commemoration of the passing over of Jesus from death to life, the Easter cycle points both backwards to the events of Jesus' crucifixion and resurrection, ascension and the giving of the Spirit to the church, and then forward to the final establishment of the kingdom of God.

There is some debate about the center of the second principal cycle of the Christian calendar. By the beginning of the fourth century, the Epiphany ("manifestation") of Christ was celebrated in the majority of Christian churches on January 6. It originally marked not only the birth of Jesus, but also the annunciation, the visit of the magi, the presentation of Jesus in the temple, the various miracles which witnessed to Jesus' identity, his baptism by John, and the calling of the disciples. Soon, however, as in the case of Easter, this unity fractured into individual commemorations. It began with the establishment of the new feast of Christmas, probably originating in Rome. There is some disagreement about whether Christmas was originally designed to combat popular enthusiasm for the Roman festival of the Unconquered Sun (the winter solstice),[13] but in any case it soon became the focus for the various narratives and images of the birth of Jesus. Gradually, certainly by the end of the fourth century, Christmas was the undisputed festival of the nativity. "This day," John Chrysostom said about Christmas in the year 386, "which has now been brought to us not many years ago, has developed quickly and has borne much fruit."

By the fifth century, a forty-day period of preparation corresponding to the Lenten fast, had become prefixed to the feast of Epiphany. Later this time was understood as a preparation for Christmas and called Advent. Various other commemorations split off from the Epiphany: the baptism of Jesus, the annunciation to Mary, the presentation, and the naming of Jesus. Epiphany itself remained the celebration of the visit of the magi and the miracles that attested to Christ's divinity.[14] By the beginning of the sixth century, then, the two basic cycles of the church year, the Christmas cycle and the Easter cycle, were fixed with their attendant seasons of preparation and lesser commemorations. It is worth noting that in the early period, Christians celebrated specific events in the life of Jesus, and not doctrinal concepts or ideas about Jesus. It was only much later, in the Middle Ages, that festivals such as Trinity Sunday, Corpus Christi, and the Assumption of the Blessed Virgin Mary (marking Mary's bodily ascension into heaven) began to appear.

The third major "cycle" within the Christian calendar is the cycle of saints' days, called the sanctoral cycle. In the early centuries, the death of a Christian martyr (from the Greek word for "witness") would be commemorated annually on the date of the death with a service at the gravesite, including a celebration of the Lord's Supper. Lists of local martyrs were circulated among the various Christian communities, and eventually the dates of the martyrs' deaths were marked throughout the church as a whole. After the period of intense persecutions, the names of other Christians were added to the list of martyred saints: those who had lived lives of conspicuous holiness, those who had denied or debased themselves for the sake of the gospel, and those whose saintliness was attested to by miracles of various kinds. As in the case of martyrs, a service of prayer and a celebration of Communion was held on the anniversary of the death of these holy men and women. Some of these commemorations remained local events only, while others were marked throughout the church. Eventually, the celebration of these memorials "took over" the Christian calendar, usurping not only the celebration of Sunday, but of other significant Christian festivals and seasons of preparation as well. The cult of the various saints was further promoted by traffic in relics, which became an important contributor to the economic well-being of both the local and the wider church.

All of the sixteenth-century reformers were committed to purging the Christian calendar, and many removed all saints' days and other festivals that were not explicitly "celebrations of the Lord." Others were willing to retain memorials of the disciples (including Paul), but the more radical reformers refused to celebrate even Christmas. John Wesley, for example, said "at present, holy days serve no practical end for the Methodist people," and removed all feast days except Advent, Christmas, Good Friday, Easter, Ascension Day, Trinity Sunday, and All Saints' Day. (He himself was particularly devoted to All Saints' Day, and mentions it each year in his journal.)

In the twentieth century, a host of non-biblical festivals began to encroach on the traditional Christian calendar, including Mother's Day, Memorial Day, Children's Sunday, Rally Day, and Worldwide Communion Sunday. Many people are beginning to question the value of such celebrations in the proclamation of the gospel, arguing that they are simply a part of a secular agenda. But at the same time, the modern period has also seen an unprecedented number of men, women, and children who have given up their lives for the sake of their Christian faith. Recent additions to the calendar of "group commemorations" for the saints and martyrs of Europe (February 3), of Africa (February 21), of the Americas (April 8), and of Australia and the Pacific (September 20) have become important to the worshiping lives of many Christian communities.

## The Christian Week

A second principal witness to the Christian understanding of time is the ordering of the week. For the people of Israel, the Sabbath was the seventh day of the week, set aside by divine command as a day of rest:

> Remember the sabbath day, and keep it holy. Six days you shall labor and do all your work. But the seventh day is a sabbath to the LORD your God; you shall not do any work—you, your son or your daughter, your male or female slave, your livestock, or the alien resident in your towns. (Exod. 20:8–10)

The Sabbath was not only a commemoration of God's rest at the conclusion of creation, but a continual reminder to the Jews of their own liberation from oppression by a just and righteous God (see Deut. 5:12–15), and so was also intended to be an event of liberation in its own right. In addition, the inclusion of slaves and non-Jews in the Sabbath prohibitions against work was a sign that the Jewish people were never to be a nation of oppressors. But for followers of Jesus Christ, the Jewish Sabbath was not replaced by the Christian Sunday.

Instead, the Sabbath-day commitment to freedom and justice had become a Christian Sabbath era, a Sabbath life of liberation and philanthropy. The principal day of prayer for Christians, then, was not the seventh day of the week, but the first day of the week, the day of the resurrection (see, for example, Acts 20:7). In the Christian religious imagination, just as God had begun the creation of the world on the first day of the week (Gen. 1:1–5), so too had God begun the new creation first day of the week with the raising of Jesus from the dead. Because of this, every Sunday is a "little Easter" for the Christian community.

The establishment of Sunday as the principal time of gathering for Christian worship seems to have happened very soon after the death of Jesus, among both Jewish and Gentile Christians alike (although Jewish Christians may have continued to worship in the temple and synagogue for some time). Occasionally, splinter groups have insisted that the Jewish Sabbath was not meant to be abrogated, and members of the Seventh-Day Adventists and Seventh-Day Baptists continue to observe Saturday as the day of worship. Strict observance of the Lord's Day as a divinely ordained day of rest (following the injunctions associated with the Jewish Sabbath) has been a feature of other Protestant denominations since the seventeenth century, and passed into civil legislation in many places.

## The Lectionary

Readings from the Scriptures had been an ordinary part of the synagogue service in the time of Jesus (see Luke 4:16–21), and Justin Martyr (ca. 100–ca. 165) says that when the Christian community met for worship "the memoirs of the apostles or the writings of the prophets are read as long as time permits."[15] Beginning in about the fourth century, however, specific biblical readings were appointed for the various days in the Christian calendar, and eventually collected in a book called a lectionary. From the fifth century onwards, three lessons plus a psalm were appointed for a given day: a reading from the Old Testament, a psalm, one from the Epistles, and a Gospel reading, although at certain times other combinations were indicated. (In the season after Easter, for example, a reading from the book of Acts ordinarily replaces the Old Testament reading, in order to follow the story of what happened to the earliest Christians immediately after Jesus' resurrection.) In most lectionaries the Gospel reading was the text that reflected the theme of the particular day in the Christian year, and an Old Testament lesson was chosen to complement it. The Epistle was not usually chosen to reflect the theme of the Gospel and Old Testament lessons for the day, and the various Epistles were read in a more or less continuous fashion (called *lectio continua*) through the year. But whatever the shape of a given lectionary, its intention was to guide the preacher and congregation through the central themes of the year, and to give the Christian community a nourishing diet of Holy Scripture.

In many Protestant churches, the lectionary was abandoned in order to give the preacher the freedom to choose a timely text on which to base the sermon. But by the end of the twentieth century the deficiencies of this practice had become apparent. In many cases only a limited range of texts were actually chosen, and the preacher could often avoid difficult or idiosyncratic texts. Recently, therefore, there has been a return to the use of the lectionary, and a number of new lectionaries have been devised by various groups. Although lectionaries running on two-year, three-year, and four-year cycles all have been developed, there has been a certain degree of ecumenical agreement on a three-year Common Lectionary. This lectionary has taken seriously the observations of some biblical scholars, who objected to tying the Old Testament reading invariably to the Gospel reading, arguing that it failed to take either text seriously. In the Common Lectionary (revised in 1992 as the Revised Common Lectionary[16]) the Old and New Testament readings remain thematically linked during much of the year, but during the season after Pentecost (that is, the summer months) the Old Testament lesson floats free. This allows for the great Old Testament sagas—the stories of Abraham, Noah, Moses, and Joshua—to be told in their entirety over the course of a number of weeks.

Some critics still argue that the lectionary unnecessarily constrains the preacher, but even those who favor the use of the lectionary generally argue against its current formulation on several grounds. Feminist scholars decry the absence of pericopes that feature strong women characters, and many concerned with interfaith dialogue have remarked on the inherent anti-Semitic bias in the choice of texts to be read. Biblical scholars have pointed out that the lectionary, by its very nature, distorts the meaning of certain texts by juxtaposing them unhelpfully with other texts, and that key verses in some biblical books are left out of the lectionary altogether. Despite these often accurate observations, most preachers agree that the use of the lectionary helps their preaching enormously by forcing them to confront texts that they might otherwise avoid, and that it also helps members of their congregations by giving them a varied and nourishing diet of Scripture on which to feed. The lectionary also gives a thematic framework around which to organize the service as a whole.

## RITUAL

Unfortunately, the word ritual has come to have a negative connotation for many Christians. An "empty ritual" is something that is devoid of real significance and sincerity, and "ritualism," the obsessive or rigid formality we sometimes experience in worship, is something which is looked upon as a perversion of true Christian worship. Both of these perceptions signal a very real danger in the use of ritual, namely that it may become detached from its roots, from its meaning, from the experience of faith, from the memories and aspirations of the community that uses it. If a community or individual engages in Christian ritual simply to try to recover a lost sense of religious feeling, or a past experience of faith, then it does indeed become "ritualism." But the word ritual is derived from the Latin word *ritus*, which simply means "the form and manner of religious worship; a religious ceremony or custom." This more neutral definition implies that all worship, from the most formal to the least formal, is actually "ritual." We worship in patterned ways and we know immediately if those patterns are being violated. For example, if we begin the service with a sermon instead of with a hymn, we know that the pattern, the ritual, is not being followed.

The most common definition of ritual describes it as an "established structure of activity or pattern of movement." This definition highlights a number of things about the nature and purpose of ritual. It indicates that ritual is a human behavior, an activity. It is an action of the human body, and the interaction of human bodies with one another. Ritual takes various forms, but it is always composed of predictable patterns of activity, which are repeated by participants at certain times and under certain circumstances. Both individuals and groups engage in ritual, and not all rituals are religious. Individuals may have rituals for going to bed or for exercising, families establish rituals for celebrating birthdays or holidays, schools may have graduation rituals, and communities and nations use rituals for commemorating significant events in their history. Ritual has the capacity to shape and to renew those who use them, to give stability to life, to order and convey meaning, and to transmit to future generations the most deeply held values and ideals. In Christian worship, the use of ritual serves all of these important functions.

All worship is a creative dialogue between form and freedom, between those elements that are stable and those that are flexible. In worship we always seek to ensure both that we "do not quench the Spirit" (1 Thess. 5:19) and that we do things "decently and in order" (1 Cor. 14:40). But the stable elements of worship not only give us a sense that things are being done "decently and in order." They become patterns we know and trust, rituals that we depend upon to give us the sense that our worship is done "rightly." Rituals also draw us into a mode of human communication in which words are unnecessary. Rituals at their best speak for themselves, and they speak volumes. If I engage in the ritual of placing a bouquet of flowers at the Vietnam Memorial, for example, how many words would it take to express fully the love and devotion and gratitude and sadness and idealism which is embodied in that single ritual act? When we break the bread at the Lord's Supper, the ritual action speaks all at once of sharing, of sacrifice, and of our continual nourishment at the hands of God; it speaks of our collective memory of Jesus' last meal and our collective memory of all the commemorations of that meal which we have shared together. All rituals are actions that point to a deeper reality, and once we feel that we have to explain a ritual, it has lost much of its power.

Several specific rituals have found their home in Christian worship during its history, some have become extinct over the centuries, and some ancient rituals have been revived in current practice. Many have also changed their meaning over the years. For example, the early Christian ritual of "the kiss of peace," given as a sign of reconciliation, love, and unity in the body of Christ, is attested to in the Epistles (Rom. 16:16; 1 Peter 5:14). It persisted as a feature of Christian worship for several centuries, shared among members of the congregation before they partook of Communion. Gradually, however, the ritual became truncated into a bow exchanged between the presiding ministers at the service. And in the churches that came into being after the Reformation, the passing of the peace largely disappeared for over four centuries. Recently, however, the more ancient practice of sharing a Christian greeting before the Lord's Supper has been restored in many denominations, and established as a meaningful part of preaching services as well. In some communities it retains its original meaning. In others, however, the peace is sometimes viewed today not as a ritual of reconciliation, a gesture which proclaims that no division should be present within the body of those baptized into unity in Christ, but rather as a secular greeting, a way of saying "hello" to those whom we have not seen since the previous week. So, even though an ancient ritual action is restored, this does not guarantee that its original meaning will be restored with it.

Many other rituals from the early church are being suggested for incorporation within contemporary services of Christian worship, such as the footwashing on Maundy Thursday, the imposition of ashes on the foreheads of believers on Ash Wednesday, the anointing with oil in healing services, and the lighting of the paschal candle at Easter. And a number of newer rituals such as the decoration of a Christmas Chrismon Tree and the lighting of the Advent wreath give shape to our current religious sensibilities. Whether old or new, rituals in the life of the church are ways of deepening and enriching our corporate life as Christians, and of giving expression to those things that bind us together. As long as care is taken to ensure that ritual does not degenerate into "ritualism," we can feel free to draw on the rich heritage of the church's ceremonial activity and to encourage the making of new rituals to express the perpetual renewal of our common life in Christ.

## ART AND ARCHITECTURE

One of the elements of Christian worship that is most frequently overlooked by those who study it is the physical environment in which it takes place. At the same time, those who know little about the Christian faith are most likely to comment on the shape of our church buildings and the ornamentation of their interiors. Over the centuries, the church's attitude toward the visual arts has gone through various phases, from lavish patronage to outright hostility. The monuments to this shifting attitude stand in every city and town in all parts of the world, since wherever Christians have gathered for worship they have built the *domus ecclesiae* ("house for the church") and furnished and decorated it in various ways. The elaborate grandeur of the medieval cathedrals and the simple beauty of a country chapel both spring from the impulse to provide a suitable setting for the worship of Almighty God.

But as beautiful as these artistic and architectural expressions of faith are, the student of Christian worship is not primarily interested in their visual effect. For students of worship the church building and its furnishings are principally viewed as the setting for the various acts of Christian common prayer. From our perspective, the baptismal font is not primarily a work of art, but a tool used in the making of new Christians; the pulpit is not a monument to the woodworking skills of our forebears, but a place for the proclamation of the Word of God. The form of these things may be important to art historians, but to liturgists it is their function that matters. The shape and arrangement of the church and its furnishings become data that can tell us a great deal about the history, theology, and practice of Christian worship.

The earliest Christians did not gather in specially constructed buildings, but in ordinary domestic dwellings, sometimes adapted for the requirements of Christian worship. A tub or pool was needed for baptism, a table for the celebration of the Lord's Supper, a space for people to gather for the hearing of the Word were all that was necessary in these earliest "house-churches." A remarkable example of an early Christian house-church survives in the Syrian desert at Dura Europos. Dated at around 232 and discovered and excavated in the early 1920s, this converted house stood in a row of buildings alongside a Jewish synagogue and a pagan temple. Space for the congregation to gather in the house-church at Dura Europos was made by removing a partition and turning two ordinary rooms into one. In this large room there is a raised platform, which scholars say was the location of the altar-table, and in a third room a baptismal pool was built into a side wall. Around the pool there are wall paintings depicting Christ the Good Shepherd carrying a lost sheep across his shoulders.

During the third century Christian worship gradually moved out of domestic settings and into purpose-built edifices. The earliest examples of these were adaptations of secular buildings, and this trend was heightened after Christianity became tolerated within the Roman Empire in the early-fourth century. The place for ordinary legal and financial transactions was a building called a "basilica," from the Greek word *basileus* meaning "king" or "emperor;" the basilica was the seat of imperial authority. Most often the basilica was a rectangular building which one entered through a narrow narthex or porch. The interior consisted of a central gathering space, called a nave, and a narrow aisle ran along each side. At one end was the apse, a semicircular niche within which was placed a chair for the person presiding over the proceedings. The apse was usually in the east end of the building, and a table or bench was placed in front of it. In the center of the nave was the ambo from which documents were read and proclamations made.

Christians made use of all of these features of the secular basilica. The people gathered in the nave and the presiding ministers for the service sat in chairs in the apse. Reading and preaching were done from the ambo, and the table was used in the celebration of the Lord's Supper. Even the names of the various parts of the building have remained in use as technical descriptions of the various elements of church architecture, and the "liturgical east end" of any church building is always the end in which the altar-table sits, no matter what actual geographical direction the building faces.

As Christianity came to dominate the social and political landscape of Europe, so too did church buildings become more imposing features on the physical landscape. Christian nobles built churches and endowed their upkeep; the decoration and enhancement of places of worship was considered a meritorious act, a holy endeavor. It is often said that the pictorial representations of biblical scenes in stained glass and wall paintings in medieval churches served as a form of religious education for a largely illiterate population. But although some learning surely took place in this way, there was a more important motivation for the decoration of the interiors of churches. It was generally believed that when one looked at something, the image of that thing penetrated the eye and imprinted itself on the soul, thereby transforming the soul for better or for worse. If a person gazed upon an ugly or impious object, then the soul would be damaged. On the other hand, if a person fixed attention on a beautiful or holy object, the soul would be nourished. These dual motivations, then, merit for the patron and soul-building for the worshiper, led to the creation of a visual environment for worship which increased in its elaborateness throughout the Middle Ages. Even in small, rural churches wall painting and colored glass were seen to be necessary decorative requirements. Often these were augmented by altarware made of precious metals, intricately embroidered liturgical vestments, books bound in fine leather and encrusted with gems, and images carved of wood and stone. The message sent by the environment for worship in this period was that seeing was much more important to the experience of Christian worship than hearing. Most of the words of the service would, in any case, have been spoken softly by the presiding minister in an antiquated language; preaching was irregular, and in ordinary services no music was sung. Until the fourteenth century there were no pews in churches, and so the congregation could move to whichever location in the church the liturgical action was taking place.

With the Reformation, however, this visual emphasis changed with changes in worship, and hearing would become the dominant factor in the design of an appropriate environment for public prayer. In order for the congregation to hear the sermon, the reading of Scripture, the hymns, and the prayers, they had to be gathered near the source of the sound. And since much of the sound in a reformed service of Christian worship emanated from the front (that is, from the pulpit, the prayer desk, the altar-table), as many people as possible had to be seated as close to the front as possible. Galleries were added to the interiors of many buildings, and sounding boards were erected over the pulpits in order to direct the sound into the congregational space. With this principle in mind, John Wesley recommended an eight-sided building as the shape most conducive to hearing, and under his influence Methodists built a number of octagonal chapels.

In the new American colonies, those who had in their homelands been forced under persecution to worship in private houses and other unobtrusive buildings now created a form of church architecture which looked very much like an enlarged domestic dwelling. But now, instead of being hidden away in a back street, the building for worship formed the centerpiece of the new town plan. The New England meetinghouse of the seventeenth century was simple and unadorned, filled with light and dominated on the long side by a central pulpit surrounded by box pews for the congregation, attesting to the centrality of preaching. But changes were inevitable, and the rebuilding of many of the London churches by Christopher Wren after the disastrous fire of 1666 gave the increasingly confident American Christians a new and more sophisticated form of church architecture. Soon the exterior was dominated by the classic church spire, and the interior was reoriented so that the pulpit became the focus of the short side of the rectangular building, with pews either side of a long central aisle. This continues to this day to be the quintessential "American church."

As time passed, changing tastes in architecture not only affected the way church buildings looked on the outside but also the way they worked on the inside. In the nineteenth century, the revival of styles of architecture from the past, particularly imitations of classical Greek and medieval Gothic buildings, gave shape to the experience of Christian worship. Each of these styles began as attempts to provide suitable expressions of a particular understanding of Christian worship: the lightness and simplicity of classical design for those who saw worship as a rational and well-ordered form of public service, and the lofty mystery of Gothic for those who viewed worship as a transcendent experience of divine-human encounter. In all periods of Christian history, however, many congregations have built churches in a particular architectural style simply because they liked the way it looked, rather than because it suited their theology and practice of worship.

It sometimes happens that a building designed for one form of Christian worship becomes unsuitable when worship undergoes significant changes. The renovation of medieval church buildings to accommodate an emphasis on the spoken word in the sixteenth and seventeenth centuries, and the more recent adaptation of neo-Gothic buildings to accommodate contemporary, more participatory, forms of worship are evidence of the persistent priority of worship in setting the church's architectural agenda. Just in the past half-century, important changes in Communion practice, in baptismal theology, in the role of music, and in our understanding of the nature and mission of the Christian community have shaped and reshaped the setting in which Christian worship takes place.

Often Christians have thought of their church buildings as "sacred space," and it is important that we give some attention to this concept. What does it mean to call a particular place a sacred space? Most of us recognize that the holiness of a particular place is not self-evident, that it does not rest on its beauty or majesty, on a quality of the light or on some memory of a religious experience that took place in it. Both peaceful places and busy places can become special to those who use them, both makeshift storefront churches and cathedral-like edifices can be places of encounter with the Living God. If the idea of a particular church building being a sacred space means anything, it means that a faithful Christian people who are striving to live according to the gospel, who gather there to hear the word of God and to learn what it means to act upon it, and who seek a ministry of reconciliation have drawn their building into that ministry in the name of Jesus Christ. This means that each Christian community bears a real responsibility for the sacredness of its space, and that each Christian community needs to be involved in the task of handing on the sacred use of whatever space it inhabits to future generations of Christians.

# 3

# The Nourishment of the
# Christian Life 1

In many and various ways, worship sustains and nourishes the Christian life. It builds up faith, creates the bonds of community, encourages the clarification of values, and forms an arena for the creation of meaning and the growth of understanding. Many of the worship structures we will discuss in the following two chapters are not specific to Christianity, however. Various religious traditions mark the initiation of new members, hold regular communal meals, pray daily, designate persons for diverse forms of service by acts of worship, and celebrate the restoration to full fellowship of those who have returned to the prescribed manner of life and belief after a period of waywardness. But in this section we will discuss the particular ways in which Christianity has shaped those kinds of events and the ways in which those events, in turn, have shaped the experience of Christian believers. Taken together, Christian initiation, the Lord's Supper, daily prayer, penance (also called reconciliation), ordination to the various public, professional ministries, and the ordinary Sunday Service all serve to strengthen and feed the minds, hearts, and souls of the Christian people as they strive to attain to the "full stature of Christ."

## CHRISTIAN INITIATION

Throughout the centuries, the experience of the church has been that "Christians are made and not born." Whether we have been nurtured within a Christian family from infancy or have encountered the Christian faith only later as adults, various forms of worship mark our incorporation into the Christian community and celebrate our relationship with the crucified and risen Christ.

The rites of Christian initiation historically have included a number of different types of activities: washing with water, anointing with oil, the imposition of hands on the head of the candidate, forms of instruction, affirmations of faith, and naming ceremonies. In addition, to study Christian initiation is to study a rich tapestry of theological interpretations, ceremonial elaborations, political and social influences, and biblical images. At every stage of its history, the interplay of these elements has shaped the experience of the church as it celebrates and affirms its own identity in baptism.

From the beginning, Christian communities seem to have taken it for granted that baptism was the way that new Christians were marked out and incorporated into the body of Christ. In the book of Acts, for example, there are no debates about the necessity for baptism, no questions raised about whether baptism was a proper mode for initiating new believers, and no theological discussions about the meaning of the rite. Most of these early references to baptism are simple and straightforward: in Acts 8 the Ethiopian eunuch asks Philip, "What is to prevent me from being baptized?" The passage goes on to say that Philip "commanded the chariot to stop, and both of them, Philip and the eunuch, went down into the water, and Philip baptized him" (v. 38).

But within the simple act of baptism, even in this early period of Christian history, is contained a wealth of theological meaning and symbolic interpretation. Many of the patterns of interpretation of Christian initiation are not native to Christianity, however, but can be traced to forms of religious practice found in pre-Christian Judaism. Indeed, there are at least four Jewish antecedents that contributed to the later Christian understanding of initiation.

The first is circumcision, the ritual removal of the male foreskin, normally performed on the eighth day after birth (Gen. 17:12; Lev. 12:3). Although ritual circumcision was not unique to Judaism, for Jews it was the principal outward sign of a man's inclusion in the covenant community, the sign that God accepted him as a member of the people of Israel.[1] It was performed not only on the children of Jewish parents, but also on converts, slaves, and their children. In order for a circumcision to be valid at least one drop of blood had to be shed, since it was the shedding of blood that served as a sign of the covenant relationship. The blood shed at circumcision was directly linked to the blood shed in the temple sacrifices, the blood sprinkled on the altar for the purification of the covenant community, and to the blood of the Passover lamb smeared on the doorposts on the night of the exodus so that God's vengeance would pass over the houses of the Jews (Exod. 12:13). Like the blood of sacrifice, the blood of circumcision was to remind God of the covenant promises to save and to redeem. For the people of Israel, salvation was a radically communitarian enterprise. One could not be saved by oneself; one was saved only through inclusion in a community that is already being saved by God. Circumcision, then, had social and economic as well as spiritual consequences. The uncircumcised could not join in the Passover meal, own property, nor participate in the pilgrimage feasts. One of the earliest Christian theological debates concerned whether circumcision was a necessary prerequisite for Christian baptism. In Acts 11, Peter is confronted by the Judaean Christians who demand to know why he has been eating with and baptizing the uncircumcised Gentiles. Having had a vision of the abolition of "clean" and "unclean" as fixed religious categories, Peter argues that the Holy Spirit is available to all persons equally, regardless of their previous religious affiliation.

The second Jewish antecedent of Christian initiation was the ritual washings which punctuated the life of the pious Jew. One could become ritually impure in a host of different ways. Touching a dead body, coming into contact with shed blood, tombs, diseased persons, or "unclean animals" would all result in ritual impurity. Some people, priests for example, could never allow themselves to be defiled. (This is the force behind the story of the Good Samaritan, which is much more about ritual purity than about comparative niceness.) Others could be defiled, although they were not anxious to do so since it made them temporarily unfit for a holy relationship with God and the community. They could repair the situation, however, by means of a ritual bath. This type of washing was for women, men, and children alike; women had to do this routinely because they were rendered ritually unclean by their menstrual period. Objects, too, could become defiled by contact with blood, and there is some historical evidence of ritual washings of battle dress and weapons. The sense of the power of washing in water as a sign of cleansing and purity is not unique to Judaism, but is found in many religious traditions in the ancient Near East, and images of Christians being made clean from the stain of sin are abundant in the later New Testament documents.

The third antecedent of Christian initiation is the washing in water of converts to Judaism, called proselyte baptism. Unlike circumcision and ritual washing, baptism was a practice that came rather late to Judaism, and may have begun as the first ritual bath for purity before the new convert offered sacrifice in the temple. As a separate rite it was probably connected with the expansion of Judaism outside the borders of Israel. There were several components to the rite of proselyte baptism: (1) instruction in Jewish history and in the Torah for all converts; (2) circumcision for males; and (3) for men, women, and children alike the *tebillah*, or water bath. In some places, especially in hellenized Judaism, baptism rivaled circumcision in importance as the central act by which Gentile converts adhered to their new faith. Part of the reason for this was that circumcision was not an immediately accessible or understandable symbol, while the meaning of washing as a sign of the inauguration of a new state of being was more transparent. In addition, it was a form of initiation in which both men and women alike could participate, and so something of a "baptist movement" had arisen in Judaism in the first century. The ideal for proselyte baptism was probably total submersion in cold, running water. Because water had to come into contact with the whole body, nakedness was required on the part of the convert. During this period, there was a growing theological interpretation of the initiation of converts to Judaism as "new birth." "One who separates himself from uncircumcision," the early rabbis said, "is like one who separates himself from the grave." For the pious Jew, the waters of baptism were likened to the waters of Noah's flood, a sign of rebirth into new relationship with God.

Finally, the fourth precursor to Christian initiation was the activity of John the Baptizer. Although it may have been a part of this more general baptist movement, there were several distinctive features of John's baptism that are important for the future of Christian initiation. John's baptism was not a way of making Jews out of Gentiles, nor was it a ritual bath for the repair of physical defilement. It was rather a cleansing from sin as a preparation for the coming of the Messiah, and it was bound up with preaching of the kingdom and repentance. This was a one-time event for Jews waiting expectantly for God's salvation, not for new converts or outsiders. When Jesus submitted to the baptism of John, various other images come into play: the anointing with the Holy Spirit, the expectation of the messianic era transformed into its fulfillment as present messianic activity, and the relationship of baptism to betrayal, suffering, and death. (In Mark 10:38, Jesus asks James and John "Are you able to drink the cup that I drink, or be baptized with the baptism that I am baptized with?")

All of these ritual activities taken together begin to indicate a shape to a theology of initiation within Judaism that involves:

(a) inclusion in the covenant community
(b) new birth metaphors
(c) forgiveness of sin
(d) entry into the Messianic era
(e) association with sacrificial blood
(f) repentance

We can see the ways in which these various motifs work themselves out in the theology and practice of Christian initiation in the New Testament period. So, for example, washing images are embedded in the Greek word *baptizein* itself, which originally had a root meaning "to plunge into water." (In the New Testament texts it has already taken on the technical meaning "baptism.") For the earliest Christians, baptism was a sign of inclusion into the new covenant that God had established in Jesus Christ, and at the end of the first century Clement of Rome could speak of Christian baptism quite confidently and without much explanation as circumcision. Just as circumcision incorporated the Jew into the sacrifice of the Passover lamb, Christian baptism engrafts believers into the sacrifice of Christ. Paul implies this relationship when he says to the Christians at Rome, "Do you not know that all of us who have been baptized into Christ Jesus were baptized into his death? Therefore we have been buried with him by baptism into death . . ." (Rom. 6:3–4).

If in baptism Christians are joined with Christ in his sacrificial death, they are also joined with Christ in being raised, reborn to new life. "For if we have been united with him in a death like his, we shall certainly be united with him in a resurrection like his" (Rom. 6:5). In later centuries the newly baptized were clothed in a white garment as a sign of being clothed in Christian forgiveness, of "clothing yourself in Christ" as Galatians 3:27 says. It was clear that the baptismal *metanoia*, the turning toward Christ of the whole heart, mind, and soul, was a turning toward a life of reconciliation with God and with others. And since sin was seen as the primary thing that kept reconciliation from being complete, then the washing away of sin in baptism was a necessary component. To say that after baptism the Christian believer is a "new creature" has tended to mean that in baptism sins are washed away and the believer is reborn into a life of purity and holy joy. This has been the subject of much theological debate in the church, since it raises the question of why there is any post-baptismal sin at all, and whether the church should allow the opportunity for repentance in such cases. (Indeed, the writer of Hebrews seems to be caught up in just such a controversy, taking something of a hard line in the matter in Heb. 6:1–8.)

Because baptism incorporated the believer into Christ, it also incorporated the believer into Christ's body on earth, the church. "For in the one Spirit we were all baptized into one body," Paul tells the Corinthian church (1 Cor. 12:13). This is why it became traditional to place the baptismal font near the door of the church building, in order to signify that we enter the community of faith through the waters of baptism. In addition, baptism was understood to empower Christians for their participation in the mission and ministry of the whole church. Because of this it has been spoken of as the "ordination rite of the laity."

Inasmuch as baptism engrafts the Christian into the body of Christ, within which the Spirit is operative, it is also understood in the New Testament as the rite by which Christians are given a share in that same Spirit. Christians could not be a part of the Spirit-filled community without being filled with the Spirit themselves. The question of the relationship between baptism and the gift of the Holy Spirit has resulted in a debate that has colored the theology and practice of Christian initiation to the present day. Many of the New Testament accounts of baptism follow the sequence of events found in Acts 19:5–7: "On hearing this [news about the deficiencies in John's baptism] they were baptized in the name of the Lord Jesus. When Paul had laid hands on them, the Holy Spirit came upon them, and they spoke in tongues and prophesied . . ." The candidate was baptized, and the Holy Spirit was given when hands were laid on them. As a testimony to the presence of the Spirit, the gifts of the Spirit (such as speaking in tongues and prophesy) were often displayed. But at other times, the Spirit arrived before baptism. In Acts 10:44–48, for example, Peter is preaching to a group of Gentiles and as he was preaching the Holy Spirit came upon them. "'Can anyone withhold the water for baptizing these people who have received the Holy Spirit just as we have?'" he asks. "So he ordered them to be baptized in the name of Jesus Christ." In still other passages, the Holy Spirit is given sometime after water baptism and the laying-on-of-hands.[2] In any case, what seems clear is that the three events taken together— proclamation of the crucified and risen Christ, water baptism, and the outpouring of the Holy Spirit signified by the laying-on-of-hands—constitute full initiation into the community of faith which is the church.

The second question that arises out of the New Testament evidence about baptism is who, precisely, is being baptized? Is it adults or is it children? To begin with, it must be recognized that the New Testament documents were written within a missionary situation, and because of this we find much more information about such experiences as conversion and full participation in the mission of the Christian community than about the ordinary lives of believers (including preaching and the Lord's Supper). This tends to distort the evidence about the kinds of candidates being baptized in the earliest period of the church. Obviously in a missionary situation the stories of adult converts, those who have made a mature and responsible decision for Christ, were very effective. Those who had a "faith story" to tell were more likely to be given attention in the documents than those (such as babies) who were merely carried into the faith along with their Christian families. We have no direct evidence, therefore, that any persons other than adults were baptized in the New Testament period.

But many people have argued that babies were indeed being baptized at the time. Part of their argument hinges on the interpretation of the Greek word *oikos*, which is usually translated "household" or "family." There are several New Testament passages that say that people were baptized "with their entire household/family," the most significant of which is the story of the Philippian jailer in Acts 16:25–34. We know from non-Christian sources that the "household" was a fairly broad social unit, centering on the head of the family and the nearest relatives, but also including domestic servants, slaves, concubines, and their children. The understanding of children having an independent social status is a fairly recent development in the history of the family, and would not have been a part of the thinking of the New Testament writers.

A second argument in favor of infant baptism in the New Testament period rests on the thematic association between baptism and circumcision. It was a part of the mindset of Judaism that the children of believing parents were automatically drawn into the covenant with them by circumcision. At the same time, to the extent that Christian baptism was seen as the spiritual equivalent of Jewish proselyte baptism, then again children would have been appropriate subjects, baptized as a part of the household of the convert. The believing community was understood as the principal arena within which a person's active faith was nurtured after his or her circumcision or baptism as a baby. However, we do not find any explicit description of the baptism of small children until the early part of the third century (although in about the year 200 Tertullian argues against the practice of infant baptism, which is a fair indication that it is being practiced). Certainly through the first five centuries of the church's life, the baptism of believers upon a mature profession of faith is the norm, both the theological and the practical norm. In other words, while children may have been baptized in this period along with their believing parents, this was neither a source of theological reflection, nor of practical necessity.

The third significant question that arises out of the New Testament evidence about baptism concerns what the rite of Christian initiation might actually have consisted of. Can we determine anything about what was said or done? Although some accounts of baptism in the early New Testament documents simply report that "so-and-so was baptized" (as in the case of Paul himself, Acts 9:18), in others we are told that baptism is "in the name of the Lord," or "the Lord Jesus" (Acts 8:16; 19:5), or "in the name of Jesus Christ" (Acts 10:48). But of course, it is uncertain whether these words were actually said at the time of water baptism. In the Gospels we have evidence of the use of a trinitarian formula for baptism, and the followers of Jesus are exhorted to "make disciples of all nations, baptizing them in the name of the Father and of the Son and of the Holy Spirit" (Matt. 28:19). But again, whether these words were actually said as people were being baptized is uncertain.

There has been some suggestion that the kind of short creedal statements found in, for example, Romans 10:9 ("if you confess with your lips that Jesus is Lord . . . you will be saved"[3]) may have been a part of the rite of baptism, and these kind of formulas have been linked to the beginnings of a baptismal creed. There is also some agreement that 1 Peter may have begun its life as a baptismal sermon. It addresses its audience as those "born anew, not of perishable but of imperishable seed, through the living and enduring word of God" (1:23), and goes on to refer to them as "newborn infants" (2:2), exhorting them to behave "like obedient children" (1:14). The story of the baptism of the Ethiopian eunuch in Acts 8 adds further information, indicating that in at least some cases new converts were baptized in a considerable quantity of water ("Philip and the eunuch went down into [*eis* in Greek] the water") and that pre-baptismal instruction was included.

The first piece of extra-biblical evidence we have for baptism is from a document called *The Teaching of the Twelve Apostles* which is often referred to by the Greek word for "teaching": *didache*.[4] The *Didache* is one of a class of documents called the "Early Church Orders" which were used as guidebooks for regulating life in the earliest Christian communities. This particular church order was probably written in Syria about the year 90. It seems to have been intended for a community of Jewish converts to Christianity and it has quite a lot to say about Christian initiation. New converts are given instruction about the difference between the "Two Ways": the way of life and the way of death. Both the candidate and the one who was to administer baptism are instructed to fast along with "any others who are able," and at baptism candidates are to be washed in cold, running water, which the document calls "living water." If "living water" is unavailable, any other water will suffice, but it is preferable that it be cold and plentiful. Having been baptized in the name of the Father, the Son, and the Holy Spirit, the new Christians begin to live the rather ascetic life of the community, including fasting, prayer, and regular participation in the Lord's Supper. There is no evidence about whether candidates were adults or children, but the emphasis in the document on the ethical requirements of faith in Jesus Christ seems to indicate that adult baptism is the norm.

About fifty years later, Justin Martyr bears witness to a more highly developed theology of baptism, as well as a more highly developed baptismal ritual. In his *First Apology*,[5] Justin described for a non-Christian audience the structure and meaning of the rites of Christian initiation as he knew them in hellenized Palestine. According to Justin, those wishing to become Christians are taught to pray and to fast "for the forgiveness of their sins." Then they are led to a place where there is water and "are reborn after the manner by which we were also reborn" by being washed in the water in the name of the Trinity. After this, the initiates are brought into the place where the community is assembled and they make their prayers in common for the first time. This is followed by the sharing of a kiss of peace and the Lord's Supper.

At the turn of the third century, Tertullian tells about baptism as it was practiced in Rome and North Africa. There was a rigorous discipline for those who wished to be baptized, including prayers, fasts, and vigils, and "the bending of the knee." The most solemn occasion for baptism was the Great Vigil on the eve of Easter, but Pentecost was also deemed to be appropriate. The bishop normally presided over the rite (although with the bishop's permission elders, deacons, or laypersons could baptize). Just before baptism, candidates made a formal renunciation of "the devil, his pomps, and his angels," and were then interrogated about their faith in Christ and immersed three times in water. When they arose from the water they were anointed "with the blessed unction such as Moses used to anoint Aaron to the holy priesthood" (again, an indication that baptism was regarded as an ordination to the ministry of the laity), and had hands laid on them in blessing "inviting the Holy Spirit." The newly baptized were given a mixture of milk and honey to drink, probably in place of the eucharistic bread and wine, as a symbol of their entry into the new promised land.

For Tertullian, everything that happened in the rites of baptism had a counterpart in the spiritual realm, and he makes extensive use of Old Testament imagery to help him explain the meaning of baptism.

> [T]he flesh is washed so that the soul may be made spotless; the flesh is anointed so that the soul may be consecrated; the flesh is signed [with the cross] so that the soul may also be protected; the flesh is overshadowed by the imposition of hands so that the soul may also be illuminated by the Spirit; the flesh is fed on the body and blood of Christ so that the soul as well may be made full of God.[6]

A preparation of fasting and prayer, profession of faith, renunciations of the devil, water baptism by submersion in the name of the Trinity, anointing with oil and the imposition of hands, and inclusion in the celebration of the Lord's Supper: all of these together make up the full initiation into the Christian community as Tertullian would have known it at the turn of the third century.

A more fully developed description of Christian initiation is found in another of the Early Church Orders, a document first composed in or around Rome in about the year 215. It is given the title *The Apostolic Tradition* and is attributed by many scholars to an elder of the Roman church named Hippolytus.[7] Since its discovery in the late-nineteenth century, it has been an important document for students of Christian worship, since it offers not only descriptions of what is done, but also indicates the proper words to be said for certain occasions. *The Apostolic Tradition* gives instruction to a Christian community about the selection and ordination of ministers (as well as the appointment of confessors, widows, readers, and sub-deacons), about teaching and initiation, about the celebration of the Lord's Supper, and various instructions for the proper conduct of the Christian life. Although some studies have suggested that the rites described in *The Apostolic Tradition* may never have been actually used by a Christian community, it does provide the earliest full account of the process of Christian initiation as some might have experienced it in the early third century.

The overwhelming impression given by this document is that Christian initiation was not an isolated event in the life of an individual, but rather a way of conversion that began with the decision of the candidate, and moved through various stages of faith commitment. At every stage the candidate was supported by the prayers and admonitions of the congregation, and appropriate rituals signified the transition from one stage to the next. Once the candidates became full members of the community through baptism, they played a crucial role in the progress of conversion-initiation of others, so the whole community of faith was understood as the arena within which the process of the making of Christians took place.

What else does *The Apostolic Tradition* tell us about Christian initiation during this early period? The author begins his discussion by listing those trades and professions which would disqualify an inquirer from consideration for baptism.[8] Sponsors would be asked to vouch for the sincerity of the candidates and their mode of living, and if these were found to be satisfactory, men and women (and their dependents) were accepted as "hearers of the Word," and enrolled in the catechumenate (from the Greek word *catechumenoi* meaning "those who are instructed") as candidates for baptism. There followed a period of instruction and discipline that normally lasted for three years. During this period the candidates attended the first part of the service of Sunday worship for the reading of the Scriptures and preaching, but were removed from the congregation just before the intercessory prayers and the celebration of the Lord's Supper. They received teaching in Christian doctrine (*catechesis*), in prayer and, since purity of intention was essential to the process, they were exercised of evil spirits from time to time.

The ordinary time for baptisms was at the vigil service on Easter eve, which lasted from about 2:00 a.m. to sunrise on Easter Day. It seemed right and proper to celebrate the new birth of individual believers in baptism as an integral part of the celebration of the resurrection. Once a candidate had been examined and was declared to be ready for baptism in a given year, instruction was intensified and his or her life was examined. During the final week the candidates were exorcised daily by their teachers. On the Thursday before Easter, the candidates bathed themselves, on Friday they abstained from food, and on Saturday they met with the bishop for a final exorcism and special prayers. The rest of Saturday night was spent in prayer until 2:00 a.m., when they were brought to the place apart from the congregation where the baptism was to be performed. Those to be baptized took off their clothes and were anointed with oil, after which the presbyter baptized them: first the children, then the men, and finally the women.

Each candidate was submerged in the water three times. At each submersion, the candidate was asked a question: "Do you believe in the Father?" for the first submersion; "Do you believe in the Son?" for the second; and "Do you believe in the Holy Spirit?" for the third, the answer to each being, "I believe." The candidates came out of the water, were anointed with oil, dressed, and led back to the congregation, which was praying for them with the bishop in the main worship space. The bishop laid hands on the newly baptized, anointed them with oil, and gave them the kiss of peace. Then, for the first time since they began their instruction, the candidates shared a kiss of peace with the congregation and brought gifts of bread and wine to the altar for use in the Lord's Supper. During the Communion, they were given milk and honey, both as a sign of entry into the new promised land and as the proper food of infants in the faith.

A number of things are of interest here to students of Christian initiation. During the period in which *The Apostolic Tradition* was composed there was some threat of persecution against Christians, although it was always localized and sporadic. Even though the "hearers of the word" were not full participants in the Christian life and faith during the period of instruction before baptism, they were putting themselves in a certain amount of danger simply by enrolling as a candidate for baptism. Lists of candidates were sometimes offered to persecutors in exchange for a promise that the larger community would be spared from harm. Also, unless the process for the selection of candidates was quite rigorous, the entire congregation could be placed in jeopardy. Therefore sponsors had an important role in vouching for the candidate's good intentions.

Although the normative candidate for baptism was still an adult in this period, for the first time in this document we have direct evidence that children ("those unable to answer for themselves") were also being baptized along with their parents. The long period of instruction could be shortened if the candidate were particularly keen, and sponsors continued to be a part of the process of the candidate's faith development. The time of preparation for baptism was punctuated by periodic anointings with various kinds of oil and layings-on-of-hands for strength, power, and endurance, and exorcisms for the cleansing from evil. The Great Vigil of Easter, the high point of the whole Christian year, was replete with baptismal imagery and associations: putting off the old Adam and putting on Christ, being raised from death to life in baptism, released from the slavery of sin and drawn forward into the promised land of God's kingdom. It is also important to recognize that although Christian initiation in this early period consisted of a number of identifiable component parts, and the various rites and processes were staged over quite a long period of time, it is essentially a unity.

A great deal of attention could be devoted here to the shifts in initiation practice that took place during the third and fourth centuries. Changes in the number and type of anointings, changes in the form of renunciations of the devil and adhesions to Christ, and in the kinds of images used to convey the richness of baptismal meaning all form part of the history of Christian initiation. But throughout this early period, we see over and over the fundamental pattern consisting of instruction, water bath, anointing with oil accompanied by the laying-on-of-hands, and celebration of the Lord's Supper as the core of Christian initiation. Beginning in the fourth century, however, this unified core began to disintegrate, as the individual elements were separated, realigned, and reinterpreted. One of the chief factors in this disruption, although not the only factor, was the gradual Christianization of society as a whole, and more particularly the significant changes in the relationship between church and state in the Roman Empire which took place in the early fourth century.

The impact of Constantine the Great (ca. 288–337) on Christianity is complex and subtle. By many he is seen as the great Christian emperor, who put an end to the wickedness of persecution and aided (or perhaps in some cases compelled) the spread of the Christian faith to all parts of the Roman Empire. Others contend that had it not been for Constantine, the church might have maintained the vigor and purity of its early missionary vision, and would have avoided taking the first steps along the road to the decay and spiritual decline of the Middle Ages. As with most things of this kind, the truth probably lies somewhere in between. Constantine was, in one sense, as much a symptom of the increasing Christianization of society as a cause of it. In between outbreaks of persecution, Christians had enjoyed a certain measure of public support in the second and third centuries, and by the end of the third century influential people, well placed in positions of power in the imperial system, had been adhering to Christianity in large numbers. Christian communities had begun to gather for worship in public places rather than behind closed doors in private houses and had become generally quite visible.[9] So when Constantine embraced Christianity in about the year 312, and when in the later fourth century the Emperor Theodosius (emperor from 379–395) outlawed paganism and made Christianity the official religion of the empire, it was as much a part of a strategy for delaying the decline of Roman civilization and discouraging social disintegration as it was a faith statement.

The formal alliance between church and society had important consequences for worship, for church administration (the diocese, for example, is a Roman administrative term), and for ritual, as higher clergy took on the symbols and honorific ceremonies previously reserved for government officials. But it had particularly serious consequences for Christian initiation. Gradually, being a Christian became not only a respectable religious option but a positive social advantage, and there began to be an increasing demand for initiation. This put a certain amount of pressure on the rites themselves. As people began to seek to become Christians as a part of a pattern of social or political advancement, the rites by which they adhered to the faith became more elaborate and awe-inspiring. It has been suggested that by making the rites of adherence to the Christian faith a particularly dramatic moment in the lives of converts, people would be drawn more fully into the new Christian life: the voice of the rites of Christian initiation was attempting to speak more loudly than the voice of society at large.

The apex of this trend was reached in the late-fourth century, with what have been described as the "spine-chilling rites" of Christian initiation. These rites retain the basic shape which we saw above—teaching, water bath, laying-on-of-hands by the bishop, Communion—but at each stage the ceremonies are emotionally- and visually-charged events, filled with mystery, secrecy, and colored by graphic descriptions of the works of the devil and the joys of heaven. They were powerful, multisensory experiences designed to push candidates to the brink of emotional endurance.

Here we begin to see the practice of the *disciplina arcanae* (the "arcane" or "concealed" disciplines), in which certain key elements of the faith are withheld from the candidates until the day of baptism itself, and all kinds of precautions are taken to preserve the liturgy in secrecy. So the creed, the Lord's Prayer, the words said over the bread and wine at the Lord's Supper, the ceremonies of baptism itself were all only witnessed for the first time by candidates on the day of their baptism. (It is this sort of complex and ritually elaborate rite of initiation that is described in the works of Ambrose of Milan [ca. 339–397], Theodore of Mopsuestia [ca. 350–428], and Cyril of Jerusalem [ca. 315–386].) In the days following baptism (that is, in the week after Easter), during which time the newly-baptized wore white garments as a sign of their rebirth, the rites and ceremonies which they had experienced were explained to them in a series of sermons by the bishop. There are several collections of these early post-baptismal sermons extant, from bishops of the stature of John Chrysostom, and as a genre they are called the *mystagogical catecheses*, the "instructions in the mysteries."

There was another significant change in Christian initiation that occurred during the late fourth and fifth centuries. Because of the rigor of pre-baptismal preparation, the disbarring of candidates from certain types of professions, and the unwillingness of the Christian community to forgive post-baptismal sin, many people postponed baptism until late adulthood. (We see this when we look at the lives of such people as Ambrose, Augustine, and Chrysostom who, although they were the children of believing parents, were not baptized as infants, but only later in life.) But because, as we have seen, being Christian was of considerable social advantage during this period, there was felt the need of some sort of rite which would connect a person to the Christian faith and still leave room for maneuver. In response to this need, a set of elaborate ceremonies for enrolling a person as a candidate for baptism were developed, and these began to be seen not as the first step in preparation for baptism, but rather as entry into second-class membership in the Christian community. This rite of enrollment included marking the forehead of the candidate with the sign of the cross, the placing of salt on the tongue (signifying both the preservation from evil and the seasoning of wisdom), the laying-on-of-hands, and exorcism.

With this we see the first rupture in the integrity of the rite of Christian initiation: the separation of instruction in the faith from water baptism by so many years that they no longer bore any relation to one another. This disintegration was accelerated by the rise of Latin theology in the fifth century, and is particularly associated with the theology of Augustine. Unfortunately in the case of baptism, much of the difficulty is caused by a basic misunderstanding of Augustine's theological intentions in the matter. In much of his theological work, Augustine took Christian worship as a starting point, saying if Christians pray in this or that particular way, what does it say about what they believe? At a rather decisive point in his career, Augustine reflected upon the rites of Christian initiation and asked, "Why does the church baptize infants?" If baptism is related to the forgiveness of sin, what sort of sin is forgiven in the baptism of small children? His answer was that there was some human sin that was not the direct result of a willful violation of a known moral law, but was rather inherent in the human condition, the "sin of Adam" or "original sin," and that baptizing infants bore witness to the cleansing from this type of sin in the waters of baptism.

Those who followed Augustine, however, reversed his conclusion and proposition. Where Augustine had said, "Since we baptize infants, there must be some sort of involuntary or original sin," his successors said, "Since there is involuntary or original sin, we must baptize infants." And quite quickly the fear of dying unbaptized and thus being condemned to eternal perdition because of original sin led to the baptism of babies as soon as possible (*quam primam*) as the normal practice.

It is difficult to overestimate the magnitude of this change. Even though the church had baptized babies, perhaps from New Testament times, the baptism of infants was never the theological or ritual norm for Christian initiation. Each component part of the service itself presupposed a relationship with Jesus Christ that could be articulated in a mature and reasoned way, and baptismal theology up to the fifth century was based on a self-conscious adherence to Christianity as a system of belief and behavior. "There was little if any theological or ritual importance attached to the baptism of infants, and nothing in any of the rites of baptism made allowance for the special needs of children."

When the baptism of infants became the church's normal practice, however, important consequences followed. The most important of these was the virtual disappearance of the catechumenate, the period of preparation and teaching before baptism, which no longer served any purpose in the initiation of infants. At about this time the church in the West was becoming not only an urban, but a suburban and rural institution, and the pattern of organization which pertained in the cities had to be adapted. Where in the past one local church had been served by one bishop as the head of the community, now his support staff, the elders (presbyters), began to be sent out to look after small churches in the countryside, while the bishops remained in the city.

Quite early on, as we have seen, presbyters had been the ministers of baptism, and they continued to do so in their new charges. But anointing with oil and imposition of hands on the newly baptized were still reserved as a liturgical ministry of the bishop. The unity of these actions could be maintained as long as the bishop and presbyter were in the same place: the presbyter baptized with water and led the candidates into the assembly where the bishop immediately laid hands on them, anointed them with oil, and invited them to share in the Lord's Supper. But a geographical separation between presbyter and bishop resulted in a separation in time between a presbyter's ministry of water baptism and the bishop's ministry of imposition of hands, anointing, and Communion. Since infants were now the principal candidates for baptism, it might be months or even years before the child was brought to the bishop for the second part of the ceremony. The result was a reversal in the ancient sequence of water baptism, anointing with the laying-on-of-hands, followed by participation in the Lord's Supper. Now baptism and communion came together (as late as the twelfth century infants were routinely given communion at their baptism) followed by a long delay before the bishop administered the part of the rite for which he was responsible. Within a short time, a theological rationale for the laying-on-of-hands and anointing as a separate event was deemed to be necessary. As early as 416, Pope Innocent I suggested that the bishop's role was to "seal and deliver the Holy Spirit," and that only a bishop, as successor to the apostles, had the right and power to do this. By the mid-fifth century, the term "confirmation" began to be applied to the bishop's post-baptismal liturgical ministry, and it was said to confer the "seven-fold gifts of the Holy Spirit" to the baptized, in order that they may be strengthened for spiritual combat in the world.

By the early Middle Ages, however, there was widespread neglect of the rite of confirmation. Many bishops were not resident in their dioceses, and even when they were, parents were unwilling to make the long and dangerous journey to the cathedral city, and so by the mid-thirteenth century, virtually no one was being confirmed (except for those living in the cathedral precincts and members of noble households who had their own private chapels and bishops on call). So in 1281 it was decreed in canon law that no child could be admitted to Communion without first having been confirmed, and with this the disruption and reordering of the component parts of Christian initiation in the Western church was nearly complete. From a composite unity of adult catechesis, baptism, anointing with the laying-on-of-hands by the bishop, and participation in the Lord's Supper, the church has moved to the baptism of infants soon after birth, confirmation of older children (if and when a bishop was available), which admitted them to Communion. Many baptized Christians died without having been confirmed, and at least some of those never received Communion, having not passed through the prerequisite confirmation rite.

There also grew up in the Middle Ages a certain amount of superstitious and magical thinking, which in most cases coexisted happily with religious thinking, with regard to baptism, and particularly the water used in the rite. It was said that water that had been blessed for baptism could cure all sorts of diseases, and was an effective agent in potions and spells. The effects of this are visible in many churches to this day. As a deterrent to those who contrived to steal the water from the font for illicit purposes, heavy wooden or iron covers were required to be placed on the fonts and locked, and over the centuries these covers became more and more elaborate and decorative. Although the original purpose of such font covers has been largely forgotten, they are still considered a necessary item of church furniture, sold with fonts by church goods suppliers.

Beginning in the early-thirteenth century, plague became a regular feature of medieval life, and the fear of death has been identified as one of the significant shapers of the medieval mind. It also left its mark on the rites of Christian initiation. Graphic depictions of the tortures of the damned, forever burning in hell, and theological speculation about the necessity of a period of time after death spent in purgatory making restitution for various sins because one had been snatched away unprepared, made parents even more anxious to bring their children to baptism as soon as possible after their birth lest they die unbaptized, condemned on account of original sin. This made a profound impact on Christian initiation, since it detached the rites of initiation from the ongoing life of the community. Baptisms became private affairs for the family and clergy, celebrated not in a spirit of communal joy and thanksgiving that a new member was being brought into the body of Christ, but with a sense of dread and urgency. It was difficult to discern in medieval initiation theology and practice any sense of baptism as the beginning of an ever-growing and deepening relationship with the God who pledged fidelity in baptism, and the beginning of the life of faith and service. For example, most women were not present for the baptisms of their children, since the child was taken away to the church almost immediately after birth by the father and godparents. This detachment of baptism from both the life of the community and the life of faith would provoke much serious thought about Christian initiation by all those who sought to reform the church beginning in the sixteenth century.

One might think that with Martin Luther's theological emphasis on justification by faith alone, infant baptism would have been an early casualty of the German Reformation. But Luther's past as an Augustinian monk colored his baptismal theology, and the concept of original sin was an integral part of Luther's religious imagination. But although he retained the baptism of infants, Luther did make some important changes that would be reflected in the work of later Reformers, both continental and English.

First and foremost, Luther moved baptism to the center of his own spirituality. He speaks of moistening his fingers with saliva each morning and signing himself on the forehead, saying "Whatever befalls me today, at least I have been baptized."[10] The centrality of baptism in the common life of the church is reflected in Luther's liturgical proposals. He restored baptism as a public event, to be celebrated in the midst of the gathered community at the main weekly service. Baptism, for Luther, was God's promise to the baptized, sealed and signed in water, a covenant-making event, in which God promises that sins will be forgiven. One of Luther's most beautiful prayers is the so-called "Flood Prayer" which is the centerpiece of his baptismal rite from 1523, the "Order of Baptism Revised." In this prayer, God is praised for all the ways in which water has served as a sign of redeeming love: the flood as a sign to Noah that he would be saved, the parting of the Red Sea, the birth of Jesus from the waters of a mother's womb, the water flowing from his side at the crucifixion. Then it goes on to ask that the water to be used in this baptism might be used by God as a vehicle for that same saving power. This prayer is one of the masterpieces of liturgical prose, and appears in various guises in baptismal rites of all denominations to the present day. Luther could find no scriptural warrant for viewing confirmation as a sacrament. But he kept the idea of a second stage of initiation, which included the recitation of the catechism and a form of blessing for those who had learned the basic doctrines of the faith. In other words, confirmation had found a new identity as a "graduation exercise" for those who had gained Christian maturity.

The other continental reformers made similar changes in the rites of Christian initiation. John Calvin further simplified the baptism service, but added long and didactic exhortations to the parents and the congregation. All agreed on three things: that rites should be simplified, that there be no superstition implied, and that the baptism of new Christians should always be public celebrations, held "in the face of the congregation." For most who followed Luther, confirmation became a way of insuring that children were instructed in the faith.

But for some of the reforming spirit, these changes did not go far enough, and the first important fracture in the Reformation was over the issue of baptism. In Germany, a priest named Balthasar Hubmeier (1485–1528) led a group that alleged that the baptism of infants was unscriptural and unreasonable, and that a truly reformed community should abandon the practice immediately. Hubmeier and his followers sought to create through baptismal discipline a pure and undefiled Christian community, and in this endeavor the baptism of believers only was the cornerstone. Baptism for these so-called "Anabaptists" (meaning "those who baptize again") came to be the sign by which the true church could be distinguished from the mass of those who had been indiscriminately baptized as infants. Moreover, Hubmeier taught that all infant baptisms were invalid, had meant nothing in the sight of God, and so his followers began re-baptizing. Because there were not only religious but political dangers in this deviation from ordinary practice, severe persecutions of those on the radical wing of the Reformation ensued. Tens of thousands from the various branches of the radical Reformation, (including the Mennonites, Amish, and Hutterites, for example) were martyred, often by drowning. This persecution continued throughout the sixteenth century and into the seventeenth century in many places. The hymns, which were written as a response to this experience of persecution, are among the most moving in all of Christian hymnody, and are still sung in Anabaptist services today. These hymns declare the power of the Spirit, and the water of baptism, and the blood of those who have died for the faith, all of which together bear witness to an unshakable faith in the Living God.[11]

Still later, the Reformers in England produced a baptismal rite which bore all the hallmarks of their predecessors on the Continent: simplicity, the absence of any element which might lead to superstitious interpretations, and the requirement that baptism be public, except in cases of emergency. (A special set of instructions was provided "For them that be Baptized in Private Houses in Time of Necessity.") Each child was to have three sponsors: two women and a man for female children, and two men and a woman for male children. Confirmation was administered to those who could say "in their mother tongue," the Articles of Faith (the Creed), the Lord's Prayer, the Ten Commandments (all of which churches were required to display publicly), and a short catechism. It was considered useful and expedient that a bishop preside at this service, since it would allow the bishop to see the various parishes in the diocese, lend special dignity to the rite, encourage vigorous instruction (since the examination on these elements would be done by an outsider), and it would serve as a sign of the unity of the church.

Throughout the succeeding centuries, the rites of Christian initiation remained little changed, but the debates surrounding the meaning of those rites were vigorous and often divisive. What did it mean to say that in baptism persons are "born again and made heirs of everlasting salvation"? Many of those who undertook revisions (both authorized and unauthorized) of the Church of England's 1662 Book of Common Prayer omitted this sentence from their experimental rites, along with the sign of the cross, which was objected to strenuously by the Puritans and their followers. During the eighteenth century Enlightenment, as "rational religion" came to dominate the theological arena, the sacraments were often pushed to the margins of the Christian life, and baptism was no exception. Baptism was seen as the performance of a duty to God, a duty demanded by Jesus and attested to in Scripture, rather than as an effective sign of our adoption as sons and daughters, or a dynamic encounter with the Living God who in baptism fulfills a covenant-making promise.

Perhaps the most radical approach to Christian initiation can be seen among the Society of Friends (Quakers). They take as their baptismal mandate the words of John the Baptizer (in Luke 3:16): "I baptize you with water; but one who is more powerful than I is coming; . . . He will baptize you with the Holy Spirit and fire." With the inauguration of the new covenant, the time had come for the true worshipers to worship God "in Spirit and truth" (John 4:23–24); outward and visible signs were no longer necessary. All people had equal access to what the great Quaker teacher Robert Barclay (1648–1690) called "the pure breathings of God, which is the Inner Light," and the core of all Friends' corporate worship, is the silent, patient waiting for the stirrings of the Spirit. For Quakers, baptism, like the Lord's Supper, is a spiritual rather than a material reality.

Baptism as an event of spiritual rebirth is also attested to among the Pentecostal churches. While most of these churches baptize adult believers in water upon profession of faith, they also attest to the necessity of a "Second Blessing" or "baptism of the Spirit" in which various gifts and manifestations of spiritual power are given to individuals. Taking the book of Acts as their guide to the kinds of gifts which can be expected as counterparts to the "second blessing," Pentecostals see baptism as a two-stage event in which the water-baptized believer is anointed with the Spirit as a witness to the renewal and transformation of body, mind, and soul. The gifts of the Spirit, including healing, glossalalia, and prophesy are seen as evidence that this second blessing has been received. Other groups not historically linked to the original Anabaptists, including Baptists and the Christian Church (Disciples of Christ), argue on biblical grounds for the necessity of baptism only on mature profession of faith.

As with many other aspects of life, nineteenth-century industrialization had an important effect on Christian initiation. The world was suddenly and rapidly changing, and issues of what it meant to be a Christian in a society that was propelled more and more by commercial and secular values came to the fore. In the later nineteenth century, those engaged in biblical and historical research added to the fund of knowledge about the foundations of Christian worship, and especially the rites of Christian initiation, and in this way attempted to answer the pressing question, "Who is a Christian?" In the 1930s, concerns about the relationship between infant baptism and responsible Christian faith and living began to be addressed, especially by German and Swiss theologians who sought a way of understanding what was happening in the "Christian" German nation under Hitler. At the same time, serious questions about the relationship between baptism and confirmation arose. If baptism was an act of God in which a child is claimed as God's son or daughter, what is it that needed to be "confirmed"? Was baptism not full initiation into the Christian life and hope? Did not the earliest evidence show that baptism with water and the giving of the Holy Spirit were inseparably linked? All of these debates were at a crucial stage when in 1959 Pope John XXIII called for a Council of the (Roman Catholic) Church to be convened in the Vatican. The first such event in over ninety years, the Second Vatican Council had the benefit not only of mature thinking about initiation by the best theologians of the century, but also of two generations of biblical and historical research. By the time the delegates had finished their work in 1964, a complete rethinking of theology and practice of Christian initiation had taken place and a mandate for a revised set of rites had been given. These would be the first new services in nearly four hundred years.

The new Roman Catholic rites of Christian initiation became a model for all other denominations that sought to renew their understanding of baptism and confirmation. These rites respond to the situation of religious pluralism and a growing population of unchurched adults, and they embody a number of theological presuppositions:

1. Baptism and confirmation are signs of conversion.
2. Conversion is an ongoing process which begins with one's initiation into the Spirit-filled community and which ends with one's death.
3. Because of this, the normative candidate for baptism is one who is conscious of his or her faith and belief.
4. Infant baptism is regarded as a "benign abnormality," tolerated as long as is it to be accompanied by a clear promise that the child is to be nurtured in the faith of the church.
5. The rites of Christian initiation are a unity, consisting of catechesis, water baptism, the laying-on-of-hands with anointing, and the receiving of Communion.

One of the most notable features of the new Roman Catholic provisions in the area of initiation is the Rite of Christian Initiation of Adults (RCIA). It was perceived that in the social and pastoral situation in which the church found itself, a special set of rites designed for unbaptized adults was needed. The RCIA provides a set of rites (some quite dramatic) for each stage of the process of initiation, from enrollment in the catechumenate to a post-baptismal profession of faith and reaffirmation of baptismal vows. These rites are, in a sense, responding to the same problem faced by the Christians of the fourth century: How do we make adherence to the Christian faith significant and fruitful in a rapidly secularizing society?[12]

Much of the other work on revision of baptismal theology and practice in the late-twentieth century has been an attempt to reach back into the earliest layer of baptismal history, and to recover all of the images and many of the practices which would have been prominent. Discussions have not only been held within individual denominations, but in bilateral conversations (such as the Roman Catholic–Methodist and the Lutheran–Orthodox dialogues) and in wider ecumenical arenas. One of the most significant of these discussions resulted in an important consensus statement on baptism, *Baptism, Eucharist and Ministry* (WCC Faith and Order Paper 111, 1982). In this document such things as the unrepeatability of baptism (IV:13), the necessary relationship between baptism and either active or potential Christian faith (111:8), and the special significance of water as a sign of cleansing and renewal (V:18) are affirmed. All of the member churches of the World Council of Churches have submitted responses to BEM, which provide much food for reflection by those concerned with the place of Christian initiation in the quest for Christian unity.[13]

There has never been a time in the church that was free of controversies surrounding the theology and practice of Christian initiation. Is Christian baptism for babies or for adults? Is there an alternative to baptism in the name of Father, Son, and Holy Spirit? Can re-baptism ever be permitted? Is confirmation necessary, and who is the proper minister of confirmation? How much water is needed for baptism? Can one partake of the Lord's Supper before being baptized? All of these questions continue to arise in denominational and interdenominational discussions, in congregations, and in households. In such matters as these, a creative balance between pastoral care and sensitivity, historical understanding, denominational discipline, biblical interpretation, and rigorous theological reflection is particularly important.


## THE LORD'S SUPPER

The communion of Christians with one another and with Jesus Christ during a shared meal of bread and wine has been a principal form of nourishment of the Christian life in every age. Whether this event happens daily, weekly, or monthly, whether it is called the Lord's Supper, the Eucharist, or the Holy Communion, whether it is an elaborate liturgical event or a simple act of remembering and sharing, the eating and drinking of bread and wine as a memorial of all that God has accomplished for us in Christ forms the core of the church's self-identity. But a history of changing interpretations and modes of practice makes the study of the Lord's Supper a complex endeavor. It must be set within the context of Christian theology and politics, it must be seen in the light of human ritual activity and biblical hermeneutics, it must take account of the difficulties with ancient texts and the difficulties of contemporary pluralism. All of these, and more besides, give the student of Christian worship much to digest in the matter of the Lord's Supper.

The famous liturgical scholar Dom Gregory Dix (1901–1952) remarked in 1945, that "the most important thing we have learned about the liturgy in the past fifty years is that Jesus was a Jew." On one level, of course, we had always known this, but what had become crystal clear to Dix and others was that many aspects of Christian worship were largely unintelligible without a clear understanding of the Jewish liturgical matrix out of which it arose. In the case of the Lord's Supper the truth of this insight is immediately apparent. Christians universally claim that the origin of the church's eucharistic action was a Jewish ritual meal presided over by the Jewish rabbi Jesus of Nazareth on the night before his execution in the context of the Jewish feast of Passover in the Jewish Holy City of Jerusalem. And so to understand what that action would have meant in those terms is a necessary first step, no matter how thoroughly later Christian communities may have reinterpreted or reframed that point of reference.

In one sense, every meal was a sacred occasion, a religious occasion, for the pious Jew. The prohibitions surrounding meals, the observance of the dietary laws, concern for the proper preparation of foods and prayers before partaking, and the restrictions on eating with strangers, sinners, and unbelievers, rested on the notion that in the meal, in the taking of nourishment to sustain life, God's presence was made especially tangible. The whole force of Jewish history was behind this notion: the corporate memory of the feeding of the community with quail and manna in the desert (Exod. 16:4–27), the provision of the bread of the presence (Exod. 24:12), and the festal meal associated with the Passover itself (Exod. 12:1–28). Every meal served to cement human relationships within the community of faith and served to cement the relationship between the human being and God. The sadness and outrage expressed by the psalmist in Psalm 41, for example, is not primarily that he has been betrayed, but that he has been betrayed by someone who "ate of [his] bread." Someone in radical solidarity with him, the solidarity engendered by partaking of a meal together in the name of God, had broken faith with him.

Given the importance of meals in this scheme, it is not surprising how often we find Jesus at the meal table. Again and again we find references in the Gospel accounts of Jesus participating in the religious act of sharing a meal.[14] But with whom do we find him? With prostitutes and sinners and tax collectors, the very people who were always prohibited from eating a meal with a Jew who wished to keep from being defiled. In the sharing of the meal Jesus was declaring himself to be in solidarity with the disenfranchised, those on the margins of social and religious life, and declaring them all to be in solidarity with God. In the sharing of a meal with these persons Jesus was restoring an avenue for communion with God which had been lost to them, making God's persistent love and presence transparent to them, making God's search for relationship with them visible. And over and over again when he is questioned about this he replies, "Those who are well have no need of a physician, but those who are sick" (Luke 5:31, for example).

At every meal, there was an established ritual way of giving thanks to God. This "blessing" or "thanking" (in Hebrew, *berakah*) of God on the occasion of a meal involved three things:

1. Blessing the God of creation for food, which was a manifestation of God's goodness and mercy.
2. Blessing the God of the exodus for God's saving acts in history.
3. Petition to God of saving power to act again in the present age, to send the Messiah, to free the people from whatever bondage they happened to be experiencing.

This is the pattern of prayer pious Jews used to give thanks every time they sat down for a meal, more elaborate at the weekly meals marking the beginning and end of the Sabbath (Friday and Saturday evenings), and more elaborate still at the annual celebration of the Passover. The food on the table was not incidental to this, but was the occasion for praising God, for remembering what God had done, and for maintaining the covenant relationship. The food was a pointer to deeper realities about the nature of the relationship between God and the people of Israel.

This is especially true of the Passover meal (Seder). The food and the recitation of the Passover prayers and stories (called the Passover *haggadah* or "order of the ritual") became ways of remembering and making present the events of the exodus. The Passover *haggadah* is an anthology of passages from the Scriptures, the Talmud, the Midrashim (homilies on the Torah) along with prayers, songs, games, and anecdotes all woven together with the Passover theme. In its full form it is quite long, and has a festal meal inserted in the middle. But the meal is not seen to be an interruption of the action, even though the central hymn of praise, the *Hallel*, is broken off half way through in order to serve the food. This is again to emphasize the idea that eating, like praying, is a holy action; the prayer and the meal were considered one continuous act of praise. The climax of the Passover Seder is reached with the words, "In every generation we ought to regard ourselves as if we personally had gone out of Egypt . . . not our ancestors alone did the Holy One redeem, but also us has he redeemed with them." This is the whole purpose of the Passover Seder: to see the redemption from bondage in Egypt not as an event of the remote past, but as an event which lays claim on every single Jew in every generation. So each Jewish man, woman, and child could say to God: "You have bought *me* out of bondage, and you have made *me* a child of the covenant in the events of the exodus." Until we understand this kind of thinking, it is difficult to appreciate what Christians can possibly mean when they say, "Jesus died for *me*; not only for those who knew and followed him in the first century, but for *me*" or "the blood of Christ, shed for *me*." This collapsing of history, this sense that by retelling the story, by remembering past events their power can be available in the present is central to both Jewish and Christian spirituality. At the end of the Passover Seder the members of the family greet one another with the words, "Next year in Jerusalem!" Next year, in other words, we will celebrate the Passover in the Holy City with the Messiah as the rightful host at the meal.

It is important to keep in mind that the Passover celebration is not only about words and images, but about food and, as in every ritual meal, food takes a principal role in the drama. The food becomes an occasion for remembering the love of God, and for blessing God for maintaining the covenant, and a means of pointing to some aspect of the relationship between God and humanity. The bitter herbs, for example, recall the bitterness of life under oppression, the salt water recalls the tears shed by those in bondage. So when Jesus took the bread and wine at his last meal and said, "This is my body; this is my blood," he was not doing something entirely foreign to the nature of Jewish meal blessings. It was common to use food in this way as a pointer to deeper spiritual realities and relationships.

There is some debate, of course, about whether or not the Last Supper was actually the Passover Seder (as the chronology of the final days of Jesus' life found in the Synoptic Gospels presumes) or whether it was the meal on the evening before the Passover (as suggested by the Fourth Gospel). The disciples are described as reclining at the table, drinking red wine instead of water or ordinary wine, and eating a meal that began in the evening and continued into the night, all of which supports the idea that the Last Supper was the Passover meal. On the other hand, the use of a common cup would have been unusual for the Passover meal (individual cups were the custom), and the Greek word used for the bread that was eaten is the word for ordinary, leavened bread rather than for the unleavened stipulated for the ritual of the

Passover meal. In addition, there is no mention of bitter herbs or lamb being eaten at the meal. But whether the Last Supper was a Passover meal or not, it is clearly set in the context of the Passover, and is replete with Passover themes and Passover associations.

What implications does all of this have for our thinking about the words and actions of Jesus that Christians believe lie at the roots of the church's celebration of the Lord's Supper? What does it mean to say that Jesus' final meal with his friends was a Jewish meal and a Jewish meal intimately associated with the Passover? First, to set it within the framework of Jewish meals is to say that it is an enacted prayer in which eating and words of blessing are united into one prayerful activity, that it puts those who eat in radical solidarity with one another and with God, and that it is an occasion both for God's self-giving and for human thankfulness. To set the Last Supper within the context of the Passover is to say that it is about salvation, about release from bondage, that it is an event of remembering the acts of God in history by telling the story of those acts, and that it points forward to the coming of the Messiah. Christians who are tempted to collapse the meaning of their own celebrations of the Lord's Supper into the overly-simplistic "It's just about remembering Jesus," might profitably reflect on the richness of interpretation we have inherited from our Jewish forebears.

What do the accounts in the New Testament tell us about how the Lord's Supper was experienced by the earliest Christian communities? There are five New Testament accounts of the Last Supper, one in each of the three Synoptic Gospels (Matt. 26:17–30; Mark 14:12–21; Luke 22:7–13), one quite different description in the Fourth Gospel (John 13ff.), and one in Paul's first letter to the church in Corinth (1 Cor. 11:23–26). There is a smattering of information in the book of Acts (as one might suspect of the record of a missionary church, there is much more information about Christian initiation), some evidence in Romans and in the Pastoral Epistles. How we interpret the references to the post-resurrection meals (Luke 24:13–35; Matt. 16:12–13; John 21:9–14) and the feeding miracles (Matt. 14:13–21 and 15:32–39; Mark 6:30–44 and 8:1–10; Luke 9:10–17; and John 6:1–4) as evidence for the eucharistic practice of the earliest Christian communities is a matter of some debate. It is very likely that the descriptions of the events surrounding the institution of the Lord's Supper were colored by the way in which those compiling the Gospels were actually experiencing the Supper in their own communities. When we put this evidence together with the evidence from Acts and the Epistles, we can begin to form a picture of the general characteristics of the Lord's Supper as it was celebrated in the earliest Christian communities.

All through this period (that up to about 135 CE) Christians are gathering to partake of a full meal with a separate bread and cup ritual appended to it in some way. Probably the meal was preceded by the blessing of the bread and followed by the blessing of the cup, in the order we find it in 1 Corinthians 11 ("In the same way he took the cup also, after supper . . ."). The meal itself was generally called the "Lord's Supper" (*kyriakon deipnon*) or the "love feast" (*Agape*) and the bread and cup ritual is called either by the Jewish term "the breaking of bread" or by the Greek term "Eucharist" (*eucharistia*), meaning "thanksgiving." The meal itself seems to have been a sort of potluck supper, with each household bringing food to share with the whole community, out of which was drawn the bread and the wine for use in the bread and cup ritual. Early difficulties with this arrangement are described in 1 Corinthians. Evidently the rich were eating the food which they themselves had brought and the poor not only did not have enough to eat, but were embarrassed and humiliated as well. Paul condemns this lack of solidarity in the strongest possible terms.

It seems, however, that toward the end of this period, something is happening to the relationship between the Agape meal and the bread and cup ritual. The meal is being split off from the bread and wine rite and is becoming a separate fellowship meal apart from the Eucharist. Ignatius of Antioch, in about the year 112 CE, says that it is unlawful to hold the Eucharist without a bishop present, but also that it is unlawful to hold the love feast without a bishop presiding. Both are important to the life of the community, but they are seen as distinct events. Eventually the love feast died out altogether, probably by the fourth century, to be revived only by the Moravians and Methodists in the eighteenth century. (It is also finding some use in ecumenical settings where eucharistic sharing is difficult or impossible.)

This period begins, then, with the Eucharist as a full meal appended in some way to a bread and wine rite. By the end of the period (or about eighty years after the death of Jesus), the meal is being split off, and in the post-Constantinian period the Agape finally dies out altogether. While this is happening, questions about the relationship between Christianity and Judaism are continuing to be considered, and the need and desire to "redramatize" the Passover meal is less urgent.

How often would the Lord's Supper have been celebrated? The earliest Christians had to work out how to move from the unique and definitive action of Jesus at the Last Supper to a regular repetition of that action. Some people suggest that in the years just after Jesus' execution, the Lord's Supper was celebrated annually on the Passover as a memorial of his death, but the evidence for this is very slim. The book of Acts speaks of the church meeting daily for the breaking of bread in Jerusalem (Acts 2:46), but this could mean simply the gathering for an ordinary meal. It seems that the more regular pattern was to come together for worship weekly "on the first day of the week" that is on Sunday evening (Acts 20:7). As we have seen above,[15] it is very likely that this meeting for worship took place in private houses.

Even though Paul is very concerned that "all things should be done decently and in order" (1 Cor. 14:40), he says absolutely nothing about who is to preside over the celebration of the Lord's Supper. The matter of liturgical presidency seems not to be an issue. It seems likely that the member of the community who hosted the group in his or her house, also acted as host at the meal and pronounced the blessing over the bread and wine, at least during the first seventy years after Jesus' death. But as we have seen, by the end of this period, Ignatius (112) is saying that a bishop must preside over the Lord's Supper. It is unclear how this transition took place. The questions surrounding the words that might have been said on these occasions are even more problematical. The canonical books of the New Testament tell us very little, but a few phrases have been identified by biblical scholars as having had liturgical use. We have references to "psalms, hymns and spiritual songs" being sung in worship (Eph. 5:19; Col. 3:16), and some of those hymns may be extracted from the New Testament itself, such as the praise hymn found in 1 Timothy 3:16.

> He was revealed in the flesh,
>     vindicated in spirit,
>         seen by angels,
> proclaimed among Gentiles,
>     believed in throughout the world,
>         taken up in glory.

In the second chapter of 1 Timothy there is also an exhortation to liturgical intercession, and it seems likely (although by no means certain at this early stage) that the words of institution themselves may have been said at the Eucharist. A number of documents written between 100 and 300 provide additional eucharistic information. But even if they suggest certain words for use on the occasion of the Lord's Supper, all of these early sources indicate that the presiders should "pray according to their ability" rather than follow exactly the models given in the text.

But these early eucharistic texts do indicate that the presider at the Lord's Supper should always "pray within the conventions." What were these "conventions"? What were deemed to be the essential images and ideas for these central prayers at the Eucharist? First, the prayer was centered on thanksgiving, both for creation and redemption in Christ. In 155CE Justin Martyr spoke of the importance of giving thanks "both for creating the world and all things that are in it and for freeing us from evil into which we were born" in the prayers over the bread and wine. The repetition of the Institution Narrative seems to be an almost universal feature of these prayers, and a request that the Holy Spirit act in the celebration to make the Communion with God and with the community of faith fruitful. A declaration that the congregation is offering the bread and wine as a sign of their total self-offering in union with the sacrificial self-offering of Christ is also seen to be important. The whole prayer was addressed to God the Father, through the Son, in the power of the Holy Spirit and ended with a Trinitarian doxology.

The usual ordering of these elements remained close to the pattern of Jewish meal blessings, at least for the first several centuries.

1. Thanksgiving to God for creation, telling the story of God's creative activity.
2. Thanksgiving to God for redemption, reciting the history of God's saving acts, culminating with,
3. the story of God's decisive redeeming act in the life, death, and resurrection of Jesus Christ. The story of Christ culminates in the recitation of the
4. narrative of the institution of the Supper.
5. Remembering all of this, the faithful who are united with Christ in baptism, offer themselves in union with Christ's self-offering for the sake of the world,
6. praying that the Holy Spirit will infuse this act of eating and drinking with power.
7. All this is asked of God the Father, through the Son, in the power of the Spirit in the church.

In all of this, the community knew that Christ was present in their celebration, in the power of the Spirit as he had promised before he died (Matt. 18:20; John 14:18–20). But questions about where or how or when that presence was actualized were of little interest.

By the late third century, encouragements to extempore prayer had all but died out, and a pattern similar to the one above became normative. In addition, with the intensification of theological controversies in the fourth century and the impending collapse of the structures of the Roman Empire that had ensured a certain degree of stability, the need for fixed prayers over the bread and wine at the Lord's Supper grew. More and more, authoritative texts for the eucharistic prayers were circulated, and became ways of proclaiming and guaranteeing the orthodoxy of the community that used them.

Because of this, there was also a growing tendency toward the standardization of texts for use in the Lord's Supper, and authority for these texts began to be centered at Rome. At the same time, the theology of the Eucharist began to emphasize the sacrificial aspects of the celebration, the localized presence of Christ in the bread and wine itself, and the closer identification of the bread and wine with the body and blood of Christ. Because of these trends, a sense of awe and reverence surrounding the Eucharist grew to dominate popular piety. Beginning in the mid-tenth century, the idea that ordinary people were unworthy to handle the body and blood of Christ in the form of bread and wine had begun to cause the laity to be reluctant to take Communion. Simply gazing upon the bread and wine at the moment when it was thought to be "consecrated" (transformed into the body and blood of Christ) was believed to be sufficient to produce a saving effect. At the same time, the belief was strong that the Lord's Supper (usually called the "Mass"[16]) was a representation of the atoning sacrifice of Christ, and that the effects of that sacrifice were present and active in the eucharistic bread and wine. This in turn led to the expectation that these might be practically employed to bring about certain desired objectives. Because of this, as the centuries progressed the bread and wine used for the Eucharist increasingly had to be protected from theft, since they were thought to possess supernatural powers which could be harnessed for use in magic spells and potions. By the eleventh century, this sense of the power inherent in the celebration of the Mass meant that it was almost universally believed that the entire salvation of the world was dependent upon it in some way.

The theological poles of medieval eucharistic theology can be clearly seen in the controversy between two ninth-century theologians who were monks at the monastery of Corbie, in what is now northwestern France. In the first systematic treatise devoted solely to the theology of the Lord's Supper, Pascasius Radbertus (ca. 785–ca. 860) described the way in which Christ is present in the Eucharist in extremely realistic and physical terms. Ratramnus of Corbie (d. ca. 868) was provoked to respond, and attacked this carnal view of the presence of Christ in favor of a more symbolic and spiritualized interpretation. In the end, Ratramnus' view was condemned as failing adequately to safeguard the doctrine of the "real presence" of Christ. The next three centuries saw an increasing identification of the bread (now universally referred to as the "host," from the Latin word for sacrificial victim) and wine with the physical body and blood of Christ, and an increasing distance between academic and popular understandings of the Eucharist.

These popular deviations from the "official" theology of the Lord's Supper, and particularly grossly carnal interpretations of the presence of Christ, including widespread reports of bleeding, groaning, and weeping hosts, had begun to be a cause of concern among church authorities and academic theologians. In seeking to stem the tide of these hyper-realistic explanations of the "real presence," Thomas Aquinas (ca. 1225–1274), a teacher of theology in Paris, applied the best philosophical tools of the day to the problem. Using concepts originally developed by the philosopher Aristotle (ca. 384–322 BCE), Aquinas explained that while the perceptible features (the so-called "accidents") of the bread and wine remained intact during the Eucharist, the inner reality (the "substance") of the bread and wine were transformed ("transubstantiated") into the inner reality of the body and blood of Christ. In every other case in the natural world, the "substance" of a particular thing and its "accidents" conformed to each other exactly: for example, in the case of a tree, the inner reality of a tree is always matched by something identifiable to the five senses as a tree. The elements of bread and wine at the Eucharist, according to Aquinas' view, were the only exception to this principle. What is perceived with the senses was bread and wine; if we could see their true nature, however, we would see that they were really the body and blood of Christ. In this sense Aquinas could speak of the "real presence" of Christ under the forms of bread and wine in the Lord's Supper.

By the time of the sixteenth century Reformation, several of these trends in eucharistic theology and practice had crystallized. Increasingly the Mass had become something to be seen rather than something in which to participate. (Because of the fear of defiling the body and blood of Christ, laypersons received Communion only infrequently,[17] and since 1415 Communion wine had been denied to them absolutely by canon law.) Because each Mass was thought to make present the atoning sacrifice of Christ, the number of celebrations multiplied to ensure a superabundance of saving grace. Many monasteries and parish clergy made their living from the "mass stipends" paid by groups and individuals who wished the benefits of the Mass applied to particular causes, and especially to ensure the early release of souls from purgatory.

But at the same time, biblical literacy had been growing rapidly among the laity since the invention of the printing press in the late fifteenth century, and theological tracts and books for lay people had a wide circulation. Devotion was high, and itinerant preachers were finding receptive congregations, eager for religious knowledge of all kinds. Hymns and prayers were being composed in the language of the people, and pious poems were set to popular tunes. Although the official liturgy remained in Latin, published guides to the service were available for those who wished to follow along as the clergy celebrated the Mass.

This explosive combination of heightened eucharistic interest among the laity and a high degree of neglect and irreverence of the Eucharist among clergy set the stage for the radical reevaluation of the Lord's Supper by those in the sixteenth century who sought a thoroughgoing reformation of the church. The Reformers' concern with the centrality of the Word of God, and their insistence on justification through faith alone and the priesthood of all the baptized put the Eucharist at the center of the Reformation debate. In *The Babylonian Captivity of the Church* (1520), Martin Luther (1483–1546) began the attack on the current theology and practice of the Mass. Luther was possessed of a unique combination of intelligence and passion, together with a morbid fascination with the state of his own soul, and a truly independent, albeit anguished, spirit. Earlier in his life, while he was still an Augustinian monk, he wrote in his diary, "God appears horrifyingly angry, and with him the whole of Creation. There can be no flight, nor consolation, either from without or within, but all is accusation." For Luther, even the intricate system of assured grace offered in the eucharistic theology of the day was not sufficient to assure him of his own salvation. And so, in about 1509, he turned to Scripture, and unleashed a whirlwind. Eight years later this devout former Augustinian monk was declared a "Son of Satan" by Pope Leo X.

It is difficult now to appreciate the power of *The Babylonian Captivity of the Church*; it quickly became the manifesto for the Protestant Reformation. It speaks of three "walls" that had been built around the "captive church": the denial of the wine to the laity, the doctrine of "transubstantiation," and the understanding of the Lord's Supper as an atoning sacrifice. The presence of Christ in the Eucharist, according to Luther, was like the presence of fire in a heated bar of iron, in which "every part is both iron and fire": in the same way Christ's body and blood are wholly present in the eucharistic bread and wine. With regard to receiving both bread and wine at Communion, Luther argued that since Christ gave both the bread and the cup to his disciples at the Last Supper his present-day disciples deserve nothing less. The Eucharist was the legitimate "birthright" of those who are born anew through baptism and faith in Christ. Luther wrote two services for the Lord's Supper, one in Latin (the *Formula Missae*, 1523) and one in German (the *Deutsche Messe*, 1526), in which he embodied his principles for the renewal of the Lord's Supper. In these rites it is clear that Luther is attempting to "de-objectify" the Eucharist, to reinsert it into the context of a living community of faith and to ensure that it will no longer be treated as a "thing" to be gazed upon, or used, or manipulated for gain. It was rather to be understood as an *event*, in which the whole community of faith experienced the presence of the risen Christ in and through eating and drinking bread and wine.

But others in this period desired a still more thoroughgoing reformation of the church, and thus of the Lord's Supper. Swiss reformers Ulrich Zwingli (1484–1531), Martin Bucer (1491–1551), and John Oecolampadius (1482–1531) believed that Luther's retention of the physical presence of Christ in the elements of bread and wine left too much opportunity for idolatry and practical abuse. They all moved it in the direction of a more spiritualized and memorialistic view of the Eucharist. At the Marburg Colloquy (1529), Luther (holding firm to his conservative position) and the more radical Swiss reformers were unable to come to agreement on an understanding of the presence of Christ in the eucharistic bread and wine, marking the fracture of the Reformation into distinct theological camps. John Calvin (1509–1564), the reformer of the Swiss church at Geneva, attempted to moderate the Swiss and Lutheran view, arguing that Christ is truly, albeit spiritually, received by those who partake faithfully of the bread and wine.

The various continental Reformers could agree, however, on a number of practical matters regarding the Lord's Supper. These included the necessity of everyone receiving both the bread and wine at Communion, and the reading and preaching of God's Word at each celebration. The idea of speaking of the Lord's Supper in sacrificial terms was too freighted with a history of abuse to be retained, but the Reformers did find biblical warrant for speaking of the "sacrifice of praise and thanksgiving" as a response to communion with Christ. All the Reformation services were much simpler than their medieval predecessors, and increased participation of the laity was facilitated by the fact that the service was said in their own language and by the addition of numerous congregational responses. Although the intention was to return to the practice of the primitive church of celebrating the Lord's Supper weekly, most people were so accustomed to receiving Communion infrequently that quarterly Communion was all that could be achieved in many places.

At the same time, the Catholic Reformation (sometimes called the Counter Reformation) left its own mark on eucharistic practice and piety. A council of the church convened at Trent (1545–1563) sought to curb abuses, to stem the tide of Reformation, and to settle certain questions that the success of Protestantism had thrown into question. Several of the sessions of the Council of Trent dealt directly with the Mass. One important result of the Council's deliberations was the establishment of the Congregation of Sacred Rites. Aiming at the standardization of public worship according to the Council's decrees, and with a uniform liturgy for all of Roman Catholicism the ultimate goal, the Congregation immediately undertook the reform of liturgical books. They produced a set of services in 1570, and this formed the official eucharistic liturgy of the Roman Catholic Church until the Second Vatican Council undertook revisions nearly four centuries later.

At the same time, a second generation of Reformers had established Protestant eucharistic practice in the British Isles and Scandinavia. Drawing from a variety of theological and liturgical sources, Thomas Cranmer (1489–1556) embodied a reformed theology of the Lord's Supper in successive editions of the Book of Common Prayer (1549 and 1552). The ambiguities in the theology of the Lord's Supper in Cranmer's services are abundant, so that debate about their intention has persisted to this day within the Anglican family of churches. Some argue that he was interested in maintaining much of the established medieval theology; others say that his reformation was thorough, and no trace of Catholic piety or practice remains. As in most situations of this kind, the truth probably lies somewhere in between. Symbolic of the ambiguities inherent in the reformation of the Lord's Supper in the English church is the insertion at the end of the Communion service of the famous "Black Rubric," which declared kneeling at Communion should not be interpreted as adoration of the eucharistic bread and wine. Kneeling was not forbidden, but was reinterpreted in a thoroughly reformed direction. In any case, Cranmer's execution by fire at the hands of the Catholic Queen Mary only underlines this ambiguity of intention. Having written a staunch defense of a Catholic interpretation of his work, he is alleged to have thrust his writing-hand into the fire before stepping into it, in order to indicate his remorse that the hand had betrayed the Reformation cause.

During the seventeenth century, those desiring a more complete reformation of the church believed that the Eucharist was still the occasion for much misunderstanding and abuse, and sought to remove those things that might lead to superstition. Any suggestion that the Communion table was an altar (implying that it was a place of sacrifice), kneeling or other indications of adoration of the bread and wine, the use of liturgical vestments,[18] the making of the sign of the cross, and the use of the term "priest" for the presider at the Lord's Supper were all points on which these "Puritans" (those who wanted to "purify" the church) stood fast. The Puritan view of the Lord's Supper was carried to the New World with the earliest colonists, and came to dominate much of the theology and practice of the Lord's Supper in the American colonies. The Society of Friends (Quakers), in their desire to worship God "in Spirit and in truth," understood Communion (like baptism) as a wholly spiritual communion with Christ through the medium of the Inner Light, and did away with the material elements of bread and wine altogether.[19]

The eighteenth-century Enlightenment, with its exaltation of human reason, made a profound impact on the eucharistic theology and practice of both Protestant and Roman Catholics alike. Rationalist preaching and the informed study of Scripture, as activities of the enlightened mind, came to dominate Protestant services of worship to an even greater degree than before, and the celebration of the Lord's Supper was given a subordinate role. The Lord's Supper was viewed as a way of calling to mind the virtues of Christ, and was considered a duty and obligation for those who took seriously the Lord's command, "Do this in memory of me." This practical and theological marginalization of the Eucharist continues to this day in many Protestant churches.

But this pattern of cool Enlightenment rationalism is interrupted by the Methodist movement, with its strong emphasis on religious experience, personal and social holiness, and the "warm heart." The work of John and Charles Wesley runs counter to a number of Enlightenment trends, and their eucharistic practice and piety is an example of this. In an age in which the Lord's Supper was celebrated less and less frequently (less than quarterly according to a mid-eighteenth century survey), the Wesleys argued for the absolute necessity of weekly Communion (and John himself generally tried to partake of Communion daily). To an age that had deep anxieties about any sense that the Lord's Supper could be spoken of as a "sacrifice," the Wesleys restored a powerful and beautiful sacrificial vocabulary in a series of hymns on "The Eucharist as It Implies a Sacrifice." In an age which distrusted the possibility of the material communicating the things of God, an age of rigid empiricism, the Wesleys emphasized the power of God working to heal and restore through bread and wine. In *The Sunday Service for the People Called Methodists in North America* (1784), John Wesley provided a revised version of the service of Holy Communion in the Book of Common Prayer (1662), and he stipulated that the Methodist Societies in America should celebrate the Supper weekly. Unfortunately this legacy of eucharistic devotion was squandered by his spiritual heirs in America; by the time of Wesley's death in 1791 the Sunday Service had become only a brief appendix to the Discipline, and its admonitions about the necessity of frequent Communion went unheeded, deemed to be impractical in a frontier missionary situation.

Nineteenth-century religion reacted to Enlightenment rationalism and the forces of industrialization in two ways, and each of these had a significant impact on the theology and practice of the Lord's Supper. The first of these is usually referred to as "Romanticism," which sought to restore the more cohesive religious experience of an earlier period. Many figures in the Protestant Romantic movement (like their Roman Catholic counterparts) looked to the medieval period as the golden age of Christianity, and hoped to revive the eucharistic patterns and piety of the Middle Ages, even among such groups as Lutherans and Anglicans who had quite decisively rejected it in the sixteenth century. Frequency of Communion increased dramatically among those groups affected by Romanticism, but together with this was a tendency toward the privatization of religious experience and excessive sentimentality in eucharistic devotion. But despite this inclination toward nostalgia, the concomitant search for the historic roots of Christian worship set the stage for modern liturgical scholarship.

The second major influence on Protestant eucharistic theology and practice in the nineteenth century was the evangelical revival. With an increasingly mobile population pushing westward across the American frontier and into the new industrial cities and the concomitant shifts in social and religious patterns, the need for a revival of religion became apparent to many.[20] During the first half of the nineteenth century, revivalism spread down the Erie Canal and then followed the settlers west. Camp meeting revivals were a feature of this process, and these religious gatherings would have a profound impact on the theology and practice of the Lord's Supper in America. Because the various strands of the evangelical revival were united around the conviction that salvation did not depend on the externals of religious practice, but rather on a deep and personal Christian commitment, preaching and other acts of worship that were designed to bring about conversion came to dominate public prayer. This had the effect of pushing the Lord's Supper further toward the margins of the religious experience of many Christians. At the same time, the temperance movement was also taking hold of the religious imaginations of many Christians, and imbibing any form of fermented drink was seen as both dangerous and immoral. Concern over the wine used at Communion increased. By the 1870s the scientific principles of Louis Pasteur had been applied to the pasteurization of grape juice, which could then be used as the normal substance for use in the Eucharist in many Protestant churches.

In the twentieth century, a renewal of attention to the Lord's Supper took place within many Christian denominations as part of a wider liturgical renewal. Rigorous historical and theological research led Roman Catholics to reaffirm that the Eucharist was at the heart and center of their corporate experience, the event in which the people of God gather to proclaim and make present the redeeming work of Christ. The Second Vatican Council authorized the official revision of the Roman Catholic rites for the Mass in 1963, and the Council's *Constitution on the Sacred Liturgy* applied the renewed eucharistic theology to questions of congregational life and the mission of the church. Beginning in the 1960s, the Roman Catholic liturgical agenda began to influence the revisions of Protestant services of the Lord's Supper. At the same time, historical studies and ecumenical discussions have made for a great deal of interdenominational agreement on the form and content of the Eucharist. Many churches for whom the Lord's Supper had been an occasional service have sought to reintroduce it as the main Sunday service, and in the period from 1975 to 1995 United Methodists, the Presbyterian Church (U.S.A.), and the Episcopal Church (U.S.A.), among others, undertook thorough revisions of their official services of Holy Communion.

One of the central questions in this period (and, in the end, one of the points of real ecumenical convergence) has been about what constitutes the most appropriate form of prayer at the Lord's Table. As a result of research into both the nature of Jewish meal prayers and the earliest layers of Christian Communion practice, several of the ancient elements of eucharistic praying that were lost in the Middle Ages and Reformation have been recovered in almost all of the official denominational and ecumenical texts. The recitation of the acts of God in creation and prophesy, which disappeared from the eucharistic prayer in the Western church as early as the fifth century, was reinstated. The God who is blessed in the Lord's Supper is not only the God who acted in the life, death, and resurrection of Jesus Christ, but who has also acted in the whole of the created order and all of human history. The empowering and transforming work of the Holy Spirit, which again had been for-gotten as emphasis on the atonement of Christ increased, was also restored to the prayer at the table. And finally, almost without exception, there has been the recovery of an eschatological element in these prayers. The Great Thanksgiving is an occasion for looking back to the action of God in creation and in Christ, for focusing on the present activity of the Holy Spirit, and for looking forward to the final consummation of all things at the end of history. We eat and drink in anticipation of the heavenly banquet, when Christ him-self will act as host at the feast, and our Communion will be perfected in the reign of God to come. Although some Protestant groups continue to insist that only the biblical Words of Institution (with or without a Communion meditation on some relevant theme) are needed for an authentic celebration of the Supper, the ecumenical consensus on the need for a more fully realized prayer at the Lord's Table is one of the hallmarks of the modern period of liturgical history.

What is the shape of the contemporary Eucharistic Prayer? How are these various elements arranged and ordered? Overall, the prayers at the Table of the various denominations follow a similar structure:

1. Opening dialogue—in this, the presider and congregation offer a Chris-tian greeting to one another, and indicate that they are together about to "lift their hearts to God" in prayer. The most common of these dialogues is called by the Latin name *Sursum corda*, meaning "Lift up your hearts!" Most often, the opening dialogue is phrased something like this:

    **Presider:**  Lift up your hearts!
**Congregation:**  We lift them to the Lord.
    **Presider:**  Let us give thanks to the Lord our God.
**Congregation:**  It is right to give our thanks and praise.

2. There follows a blessing of God the Father[21] for those saving acts that have brought the community to birth and sustained it. In many cases this recitation includes both Old and New Testament images and events: creation, covenant, exodus, the gift of the promised land, and prophesy all find a place in what is referred to as the preface of the Great Thanksgiving. Sometimes the particular season of the church year or moment in the life of the church is mentioned as a further occasion for thanksgiving.

3. This praise and thanks to the Father culminates in the ancient hymn called the Sanctus: "Holy, holy, holy Lord, God of power and might, heaven and earth are full of your glory, Hosanna in the Highest!" Because of the inclu-sive nature of this hymn, it is sung or said by the whole congregation together.

4. After the Sanctus, in the part of the Great Thanksgiving known as the post-Sanctus, the prayer focuses more closely on the coming of Jesus Christ to

save and reconcile the world to God, and often highlights those elements in the narratives of Jesus' life that are celebrated and preached on in the service.

5. This recitation of God's saving action in Christ leads to recalling those acts which Christians believe lie at the foundations of our celebration of the Lord's Supper: Jesus' final meal with his friends in the upper room. The Narratives of Institution used in the Great Thanksgiving are generally not taken directly from any one of the narratives in the Synoptic Gospels and 1 Corinthians, but are in various ways conflations of several of these accounts.[22]

6. The prayer then turns to ask God to accept the offering we make of our selves, our prayers and thanksgivings, and of the work of our hands, as we come together before God in an act of the faithful remembering of our redemption in Christ. The part of the prayer which speaks of our remembering is referred to as the anamnesis (from the Greek word "remember" or "re-present") and the part which asks God to receive our self-offering is called the oblation (from the Latin word for "offering").

7. The community proclaims its confidence in the God to whom it prays by making a brief acclamation, that Christ died to save, rose from the tomb, and will come again in power and glory. This acclamation usually is quite simple: "Christ has died, Christ is risen, Christ will come again!", and is said by the entire congregation.

8. Then the prayer moves on to a further petition, this time to ask if God will send the Holy Spirit to act with power to make our Communion fruitful. This epiclesis, from the Greek word meaning "to call down upon," can either ask for the Spirit to infuse the life of the community with the presence of Christ as it eats and drinks together, to allow us to "discern the body" (1 Cor. 11:29) so that we might eat and drink to our salvation, and to empower those who partake of Christ's presence to conform their lives to his for the sake of the world.

9. And finally, the Great Thanksgiving concludes with a doxology, summing up the praises of the Father, offered through the Son, and in the power of the Holy Spirit in the holy church. As a fitting response, the congregation joins in the Amen, setting their seal on the words that have been offered by the presider on their behalf.

As we can see, this form of the Great Thanksgiving returns to themes we found in Jewish meal blessings: blessing God for creation and for redemption, asking God to act again here and now with that same creating, redeeming power, and looking forward to the coming of the Messiah in triumph. And it is also self-consciously modeled on the type of eucharistic prayers that we believe Christians in the first five centuries of the church might have known. In both of these patterns, the community gives thanks to God by remembering and retelling the story of what God has done for it in history, and by offering themselves to one another and to God as they eat and drink. It must be said again that not all Christians will recognize this extensive form of eucharistic praying. In many cases, the impact of frontier revivalism, Puritan sacramental minimalism, and American pragmatism has been to reduce the prayers at the Lord's Table to a few worthy thoughts to ponder on the occasion of Communion. The ecumenical implications of this are serious, however, since divisions are often perpetuated and reinforced when one group deems the eucharistic praying of another to be inadequate.

In the consensus document *Baptism, Eucharist and Ministry*, it was agreed that five basic themes formed the core of Christian belief about the Lord's Supper: the Eucharist was affirmed as a thanksgiving, an anamnesis or memorial, the arena for the action of the Spirit, as Communion, and as a meal of the kingdom. ("Sacrifice" was clearly deemed still to be too sensitive an image to be included.) This ecumenical consensus was embodied in a eucharistic prayer referred to as the "Lima Liturgy" (since it was agreed at the 1982 World Council of Churches meeting at Lima, Peru). The Lima Liturgy is, like all ecumenical instruments, a consensus document, and designed more for study and discussion than for use in a congregational setting. But questions of eucharistic sharing between and among different Christian denominations continue to dominate ecumenical discussions, and because of real differences in discipline, order, and theology in matters concerning the Lord's Supper, no easy answers are forthcoming.

The two events that we have been discussing in this chapter, Christian initiation and the Lord's Supper, have been recognized by Christians across the denominational spectrum and throughout Christian history as essential to the nourishment of the Christian life and faith. Their designation by the church as "sacraments" or "ordinances" highlights their centrality. Although some issues of sacramental theology have been touched upon in this section, a more thoroughgoing study is beyond the scope of this book. Suffice it to say that the meeting between God's decisive action and faithful human response in the events of initiation and Eucharist, however they are interpreted, has resulted in the renewal and restoration of individuals and communities alike throughout the history of the Christian church.

# 4

# The Nourishment of the
# Christian Life 2

Although the Christian sacraments of initiation and the Lord's Supper have occupied a special place in the sustaining of Christian life and faith, other forms of worship have provided significant occasions for spiritual nourishment as well. For many Protestant Christians, the ordinary Lord's Day service is the most usual occasion for gathering for prayer and praise of God, and for others public forms of daily prayer are an important devotional resource. Coming together as a body to acknowledge our misdeeds and to receive assurance of God's willingness to forgive in public services of reconciliation (also called "penance") has also punctuated the life of many communities, and the rites of ordination to the various ministries of the church remind the whole community of its calling. In this section we shall look at each of these forms of worship in turn, in order to see how Christians past and present have understood their meaning and purpose.

## THE LORD'S DAY SERVICE

Historically, the development of the Sunday Service was, in one sense, a liturgical response to the failure of the post-Reformation churches to secure the Lord's Supper as the ordinary weekly celebration. As we have seen, there was a deep desire on the part of the Reformers to insure that Communion services would be held frequently, but only on those occasions when people who were willing and able to receive Communion were present. At the same time, an uneasiness about "worthy Communion" made ordinary Christians unwilling to partake more regularly of the elements of bread and wine. Therefore, quarterly Communion became the norm in most of the churches that have traced their roots, directly or indirectly, to the sixteenth-century Genevan Reformation. Even the vigorous eucharistic piety of John Wesley could not be transferred intact to his successors, and frequent Communion was not a normal feature of the Methodist churches, either in England or in America.

Over the centuries, the Lord's Day service has responded to many of the religious forces which were shaping the church as a whole, and it has therefore taken a variety of forms. Generally, however, Sunday worship has been centered on the reading and preaching of the Word of God, and the service has been enriched by various congregational acts of preparation for and response to the proclamation of the Word. Each of these three basic elements, preparation, proclamation, and response, may take the form of prayer (any of the various types of prayer discussed earlier[1]), music, recitation and exposition of texts, and ritual and symbolic action. Overall, two questions determine our understanding of both the historical development of the Lord's Day Service and its present configuration: What elements are essential to the ordinary Sunday Service? and In what way should the various elements of the service be ordered? As we shall see, both of these are not simply pragmatic questions, but are also theological questions, and the composition of the Sunday Service always expresses (and exposes) a particular theological agenda.

## The Gathering

Where does worship begin? It is tempting (especially for clergy) to believe that the Sunday Service begins when the minister says the first "official" words of the service. But in a most important sense worship begins with the gathering of a group of people who have the worship of God as their aim and their intention. This is why in many contemporary orders of worship the first main section of the service is called "the gathering." The gathering includes a number of elements which are designed to focus the attention of all the participants on the occasion at hand, and to help them to declare why they have gathered at this particular time and in this particular place. This often takes the form of a "call to worship" (usually framed as a dialogue between the worship leader and the congregation). The call to worship proclaims the willingness of those gathered to come before God in worship and their confidence that God is with them. In many cases biblical phrases are employed, such as, "This is the day the LORD has made; let us rejoice and be glad in it." (Ps. 118:24) or "O come let us worship and bow down, let us kneel before the LORD, our Maker!" (Ps. 95:6). The call to worship is not a prayer that we *might* be given the grace to praise God rightly, but is rather an assertion that it is our corporate intention to praise God rightly.

Sometimes this praise theme is expressed in the extended congregational singing of what have come to be called "praise choruses"; simple, easily-memorized songs which express the singers' adoration of God. Although, as their name suggests, they do normally strongly express the adoration of God, and are accessible and engaging, allowing worshipers at all levels of expertise to participate, the extended singing of praise choruses at this point in a normal Sunday Service can have a number of detrimental effects. First it can tend to focus attention on our *feelings* about God rather than on God's essential being. Second, because so many of these songs are quite subjective and personal (frequently employing the first-person pronoun "I"), they can disrupt the formation of a truly communal feeling, emphasizing not the gathering of the church in the presence of God but rather the emotional state of the individual worshiper. In other cases, members of the congregation may not be prepared to engage in the unalloyed praise of God. They may need to be addressed by the Word, to confess, and to meditate on blessings received before they can undertake the kind of radical commitment embodied in these songs. On some occasions, the "plotting" of the service may demand that the congregation work toward praise, slowly and deliberately, rather than being asked to jump into it unprepared.

If there is an opening hymn, its text often carries through this theme of praise; the hymn can either be placed before or after the call to worship. The opening collect or prayer of the day, or the pastoral prayer is centered on the theme of the service, usually by picking up images from the Scripture lessons that will be read. As we have seen,[2] there is some debate about whether the confession and assurance of pardon are properly a part of the gathering, or are more appropriate after the proclamation of the Word of God. When they are included as a part of the gathering, they too may be keyed to the lessons of the day or occasion in the church year. If the confession and assurance are placed in this position, they can be sealed with a congregational act of praise, either a canticle (such as the Gloria in Excelsis), a hymn, a praise psalm, or song, or an acclamation expressing our joy in the many blessings we have received at the hand of God.

## The Proclamation of the Word of God

The second major section in the Lord's Day Service is the proclamation of the Word of God. In many services, a prayer of illumination precedes the reading, asking that we might hear God's voice as the Scripture is read, and that our hearing may bear fruit in lives of devotion and service through the power of the Holy Spirit. As we have seen,[3] it has been the traditional practice to read three passages from Scripture, one each from the Old Testament, the Epistles, and the Gospels. But ironically, the reading of the Bible has often not been given the attention we claim it deserves in services of public worship. Sometimes only a few verses are read, serving merely as a springboard for the sermon. In other situations, the congregation is asked to follow along in their pew Bibles, rather than to focus their attention on the reader. In such cases, the dramatic impact of seeing and hearing one of their number standing before them to claim and proclaim the gospel publicly is lost. The readings themselves can be interspersed with congregational responses, such as the singing of a psalm, hymn, or repeated alleluias. In some cases, especially for children's services, the lessons can be dramatized or read by two or more people together.

⟨In a sense, the history of the Christian sermon mirrors the history of Christianity as a whole. For Martin Luther and his successors, no gathering of Christians was complete without the reading and exposition of the Scriptures, and there has never been a renewal of the church that was not accompanied by a renewal of preaching. While there is not space here to review the history of preaching, it is important to say that Christianity is not self-revealing, and the words from Romans are as valid today as they were in the first century: "How are they to believe in one of whom they have never heard? And how are they to hear without someone to proclaim him?" (Rom. 10:14). Those who claim that the traditional sermon format is obsolete in this new millennium have yet to provide the church with a viable alternative.⟩

## The Response to the Word of God

The third major section of the Lord's Day service is the response to the Word of God. Faithful Christians who have heard again the Word that has drawn them together and given them life need ways of saying "Yes!" to what they have heard. And those seeking to come to faith or to return to faith require an opportunity to express what is in their hearts and minds. The response can take a number of forms, and may be quite full. In most congregations this is the place for the prayers of the people (and if it has not already taken place, a confession of sin and assurance of pardon); oftentimes the creed is also said as a response to the proclamation of the Word. Sometimes an invitation to Christian discipleship is appropriate, or a hymn, anthem, or other musical response; the passing of the peace can be a proper response to what has been heard, and certainly this is a suitable place for the offering. In many cases, the response to the Word takes the form of a special event: a baptism, confirmation, the recognition of ministries, a marriage, or the giving or dedication of a memorial gift. Overall, this section is designed to answer the question, Now that you have heard God's Word, what are you going to do about it? How are you going to live out the Christian life, given the things that have been proclaimed? What commitment do you make?

One of the indispensable forms of congregational response in the Sunday service is the thanksgiving, which declares that whatever the specific response to the preaching of the Word of God, the general response is one of gratitude for all of God's many blessings. An extended prayer of thanksgiving or the Lord's Supper finds its place here, as well as the Lord's Prayer as the summary of all Christian praying. A hymn of thanks, or a more tangible expression of gratefulness, is also appropriate.

For those congregations that are wedded to the Pastoral Prayer, there is some question about its most appropriate placement. Many argue that the Pastoral Prayer is most logically located and helpfully as a part of the Response to the Word. In this location it can gather up the threads of the service, key into themes in the reading and preaching, and draw people forward into new levels of commitment based on what has come before. This again is a matter of the logical "plotting" of the service. What naturally follows what has gone before? Where is the climax of the service? How are people allowed to claim what they have heard and done in a meaningful way? In much of this, the traditional Pastoral Prayer, which is an amalgam of various themes and intentions, can be less than helpful. The confession included in the prayer may be most appropriate at the beginning of the service in order to open the heart to what is to be proclaimed, while the intercessions may be better left to the end, when people have been made vulnerable to the demands of the Christian conscience through the reading and preaching. Perhaps for those congregations in which the Pastoral Prayer is seen to be indispensable, it might be divided into a number of different sections, with the appropriate prayer theme addressed in its most logical place in the "narrative" of the service.

Many American congregations are accustomed to having an altar call, or invitation to Christian discipleship, as a necessary component within the Response to the Word. Often this has become an indispensable part of the ritual even in very stable congregations in which no one ever comes forward to respond. The altar call goes back to the era of frontier revivalism, when the aim of the entire service was to gather in a harvest of converts, generally after a protracted experience of "hellfire-and-brimstone" preaching designed to bring sinners to the brink of despair over their eternal fate. One of the difficulties here is that in some congregations it provides the only opportunity for a response to the Word, leaving those who do not wish to make a new commitment without an adequate way to express their own response. Whether this relic of a past age has genuine relevance in the contemporary evangelistic situation is unclear, but in every case the provision of an altar call deserves thorough consideration based on the special circumstances of the congregation and the particular emphasis and trajectory of the service.

## The Sending Forth

The Lord's Day Service comes to a close with the "sending forth." The blessing (benediction) and dismissal declare that the people who have gathered for worship are also given the gifts and graces necessary for living out the Christian faith in the world, and that they must go into that world to engage in the mission of the church. A spoken response or a hymn can confirm the congregation's intention to do this, and often an organ or instrumental voluntary concludes the Lord's Day service. But once again, the question arises, When is Christian worship concluded? Perhaps it continues as people greet one another after the service, during the "ritual of coffee," and as people make plans for the coming week.

This order of worship expresses a number of theological convictions. It says that God's love calls the church to gather, and empowers it to offer itself in prayer, praise, and acts of commitment. The congregation yields to the Word of God, and responds to it in a readiness to pray for others, to confess their sins, to make peace with one another, and to rededicate themselves to work for the good of all people. For all the acts of God on their behalf (past and present) and for the opportunity to participate in the outworking of God's will for the world, the church offers its thanks, and receives God's blessing for its labors.

Here, however, we expose a problem with the ordinary Sunday Service. The type of Christian worship described above works very well for the nourishment of the Christian faith and practice of people who are already quite committed, or who are on the way to church membership. But for those who are searching, or those who are in the very early stages of Christian faith, or those who have limited acquaintance with Christian stories, images, and values, this type of service expects a degree of participation that may cause anxiety or embarrassment. In a time of increased interest in the role of Christian worship in the task of evangelism, this problem has drawn the creative attention of many pastoral liturgists. In response, some congregations have tried to lighten the tone of the ordinary Lord's Day Service by deleting such elements as creeds and acts of dedication, in order to make it more generally accessible to "outsiders." Others have included teaching elements within the service itself, and many congregations have instituted separate "seeker services" designed for the special needs of those who are taking their first steps toward Christian commitment. But there are serious objections to these sorts of approaches to the Lord's Day Service. Some argue that it is a significant departure from the historic meaning and function of Sunday worship, which has always been principally for the spiritual nurture of faithful believers. The claim is also made that the Christian community must always take responsibility for the growth in faithfulness of inquirers, and that when devoted Christians integrate newcomers into the Sunday Service and teach them about its significance in the Christian life, they are forging a proper relationship between worship and evangelism.

Some churches concerned about the inability of seeker services to provide sufficient nurture for the community of deeply committed Christians have responded by holding such services at an alternative time to the main Sunday service, or sometimes even in direct competition with it at the same hour. Questions arise here about the role of worship in the formation of a single, cohesive congregation, about the encouragement of a "consumerist" mentality toward worship, and about the provision of appropriate mechanisms for moving "seekers" toward the center, toward the kind of commitment that is expected in a more traditional service of Christian worship. All of these issues are made even more difficult to consider rationally in the face of the massive numerical success of mega-churches, within which the model for these kinds of services was developed. The idea that growth in numbers is necessarily equivalent to growth in spiritual awareness and discipleship is all too common, and can sometimes subvert all of our best instincts about what elements make up the most nourishing liturgical diet for the Christian people.

## DAILY PRAYER

Another way in which the Christian life has been nourished by structures of public worship is in and through the various patterns of daily prayer that have been devised by Christian communities through the centuries. Called variously the "Daily" (or "Divine") Office,[4] the "Horarium," the "Canonical Hours," and the "Liturgy of the Hours," the act of marking certain times of day with such things as prayer, recitation of the Psalms, and singing has been a persistent feature of Christian practice, although it has been more significant for some Christian groups than for others. With the current resurgence of interest in various forms of Christian communal living in which daily prayer is a central feature (communities such as those at Iona in Scotland and Taizé in France), questions of the usefulness and desirability of forms of daily prayer have become more relevant.

The history of Christian daily prayer is a history of people trying to live out and manage the apostolic encouragement to "pray at all times" (Eph. 6:18). In his *Homily on Numbers 23*, Origen says:

> If we offer the sacrifice of praise increasingly and prayer without inter-
> mission, every day is a festival to the Lord: our prayer ascends like
> incense in the morning; the lifting up of our hands like an evening
> oblation.

This ideal of perpetual prayerfulness has been a feature of many religious traditions, and this ideal is often expressed in forms of daily prayer, which
becomes a way of symbolizing prayerful approach to the entire day.

Such an attitude can be seen at work in the practice of Jewish daily prayers
in the New Testament period. In the time of Jesus, the core of Jewish daily
prayer was the recitation of the confession of faith known as the Shema. On
rising and retiring to bed all males over twelve years old were obliged to repeat
the affirmation which begins, "Hear, O Israel: the LORD is our God, the LORD
alone. . . ."[5] The significance of the Shema is described in Deuteronomy 6:4–9,
and the text used in daily morning and evening prayer is composed of sections
from Deuteronomy and Numbers (Deut. 6:4–9 and 13–21, and Num.
15:37–41). Appended to the beginning and end of the Shema was a set of benedictions and prayers for morning and evening. In addition to these private
prayers, a service of public worship was held in the synagogue three times during the day (morning, afternoon, and evening), and this included prayer,
recitation of the Psalms, and readings from the Torah according to a fixed
cycle. There were also special household prayers said at the evening meal. The
prayers for the evening meals at the opening and conclusion of the Sabbath
(Friday and Saturday) were more elaborate, and were accompanied by a lamp-
lighting ceremony and a set of benedictions to mark the beginning and end of
the Sabbath. Biblical references to the times of prayer include Psalm 119:62
and 164: "At midnight I rise to praise you, because of your righteous ordinances" and "Seven times a day I praise you for your righteous ordinances."
Although these verses may simply describe perseverance as the ideal in the life
of prayer and praise of God (in other words, they may be a poetic way of saying that praying is more important than sleeping), they may also indicate
actual times of day when prayers were to be said.

Although Jewish Christians probably continued worshiping in the synagogue in addition to gathering in their own groups, gradually those who
believed that Jesus of Nazareth was the promised Messiah began to feel
uncomfortable with the synagogue liturgy. Certain synagogue regulations had
been dispensed with for Christian prayer gatherings, particularly the requirement that ten men (the *minyan*) was the minimum number needed for a service. (A warrant for this change was found in the words of Jesus, "For where
two or three are gathered in my name, I am there among them," Matt. 18:20.)
But despite this move away from active participation in synagogue worship

among the earliest Christians, some patterns of Christian daily prayer may have continued to be influenced by synagogue practice.[6]

The principal area of continuity between Jewish and Christian daily prayer in this early period is in the pervasive sense that the day itself was a potential locus for the revelation of God and God's action in the world. Where Christian weekly (Sunday) worship was focused on God's acts of redemption, daily worship tended to be centered on God's acts of creation. But there are no authoritative statements about the most appropriate form and content for daily prayer until the fourth century. And there is certainly no Christian equivalent of the Jewish Shema as the centerpiece for daily prayers. The most common feature of daily prayer in the early centuries of Christianity was praise of God and intercession for the needs of the church and the world. The recitation of the Psalms was also seen to be an appropriate element in daily common prayer, but these psalms were usually chosen for their attachment to the particular time of day, morning or evening (Psalm 63, for example, which proclaims that "My soul is satisfied as with a rich feast, and my mouth praises you with joyful lips when I think of you on my bed, and meditate on you in the watches of the night . . .").

The early services of daily prayer were designed as occasions for ordinary Christians to pray and to praise God together each day. As vehicles for "popular" devotion, designed for Christian congregations and families, these services were brief, simple, invariable, colorful, musical, thematically related to the time of day, and accessible to the participation of all. Originally there were no lessons from Scripture, no sermon, and no Christian teaching, but only praise and thanksgiving to God (in the morning) and confession and intercession (in the evening). Consisting of a few well-chosen psalms that could be memorized easily, popular hymns sung to simple tunes, and extempore prayer arising out of the particular needs and thanksgivings of the community, this type of daily common worship (sometimes referred to as the "cathedral" or "people's" office) persisted throughout the first three centuries of the church's life. Many of the early Christian teachers encouraged faithfulness in daily prayer; in about the year 200 CE, for example, Clement of Alexandria suggested that Christians should gather together for prayers in the morning and at noon, and that at the evening meal and at night prayers should be said in families or privately.

Gradually, however, other options for working out the instruction to "pray always" began to be devised. This process was accelerated with the spread of Christianity into rural areas and especially with the decline of persecution and the lessening of the threat of martyrdom at the turn of the fourth century. Certain people, wishing to live the Christian life more intensely, separated themselves from the world and went to live in the desert in imitation of Christ's wilderness experience. Among the many disciplines they imposed upon themselves was the memorizing and the daily repetition of the 150 Psalms. Other Christians gathered into small groups in order to devote themselves to prayer, communal encouragement, and acts of charity. Basil, bishop of Caesarea (also called Basil the Great [ca. 330–379]), gathered such a group around his cathedral and placed them under a discipline or "Rule." Included in this rule were instructions for a complex pattern of daily prayer, consisting of eight services or "hours": a "vigil" at midnight, "matins" at cockcrow (2:00 a.m.), "prime" in the early morning, "terce" at the third hour (9:00 a.m.), "sext" at the sixth hour (12 noon), "none" at the ninth hour (3:00 p.m.), "vespers" when the day's work was over, and "compline" at nightfall. The recitation of the 150 Psalms became the centerpiece of this scheme, and the Psalms were divided among the hours of prayer without consideration for the time of day for which they might be appropriate.

Quite soon, the prayer practices of these communities of highly committed men and women became the ideal for all Christians. But it was an ideal that was impossible to follow, since it demanded a great deal of time and attention, and a high degree of literacy and skill. Fairly quickly, the "people's office" died out, and ordinary Christians relinquished to religious professionals (monks, nuns, and ordained ministers) the mandate to "pray always." In addition, the sense that the time of day itself provides the principal thematic guide for prayer, the images and metaphors for Christian reflection were also being lost. Where there had previously been no explanation necessary for why prayer was said at certain times of the day, now with the increasing complexity of the prayer patterns, alternative forms of justification were required. The hours of prayer themselves were tied to the hours of Jesus' passion: at 6:00 a.m. the Lord was judged guilty, at 9:00 a.m. the crowd cried out "Crucify him!", at 12 noon Jesus was nailed to the cross, at 3:00 p.m. he gave up his spirit, and so on. Because these disciplined communities were striving to identify with the sufferings of Christ, a more penitential interpretation of daily prayer began to replace the sense of joyful thanksgiving that had infused the people's office.

The medieval concern with human mortality was reflected in important changes in the structure of daily prayer. Because of anxiety about the fate of the dead and conviction that the Virgin Mary played an essential role in the fate of everyone, special prayers and lamentations for the dead and a separate set of prayers and hymns dedicated to Mary were added on to the ordinary course of the eight hours of daily prayer. This made the office even longer and more cumbersome than before, and even less appropriate for anyone other than religious professionals and certain wealthy laypeople who had the leisure to pursue singlemindedly the life of Christian prayer and devotion. (In fact, even religious professionals themselves had to pay others to do their ordinary work for them so that they could devote themselves to their prayers.) As clergy became more mobile, however, and less tied to communities where the hours of prayer were said regularly, the requirement that they say the daily office became burdensome for them as well. The invention of a "portable" prayer book (called the "breviary") solved the immediate problem, but it also led to a complete abandonment of any sense of marking time with the hours of prayer. Now the set of prayers devised for a particular hour of the day could be said privately whenever and wherever it was convenient, regardless of the time of day.

Although abuses of the Lord's Supper captured the sixteenth-century Reformers' primary attention, their vision of a Holy City, a society so pervaded by the Word of God that it would be a light to all people, put the restoration of a popular form of daily prayer on their liturgical agenda as well. Martin Luther, John Calvin, Martin Bucer, and others who wished the reformation of the church produced services for public morning and evening prayer for use in congregations. At the center of these services were the reading and preaching of Scripture, and to this were added prayers, vernacular hymns, a canticle and the Lord's Prayer. This scheme passed into the first English Book of Common Prayer (1549 and 1552), which centered morning and evening prayer on the recitation of the 150 Psalms on a monthly rotation. Music for these services was written by some of the finest composers of the period, among them Thomas Tallis (d. 1585) and William Byrd (ca. 1543–1623). It remained, however, essentially a reworking of the monastic pattern of daily prayer (albeit reduced to only two "hours," morning and evening), rather than a return to a truly "popular" form of the daily office.

The Puritans, who sought scriptural warrant for each and every element of public worship, reduced daily common prayer to a lengthy reading from Scripture, a detailed exposition of the passage, and the Lord's Prayer, and particularly encouraged family prayer in the morning and evening. John Wesley's 1784 revision of the Book of Common Prayer for the Methodist societies in America left the traditional Anglican morning and evening prayer services more or less intact, but the classes and bands, the small cohesive groups Wesley organized for Bible study, mutual encouragement, and prayer, devised their own devotional schemes. The Puritan strain in much Methodist, Baptist, and Reformed worship led to a heavier emphasis on family devotions than on congregational daily prayer, and this trend persisted throughout the nineteenth and twentieth centuries.

Inspired by recent historical research into the earliest layer of the practice of daily prayer in Christian communities, certain groups have sought to restore the "people's office" as a feature of contemporary congregational life. Many have recognized that the earliest pattern of daily prayer, with services that are short, invariable, thematically tied to the time of day, colorful and musical, is just the sort of pattern which best suits the needs of busy people.

At the same time, the popularity of forms of daily prayer devised at places like Taizé and Iona have recommended themselves to many, especially because of the beauty and simplicity of the music composed for these services. Visitors to these types of monastic and quasi-monastic communities have become convinced of the necessity of corporate daily prayer for the health and well-being of their home congregations, and have adapted the forms of daily prayer they experienced while on retreat to a variety of local situations. The publication of service materials from Taizé, Little Gidding, Iona and similar places has further widened their sphere of influence. On the whole, downtown churches have found it easier than suburban or rural churches to establish daily congregational services, and many are finding that the provision of a noonday service for office workers has been very well received. Many Christian hospitals, homes for the elderly, retreat centers, schools, or vacation camps also find that daily prayer falls naturally into the pattern of Christian communal living, and have begun to think creatively about how daily prayer can be a part of the nourishing of faith, hope, and love.

## PENANCE AND RECONCILIATION

The type of worship that will be discussed in this section is called by a variety of different names: penance, reconciliation, confession and absolution, the forgiveness of sins. All of these describe a ritual event that is centered on the public acknowledgment of our alienation from both God and neighbor, and the assurance of God's persistent willingness to forgive. But Christian reconciliation happens not only in public and private services of penance, but at a whole host of other liturgical moments as well. Formal confession is typically a part of the Sunday service, the service of baptism, of the Lord's Supper, on occasion at funerals or weddings, as part of special services during Lent and Advent, and as a part of the ordinary structure of Daily Prayer.[7] Indeed, reconciliation is of the essence of Christian worship itself, whenever it proclaims that something which was crushed by sin has been released and raised up in Christ Jesus. Here, however, we will center our attention on the independent, self-standing service of public worship that is called "penance" or "reconciliation."

The question that motivates much of the early history of services of reconciliation is, Can there be any possibility of a second, post-baptismal, forgiveness of sins in the case of a serious fall? The earliest Christians had to deal with the fact that even after baptism people seemed to persist in sinning, and they were forced to ask how the Christian community should respond in these cases. There is some suggestion that anyone who sinned after baptism in the very early period of Christian history was permanently expelled from the

Christian community. Certainly with the prevailing expectation that the second coming and the final judgment of all creation was at hand, a rigorist attitude toward post-baptismal sin was almost inevitable.

But as time went on and the final consummation did not arrive, the question of how the Christian community would deal with sin after baptism became more immediate. If one committed serious sin (that is, apostasy, adultery, or murder), the sinner would be required to perform certain acts of "penance," various disciplines which would serve as signs of true contrition. But there was only one opportunity for repentance. As one early church leader states, "For if anyone should sin and do penance frequently, to such a person this penance will be of no avail; for with difficulty will he live." What would this penance have consisted of? In about the year 150 CE, Clement of Rome tells us that "fasting is better than prayer, but almsgiving is better than both. And love covers a multitude of sins."

About fifty years later we have the first direct evidence that the expulsion and the reconciliation of a penitent person took place within a service of public worship. Once it had become known to the bishop that a member of the Christian community was engaged in some kind of sinful behavior, the sinner was required to appear before the community at the Sunday service wearing a garment of goat's hair, and to sit apart from the rest of the congregation. After the reading of the Scriptures and sermon, the person concerned made a public confession before the whole congregation, asked for their prayers, and was enrolled in the "order of penitents." The bishop announced to the sinner and the congregation that certain penitential disciplines would be required (such as fasting, prayer, almsgiving, and the wearing of sackcloth), stipulated a certain period of exclusion, and exhorted them to pray and to ensure that the various penances were being performed. Then the penitent was formally expelled from the gathering. From that time onward, the sinner would be allowed to attend worship for first part of the service, in order to hear the Scriptures read and preached, but would be removed from the gathering before Communion ("excommunicated").

Unless they were dying, there was only one time in the year that penitents were publicly reconciled with the church after their penance was completed, and that was at Easter. This reconciliation could take place at the Easter Vigil, at the Maundy Thursday service, or on Good Friday, but in any case the restoration of the sinner to communion with the Christian fellowship was intended to be symbolized by participation in the Easter celebration of the Lord's Supper. The service of reconciliation itself consisted of prayer, the laying-on-of-hands by the bishop, an exhortation, and a declaration of forgiveness. A verse from 1 Peter (5:6) might also have been sung: "Humble yourselves, therefore, under the mighty hand of God, so that he may exalt you in due time." After being restored to fellowship, the sinner was still under quite severe discipline, and would be expected to lead an exemplary life, doing good works, fasting, and giving alms, under the watchful eye of the bishop and members of the church.

Not surprisingly given the rigors of the system, things began to break down as Christianity became more and more an accepted part of society at large. Public, liturgical penance had probably ceased to exist by the early part of the seventh century in most places, and a new pattern for the forgiveness of sin began to take its place. This was not so much directed toward the reconciliation of notorious sinners with the Christian community, but toward maintaining the spiritual equilibrium of the ordinary Christian. In this system lists of sins were provided (called the "penitentials"), and penances were imposed according to the severity of the transgression. The Christian would make a private confession to a spiritual adviser (in some places referred to as a soul-friend), who could be either a man or a woman, usually a member of a religious order, and this person would consult the list of sins and impose the appropriate tariff or penalty for the particular sin confessed. This type of confession and absolution spread throughout the church in the West and, except for occasions of capital offenses, penance and reconciliation as an act of the whole Christian community disappeared for the next twelve hundred years.

But the problem of post-baptismal sin persisted, and various groups and individuals recommended formal rites for the restoration of sinners to full fellowship with the Christian community. For example, like other inheritors of the Reformation tradition, John Wesley affirmed that public confession and absolution was sometimes necessary in cases of "public scandal," and that private confession was a helpful way of "disburdening the conscience" of the repentant Christian. But God's forgiveness did not in any way depend on absolution by an authorized person, and private confession could be "a dangerous snare, both to the confessor, and those that confess." The imposition of penances could also be useful as a part of ecclesiastical discipline in cases of "notorious offenders," but again, care must be taken that human works should not substitute for faith in the promises of God to forgive.[8]

In recent years there have been initiatives on the part of a number of Christian churches to recover the early church's practice of public, corporate services of reconciliation. The Roman Catholic Church has taken the lead in this area, out of acute pastoral necessity. Since penance is considered one of the seven sacraments of the church necessary for salvation, and since many Roman Catholics have been reluctant to avail themselves of private, individual confession of sin to a priest, rites of public reconciliation have been devised as a way of offering the sacrament of penance to greater numbers of people. These services consist of a lengthy examination of conscience, readings from Scripture that speak of both God's judgment and God's mercy, prayers of confession, and a statement of absolution by the presider (either a priest or bishop).

In addition to these separate services of reconciliation, the penitential character of the seasons of Lent and Advent has been reinvigorated, and special prayers of confession have been written as optional openings for services during these times. Many churches, even those for whom the keeping of the Christian year has been quite foreign, have begun to restore the tradition of Ash Wednesday services, during which penitence is a principal focus of communal attention. Weekday services for penitential meditation during Lent have been organized in many places, often by women's groups who take this on as their special Lenten offering. Much of the energy behind this return to public penance has come from the recognition that sin is a factor not only in the lives of individual Christians, but in the life of the Christian church as a whole. Theological reflection on the nature of "social sin" has also contributed to the recent interest in public services of reconciliation; it has become clear that many times we not only engage in willful violations of known moral principles, but we also collude in various ways with the overall sinfulness of society. By being willing to identify ourselves with the generalized human failure to follow the path of righteousness, we open ourselves to the love and mercy of God, and thereby begin to rebuild relationships with our neighbors, between nations, and with our Creator. Services which include public repentance and absolution have been a particular contribution of the Christian churches during times of war, when a sense of triumphalism and vainglory has seemed inappropriate in the face of human suffering on both sides of a particular conflict.

The Christian life is a continual cycle of contrition and forgiveness, repentance and mercy. For a very long time, this dialogue was understood as occurring between the individual Christian believer and God, and therefore a subject more properly placed within the sphere of Christian spirituality than within liturgical studies. But recently we have begun to revise our understanding of the nature of sin and forgiveness, and to see it not only as a matter of concern to individuals, but as something which has significant consequences for the whole Christian community. We have looked back to the teaching of the early church on the nature of sin as a wound in the body of Christ, and we have begun to understand the implications of taking responsibility for the sins we commit in common with others simply by virtue of living in contemporary society. In any case, it is clear that coming to terms with our human failings is a necessary prerequisite for health—physical, mental, emotional, social, and spiritual—and therefore a proper concern of the Christian community at prayer. Because services of reconciliation proclaim not only our deep complicity with sin but also God's unrelenting willingness to forgive, they can serve as powerful witnesses to the love of God in a world where guilt and shame disable so many. Many believe that reinstating services of public reconciliation, at least on some special occasions, may lead to a deeper understanding of the ways in which estrangement from God and one another affects the body of Christ.

# ORDINATION

All social organizations develop various forms of leadership in order that they might fulfill their essential mission, and the Christian church is no exception. Most churches agree that God calls certain people to forms of representative ministry, and that the various gifts for ministry are given by God in order that the body of Christ may be nourished, for the sake of God's mission in the world. This combination of gift and calling for ministry is seen in the earliest days of the church, when the apostles gathered communities of believers around them and ensured continuity by appointing successors to carry on the ministry of leadership, discipline, and proclamation. Of course, the whole Christian community was to be a "holy nation" and a "royal priesthood" (1 Peter 2:9), acting in Christ's name to heal and to reconcile. The vocation of apostolic leadership was to call the church continually to its priestly ministry of reconciliation, to enable a lively encounter with the gospel, and to serve as a focus of unity.

Although the New Testament occasionally speaks of the appointment of leaders, it gives few specific details about how those appointments were made, about whether there were any rites to signify the appointment, nor even about what the various ministries signified. In the book of Acts, for example, we find a description of the appointment of seven deacons to distribute food within the community, thus freeing the apostles for more essential work.[9]

The overwhelming impression one gets of ministry in the early church is that it was fluid, flexible, and adaptable to the various circumstances in which the church found itself. Together the three orders of ministers exercised both authority over and ministry to those under their care. During the early centuries, leaders for the local congregation were very probably chosen by the community itself from within its membership. Those individuals who showed evidence of the gifts of leadership and holiness and who were known for sound teaching would be brought forward for ordination. Until the early-third century, however, we have no real evidence of a "rite of ordination" for any of these offices, although there may have been some kind of service of installation.

Despite certain differences, the earliest rites of ordination we know about (from the third and fourth centuries) have a clearly identifiable core which consisted of prayers for the gifts of the Holy Spirit accompanied by the laying-on-of-hands. The service would also have included a declaration by the community that it supports the choice, the reading of Scripture and preaching, anointing for service, affirmations by the person ordained of the sense of call, an announcement of the new relationship between minister and congregation, and the celebration of the Lord's Supper. As the rite developed in later centuries, various ceremonies for the giving and receiving of the badges or tokens of office (the pastoral staff, the Bible, and the chalice, for example) were also given prominence.

Gradually throughout the Middle Ages the rites of ordination became increasingly elaborate, and prayers and ceremonies manifested a hierarchical view of the ministry and supported and enhanced the separation of clergy from laity. Ordination was declared to be one of the seven sacraments of the church, and the emphasis within the rite shifted away from prayer and the imposition of hands and toward the giving of the badges of office. From about the eleventh century onward a common feature of the rite of ordination was the singing of the Pentecost hymn "Come, Holy Ghost," the first verse of which calls on the Spirit to descend on the proceedings:

> Come Holy Ghost, our souls inspire,
> And lighten with celestial fire;
> Thou the anointing Spirit art,
> Who dost thy sevenfold gifts impart.[10]

This hymn expresses the conviction that at the heart of ordination lies the anointing of the Spirit with the gifts for ministry: wisdom, understanding, counsel, fortitude, knowledge, piety, fear of the Lord.[11]

Rites for the admission to the "minor orders" of ministry (porters or "door-keepers," lectors, exorcists, acolytes, and sub-deacons) were also developed, and institution to each of these offices was seen as a prerequisite to ordination to the "major orders" of deacon, priest, and bishop. In all cases, the only person with authority to ordain was the bishop, with three bishops usually the minimum number required for the ordination of a fellow bishop. This was a way of symbolizing the collegiality of ministers across the church, and of ensuring a continuity of apostolic teaching. The major orders were signified by various distinctive kinds of dress (or vestments) that were worn while performing liturgical duties as badges of office. These included a narrow stole running sash-like (diagonally) over the left shoulder for the deacon, a similar stole worn across the back of the neck with the ends falling in front for the presbyter, and the mitre, a pointed hat with two tabs hanging in the back, for the bishop. During the ordination rite for each order of ministry, the newly ordained person was solemnly dressed in the appropriate vestments as a mark of a changed role.

The Reformers of the sixteenth century all attempted to return to the pattern of ministry as it was described in the New Testament, and to simplify the rites by which people were ordained. Some groups retained the office of bishop; others abandoned it altogether or denied that it was a separate order of ministry. Presbyters were charged with the ministry of Word and Sacrament and deacons were restored to their original work of looking after the poor. All ministers were to test their calling in the context of the local community. In all of the Reformation churches, prayer and the laying-on-of-hands were returned to the center of the ordination service, which usually also consisted of the reading and preaching of the Word of God, interrogation of the candidate on the seriousness of his intention and sense of call, a declaration of support by the congregation, and various other prayers, psalms, and exhortations. In the Church of England and other European churches established by law as the national church, legal declarations, inquiries and examinations of the candidates, the delivery of the badges of office, and exhortations tended to overshadow the invocation of the Spirit and prayer for the gifts for ministry. John Wesley was one of those who were convinced that bishops (whom Wesley called "superintendents") and presbyters (he called them "elders") were essentially a single order of ministry, differing only in the increased responsibilities given to bishops. Because of this fundamental equality, when the Methodists of America desperately needed ministers, Wesley was able to agree that they could be ordained by their fellow presbyters.

A number of significant concerns have shaped the most recent revisions of ordination rites in the Christian churches. In the important ecumenical statement *Baptism, Eucharist, and Ministry* (1982),[12] agreement on certain key issues on the nature of ordination was expressed:

> Ordination denotes an action by God and the community by which the ordained are strengthened by the Spirit for their task and are upheld by the acknowledgement and prayers of the congregation. . . . The act of ordination by the laying on of hands of those appointed to do so is at one and the same time invocation (*epiklesis*); sacramental sign; acknowledgment of gifts and commitment.[13]

As actual reunions between different churches have taken place, the provision of new ordination rites have become a principal way of affirming the fundamental unity of the parties to the mergers. The most recent revisions of ordination rites within individual denominations have rested on historical research into the earliest layer of ordination practice, and this has led to substantial consensus among the churches on the most appropriate shape of the service and its essential components. These rites display a common commitment to a return to the centrality of prayer for the gifts of the Spirit, congregational affirmation, and the laying-on-of-hands. Since the church is a community established and sustained by grace, the celebration of the Eucharist was seen to be an integral part of the rite of ordination, as a joyful response to and proclamation of God's continuing faithfulness in providing ministers for the church.

Much recent attention has been given in many of the Christian denominations to the renewal of the ministry of deacons. Gradually over the centuries, the original sense that the deacon's work was a specialized ministry of service to the sick and the needy was lost, and the diaconate often became simply a stepping-stone to other forms of ordained ministry. As the original functions of deacons are restored to them, turning their ministry away from the shepherding of the flock and toward service to the wider world, important changes in the rites of ordination to the diaconate will have to be made. Many churches are seeking to establish a permanent order of deacons, who do not consider themselves to be "in training" for the presbyterate, but rather to be doing the specific work of service they feel themselves called by God to do.

Over the centuries the rites for the ordination of deacons, presbyters (or elders), and bishops have provided evidence of the essential understanding of the place of ordained ministry in the life of the church. New images for the ordained minister are beginning to arise (for example, "enabler" and "bridge-builder") and these will undoubtedly shape the language of future rites of ordination. In addition, as new forms of ministry emerge in the contemporary church, questions are being raised about appropriate rites for the recognition of those ministries. Perhaps we have returned to a situation not unlike that of the early church, where more flexible and fluid structures of ministry are necessary for the mission of the church to succeed.

The Christian life, like all living systems, requires continual nourishment in order for it to grow and thrive. In this chapter we have seen the ways in which the ordinary Sunday service structures the life of the church around the God's Word and our response to that Word. We have found that for many communities of faith, public daily prayer has moved people toward the Christian ideal of "praying constantly," and that others find in services of reconciliation comfort and assurance whenever the burdens of the individual and collective failure to meet the demands of fidelity to the Christian calling threaten to overwhelm. Finally we have seen the ways in which the rites of ordination have served to express the Christian community's belief that God calls certain women and men and charges them with the task of supporting and upholding us as we carry out our ministries of loving service in the name of Jesus Christ. All of these, together with the sacraments of Christian initiation and the Lord's Supper, provide a steady diet of prayer, Scripture, praise, thanksgiving, and encouragement for Christian people as they grow toward the full stature of Christ.

There are, of course, other, occasional services of public worship which nourish the Christian life. Homecomings and church anniversaries celebrate the importance of strong roots and the faithfulness of those who have gone before us. Services for the dedication of churches and church furnishings give congregations the opportunity to pray that the building and its contents might be used for the working out of God's purposes, and to thank God for those persons whose labor and commitment made them possible. Installations of church workers into their jobs, Rally Day services, and the commissioning of missionaries also fall into this category, giving strength and purpose to congregations and to individual Christians. There are also times of lament, occasions in which a disaster has befallen the nation or the community, occasions of national, local, or congregational anxiety which are brought before God in specially-constructed services of worship. All these, and many other times for gathering, giving thanks, praying for courage and wisdom, rededicating our lives, and committing ourselves to the future, serve to build up and strengthen the fellowship of Christian believers.

# 5

# Christian Worship
# through the Life Cycle

The lives of all human beings follow a similar course: we are born, we grow up, we form pair-bonds, we age, and we die. Although untimely death or commitment to lifelong singleness can give a slightly different shape to the lives of some people, for the most part we are bound together by these common human experiences. Christian worship encounters people at a number of significant points in the ordinary course of their life cycle. At birth, marriage, and death, at moments of significant physical, social, or emotional transition, the Christian community gathers to pray, to thank God, and to proclaim again the gospel of God's love for us all. We do not come together for Christian worship at such times in order to "bless" things and events that are inherently "profane." Worship at these times is called out of people because the holiness and blessedness of all of life has become transparent to them.

We saw in the first chapter the kinds of lessons we have learned about Christian worship from those who work in the human sciences. One of the most important of these lessons is that there is a universal human need to celebrate significant moments in the life cycle, to mark transitions from child to adult, single to married, living to dead. It is tempting to think of celebrations of this kind as primarily of interest and importance to the individuals most immediately concerned. But they are also events of the whole community of which the individual is a part, since by ritualizing these events, the changed role of the person in the community is defined and the community itself is enabled to re-form to accommodate the change. "I declare that they are husband and wife," or "Our sister Emily has died," may seem unnecessary statements of the self-evident at a wedding or a funeral. But they have an essential function, because to state that things are true, publicly, solemnly, and in the presence of God, somehow contributes to making them true, making them part of the structure of our experience of reality.

In this chapter we will look at the various ways in which Christian worship and the ordinary human life cycle intersect and have intersected throughout history. In all cases we are speaking of ways in which worship moves people toward holy, integrated, and meaningful lives. But because such events as birth, marriage, and death are not specific to Christians, but common experiences for us all, many of the rites we will discuss have become composites of Christian ritual and other kinds of customs and ceremonies. Christians have always borrowed elements for their worship from the world around them, and this essential "worldliness" of Christian worship contributes to its great strength and resilience.

## CHRISTIAN MARRIAGE

The marriage ceremony is not something indigenous to Christianity. Not only were there rituals for pair-bonding long before Christianity came into being, but other religious traditions throughout the world give a central place to rites by which the lifelong, mutual commitment of two people is celebrated and ratified. Despite the increasing number of civil marriages, the instinct to mark the establishment of a committed relationship between two people with a religious ritual remains strong. Many times couples express the sentiment that it "just wouldn't seem right" not to be married in church, even though they may not identify themselves as committed Christians otherwise.

Because different threads have been woven into the fabric of Christian marriage, the wedding ceremony has become an occasion when civil law, piety, family and ethnic customs, social conventions, and religious ritual intertwine and influence one another. In it we can find the echoes of pre-Christian pagan practices coexisting with prayers from the Old Testament apocrypha, stories of the ministry of Jesus side-by-side with legally binding oaths. Indeed, many students of Christian worship think that this tendency toward syncretism indicates that the church made a serious mistake when it became involved in the marriage business, and that in any case wedding ceremonies may have outlived their usefulness as a part of the Christian witness.

To decide about the appropriateness of these attitudes, it is important to look at the history of Christian marriage. In Mediterranean late antiquity, within which marriages between Christians were originally set, marriage was composed of a series of stages, each of which was marked with its own specific ritual. In Roman paganism, for example, once the partners were of marriageable age (twelve years old for a boy, and eleven for a girl), their parents could enter into a marriage contract that was legally binding on both parties, and a sooth-sayer was asked to determine the most auspicious day for the marriage. On the day of the wedding itself, the woman was veiled from head to foot in orange or yellow fabric (the *flammium*), and by the light of pine torches she was escorted by a number of female attendants to the courtyard of the groom's house. There the bride-price was formally offered and accepted, and the groom placed a ring on the bride's fourth finger to signify his possession of her. The priest then read the auguries, officially declaring this a propitious time for the wedding, and the bride's parents made an offering of corn to Zeus, asking that he would oversee the ceremony. The banqueting that followed lasted until nightfall, and seems to have consisted of a series of bawdy jokes, rude speeches, and mock arguments between bride and groom. Fertility symbols, especially walnuts, were thrown around the couple.

When darkness fell, the bride was led by virgins to the door of the house, while young men sang wedding songs. She was carried over the threshold by the groom, and the two of them lit a fire in the hearth as a symbol of their new life together. The virgins prepared the bedchamber (the presence of a number of young women, dressed very much like the bride, was necessary in order to fool any demons who might try to claim the right of sleeping the first night with the new wife) and the bride sprinkled the bed with water as a symbolic inducement to fertility. The next day, the bride received her new relatives and offered sacrifices to the household gods.

Even after more than twenty centuries, some of these elements from pagan antiquity can be detected in contemporary Christian marriage rites. Brides-maids, attired very much like the bride, the giving of a ring, the wedding reception and its speeches, guests throwing various fertility symbols (today rice and flower petals are more likely than walnuts and water, but the meaning is the same), and the groom carrying the bride over the threshold, are practices that can be traced to Roman paganism.

Marriage in pre-Christian Judaism was also a thoroughly domestic affair, without a particular set of religious "rites" for later Christians to adopt or adapt. It began with a binding betrothal, when the couple's parents exchanged letters of consent or gifts of money. (The couple could live together in lieu of betrothal.) A bride-price was paid, or the groom could work off the indebted-ness with the bride's family (as Jacob did for the family of Rachel in Gen. 29:18). On the day of the wedding (marriages took place on Wednesdays for virgins and Fridays for widows), both bride and groom would fast in the morning, and then be dressed in their finest clothes by their attendants. The bride was veiled and, as in the Roman wedding, the bride's attendants (called the *paranymphs*) would be attired in similar clothing to that of the bride, in order to confuse the demons (or *dybbuks*) who might otherwise demand the right of the first night with the bride.

A quorum of ten men (the *minyan*) was necessary to witness and validate the marriage contract,[1] and this qualification having been met, vows were exchanged by the bride and groom in the presence of the guests. There is some indication that the Jewish marriage ritual at the time of Jesus included the singing of Psalm 45 and parts of the Song of Solomon, and that the wedding feast could go on for several days. Finally, as the festivities were drawing to a close, corn was thrown at the pair as a symbol of fertility and the marriage covenant was sealed with blessings and prayers. Until the seventh century, at which time rabbis began to preside at Jewish weddings, the father of the bride seems to have been the one to say the central prayers of blessing over the couple. In all of these prayers and blessings there is the strong sense that sexuality and human love are a part of the *shalom* of God:

> Blessed art thou, O Lord our God, King of the universe, who hast created joy and gladness, bridegroom and bride, mirth and exultation, pleasure and delight, love, peace and fellowship. Soon may there be heard in the cities of Judah, and in the streets of Jerusalem, the voice of joy and gladness, the voice of the bride, the jubilant voice of the bridegroom from their canopies, and of youths from their feasts of song.

The final set of rituals took place in the bedchamber itself, and included prayers over the nuptial bed and blessings over the couple. After the marriage is consummated, seven additional days of feasting follow. In post-Christian Judaism, the wedding tended to be set in the context of a festival Seder, with blessings over the cup, the giving of a gold ring, the reading of the contract, seven blessings for a fruitful marriage (many scholars say that it was at this point in the wedding feast at Cana that Jesus turned the water into wine), and the smashing of the cup to symbolize the sealing of the covenant between husband and wife. The rituals at the marital bed were gradually abandoned, but a canopy (or *huppah*) was held over the couple during the wedding itself to symbolize the bedchamber, and this tradition continues in Jewish weddings today.

During the first three centuries of Christianity, marriages remained essentially civil and domestic arrangements, in which the church was only marginally interested. Because of this, we have almost no evidence from the New Testament to tell us how marriages between Christians in this period were undertaken. Paul testifies to a period of betrothal, and suggests that a widow might remarry as long as she marries "in the Lord," presumably indicating that her husband must also be a believer. At about the turn of the second century, Ignatius of Antioch (ca. 35–112) advised the Christians under his care that those who wished to marry should seek the permission of the bishop, in order that, again, "the marriage will be made in the Lord and not for the sake of passion." It is probable that if both bride and groom were members of the local Christian community, the leader of the congregation might be asked to give a blessing of the couple at the home or in the context of the eucharistic meal in church, but Basil of Caesarea (ca. 330–379) warns that if a person had been married three or four times before, a period of penitence might be necessary prior to marrying again. It is very likely, however, that the betrothal, the veiling of brides, feasting, the exchange of rings, and other rituals from pagan and Jewish antiquity would have been common marriage practices for Christians as well.

Beginning in the fifth century we have direct evidence of the church seeking to increase its control over marriages and the rites of marriage. At first, the clergy were simply called upon to serve as reliable witnesses (as they were for many other forms of contract), in this case to affirm that consent between the partners was freely given, that both were of marriageable ages, and that they were not closely related to one another. In the mid-sixth century, however, liturgical books begin to contain special blessings for marriages to be used in the context of the Eucharist, as well as indications that marriages should not take place during Advent or Lent, and should be conducted "according to the long tradition of the church." Throughout the Middle Ages, marriage became increasingly regulated by canon law and the rites of marriage were more clearly designated as services of Christian worship. But despite the intensifying Christianization of marriage, many things that had been a part of the old domestic rite were retained, albeit drawn into the service in church. Betrothal vows, the exchange of rings and other tokens, the making of the contract, and the veiling of the bride were all now accompanied by special prayers and blessings by the priest or bishop. Even the bedchamber became the focus of the church's prayerful attention:

> Lord, bless this bed and all who dwell in it, that there may be found in them holiness, chastity, meekness, fulfillment of the law, and obedience to God, Father, Son and Holy Spirit.[2]

Because the marriage contract had to be entered into knowledgeably by the two persons concerned, much of this liturgical material was in the common language of the people, rather than in ecclesiastical Latin, making portions of the marriage rite the earliest examples vernacular liturgy.

The force behind many of these moves to draw marriages into the orbit of the church was the increasing fragmentation of society that had begun in the seventh century. Not only was the church seen as a focus of stability and order in general, but it also became a guarantor of the legality of relationships and states of life. In a society in which rights of inheritance and proof of legitimacy were matters of real political and economic significance, the fact that marriages within noble families were routinely conducted by the church ensured that things were done in good order and that later the marriage could be proven in court if necessary. Eventually, the "church wedding" became the norm not only for the nobility but for all couples of whatever rank, and the combination of legal, contractual language ("to have and to hold from this day forward" is the form of language used for all forms of property conveyancing) and prayers of blessing became firmly established as the core of all Christian marriage rites in the West.

At the same time, the theology of marriage was also developing. Marriage was considered one of the seven sacraments of the church from the thirteenth century, although in most manuals of theology it was listed last among the seven. But there was a more important question being debated: What constituted a valid marriage? In most Roman civil law, it was the mutual consent of the parties to the terms of the marriage that made a binding contract. Others argued that it was the consummation of the marriage (as it was in Germanic law), still others that it was the giving and receiving of a ring or the words of the priest, "I pronounce you husband and wife." But for most, the mutual agreement of husband and wife (ratified by sexual union) was the essence Christian marriage, reinforcing its roots in medieval contract law. All parties to the debate were united in the conviction that a man and woman were not "married by the church (or the clergy)," but rather "married one another" in the presence of the clergy and Christian community whose function was to witness and to bless the union.

Among the continental Reformers, marriage between Christians was a holy endeavor and belonged in the context of the preaching of the Word of God. Marriage, said John Calvin, was a "good state," just as "farming, building, cobbling, and barbering are lawful ordinances of God but not sacraments." Martin Luther produced a marriage rite in 1529 that began outside the church door (where all civil contracts were ratified) with the straightforward question to the couple "Do you desire to have this person for your wedded husband/ wife?" Rings were exchanged, and the minister joined the couple's right hands together, recited the words from Matthew 19:6 ("What God has joined together, let no one separate"), and declared the couple married. The wedding party then moved inside the church building and gathered at the altar where a passage from Genesis was read and a prayer of blessing recited. In all cases, the Reformers placed the emphasis on catechesis, the reading and proclamation of Scripture, and prayer for the couple as an affirmation of the rightness of their marriage in the sight of God. For the radical wing of the Reformation, the marriage of two Christians was of a particular concern, since all forms of the covenant relationship were of the substance of the church. Members of the congregation were already "in covenant" with one another, and sometimes new converts were "re-trothed" to their spouses when they entered the community by publicly declaring their relationship before the gathered assembly on the Lord's Day. If a member of the congregation had been banned from contact with the community and later reinstated, he or she might remarry a former spouse as a part of the welcoming rites. In most of the groups of the radical Reformation, being "yoked to an unbeliever" was sufficient grounds for divorce (1 Cor. 7:15).

The English Reformers made only very few changes to the late-medieval rite they inherited, and as a result the words by which many Christians marry today are nearly identical to those used by their ancestors over six hundred years ago. In the exhortation at the beginning of Thomas Cranmer's 1549 service, three purposes for marriage are stated: (1) the procreation of children, (2) the control of lust, and (3) the mutual society of husband and wife. Cranmer's wedding rite is among the most beautiful examples of English liturgical prose, and its durability attests to its depth of insight and pastoral sensitivity. Even when serious and substantial proposals for an alternative wedding service have been made, all Christian marriage rites in English since 1549 have had to take account of the marriage rite in the successive editions of the Book of Common Prayer.

Even though the wedding rite across the various traditions has been among the most stable of all Christian liturgies, various significant changes have marked its later history. The English Puritans, who generally considered marriage to be a secular enterprise, reversed the order of the reasons for marriage, giving mutual help and society precedence over the procreation of children and the prevention of fornication, and these sensibilities were brought with the Pilgrim settlers to North America. They also eliminated the giving of rings. In a presaging of modern sensibilities, John Wesley removed the "giving away of the bride" from his modified service of 1784 for the Methodists in North America. He also shortened the traditional service in the Book of Common Prayer and (probably under Puritan influence) omitted reference to the giving of a ring. Quaker couples make promises to one another publicly in the Meeting, and without clergy to preside over the ceremony, the members of the congregation witness and sign their names to a document which is then hung in the home which the bride and groom share.

Marriage is a concern of both church and state, and so a number of legal requirements regulate the conduct of marriages. Because of anxieties about clandestine marriages, in some places there is a requirement that banns (notice of a forthcoming marriage) be read in church at the main service on three Sundays prior to the wedding, although marriage in church was not itself a legal requirement in England until 1753. Various potential difficulties (both con-tractual and physiological) with the marriage of closely-related people have led to the imposition of laws of consanguinity, which prohibit marriages between not only blood relatives, but relatives by marriage within certain degrees of affinity. In many cases, the presider at the wedding in church, usually but not always the minister, acts in a civil capacity, insuring that all the proper docu-ments are signed and that the marriage is properly registered.

Several issues have shaped the latest generation of rites for Christian mar-riage in the various denominations. Changes in the status and role of women in society at large have led many to question the inequality of the partners, which has been implicit to one degree or another in most traditional wedding rites. The ancient notion that the bride is a piece of property which is trans-ferred from one responsible male to another at the "giving away of the bride" has caused that particular element of the rite to come into disfavor, and the unilateral promise of the bride to "obey" her husband has suffered similar con-demnation. Both of these have been discarded (or made optional) in many modern rites. In addition, some wedding symbolism has suggested that in making a new family together, bride and groom submerge their individual per-sonalities into an amorphous unity, and this too is being strongly discouraged.

There is also a growing recognition that the new family is not an isolated social unit, but a part of a larger network of relationships that includes par-ents, siblings and other relatives, friends, and neighbors. Many contemporary wedding rites acknowledge the extent to which the support of all these differ-ent groups is necessary for a successful marriage by encouraging the involve-ment of the congregation in various elements in the service. Members of the congregation are invited to read lessons and lead in prayer, and many rites include affirmations and symbolic gestures of love and support to be made by the whole community together. This is not simply so that "Auntie can do a bit of the service," but so that the wedding rite as a whole celebrates God's gift of a loving community within which a Christian marriage can grow and flourish. Another way in which the social context of marriage is acknowledged is in the provision of prayers of intercession, in which the new bride and groom, as their first act of worship after they have made their vows, intercede for the needs of the world of which they are a part.

Christian pastors have also had to come to terms with the fact that more than half of the marriages they perform will end in divorce, and most of the partners from those marriages will marry again. The effects of divorce and remarriage are causing a reevaluation not only of approaches to premarital counseling, but also of the wedding service itself, seeking to avoid a glib or overly romanticized attitude toward the couple's future. But despite the statis-tics, all churches agree that the rite of Christian marriage must presume that marriage is a lifelong, exclusive commitment between two people, to be undertaken seriously and with the full intention of maintaining fidelity. Many couples also come to marriage having lived together for some time, and any rite that presupposes (in words or symbols) the virginity of bride or groom may be the cause of congregational mirth or embarrassment.

Similar questions are being raised about the appropriateness of contemporary wedding services for couples who are not committed Christians. All of the new official denominational rites are self-consciously celebrations of Christian marriage, replete with biblical imagery and resting on the presumption that the marriage relationship is a community of Christian love, and a sign and foretaste of the reign of God. Some people argue that to ask a couple to tell lies in church at such a significant moment in their lives is neither good evangelism nor good pastoral care. They say that there would be real benefit in returning to the practice of the early church, with a civil ceremony the normal marriage rite for everyone, followed by a blessing in church for committed Christians.

Marriages between committed Christians of different denominations and between people of different faith traditions also present special pastoral and liturgical problems. Clergy from each tradition should be invited to participate in the service, and respect for the family, ethnic, and religious customs of both bride and groom is imperative. In some cases the wedding service is an adaptation of the existing rite of one partner's tradition; in other cases it is a composite, amalgamating the two rites into a new liturgical entity. Ecumenical bodies such as the Joint Liturgical Group of Britain and Ireland and the Consultation on Christian Unity in the United States have produced new wedding ceremonies for marriages between Christians of different denominations. In cases of interfaith marriages special sensitivity is required, and the advice of clergy from the religious traditions concerned should always be sought early in the planning process.

The question What is the essence of Christian marriage? has not gone away, and is being debated not only within individual denominations but by ecumenical groups as well. Even though throughout most of its history marriage has been understood as a contract between two people, with its terms and conditions clearly set out in the marriage vows ("from this day forward"; "in sickness and in health"; "forsaking all others"), new images are being explored which are more strictly religious and less juridical in nature. Many theologians have spoken of Christian marriage as a covenant, modeled on the covenant between God and God's people, or as the "church in microcosm," with union in Christ forging the bond of fidelity and peace between husband and wife. Others are exploring the Jewish notion that at their wedding each couple stands in the place of Adam and Eve, with the potential for starting again, for restoring in their union the damaged relationship between men and women, and reestablishing Eden in their home. At the liturgical and theological heart of many of the contemporary wedding rites is the nuptial blessing, the central prayer of the service that asks God to fill the marriage with joy that it might be a sign to the world of the love of Christ. But whatever images are used, there is a consensus that marriage is a true Christian vocation, intended not only for the mutual support of the partners, but as a part of a wider ministry to the world in the name of Jesus Christ.

## THANKSGIVING FOR THE BIRTH OR ADOPTION OF A CHILD

In many cases, Christians express a desire to mark the birth or adoption of their child with a religious ritual, but do not feel moved to request Christian baptism. Sometimes they themselves have not yet been baptized and feel their children's baptism should be postponed until the whole family can come to the font together. Others are committed to believers' baptism and wish to wait until their child is ready to make an independent profession of faith. In still other cases, the baptism has been scheduled, but before it takes place the parents wish to give thanks for a safe delivery (especially if there has been a history of miscarriage or pregnancy complications). The adoption of a child who has already been baptized is also an appropriate occasion for a service of thanksgiving in church, as is the adoption of the children of a previous marriage by a stepparent.

One rite which for generations had had a very important place in the lives of women, but which has largely died out in the modern period, is the "Churching of Women." This rite has its origins in the medieval order for "The Purification of a Woman after Childbirth before the Door of the Church," which was the Christian outworking of the Old Testament principle that a woman is unclean after childbirth and must not come for worship until she has been ritually purified (Lev. 12). Later revisions placed more emphasis on thanksgiving for safe delivery from the dangers of childbirth and the theme of impurity dropped out, so that by 1662 the rite in the Book of Common Prayer is entitled "The Thanksgiving of Women after Childbirth, commonly called the Churching of Women." Much of the anxiety about the perils of childbearing experienced by our Christian forebears has receded, and there are no contemporary rites for the "Churching of Women." But the desire to give thanks to God for the birth of a healthy child and the well-being of its mother remains, and a public service of prayer and thanksgiving may be appropriate for many parents, especially if the congregation has been united in its concern for the family during the pregnancy. Some women also feel that in giving birth they have been to a "holy place" at the boundary-zone between life and death, and they may wish to acknowledge that experience in a service of Christian worship. Contemporary services of "Thanksgiving for the Birth or Adoption of a Child" can be adapted for all of these circumstances.

Many times this type of liturgical celebration on the occasion of a birth is deeply desired, but various social conventions prevent people from requesting it. A single parent or the parents of a disabled child may be in particular need of assurance of the love of God and the support of the congregation, and in these situations a service of thanksgiving can be the most powerful form of pastoral care the church has to offer. Whenever it is celebrated, the service of thanksgiving for the birth or adoption of a child is a way of bringing before God the hopes, desires, and (perhaps) anxieties of parents for their child; of expressing the joy at new beginnings; and of giving voice to the Christian community's prayers for the family.

## THE ANOINTING OF THE SICK

The marriage rite speaks with true Christian realism about making a commitment to another person "in sickness and in health." Sickness is an undeniable feature of the human condition, and it cannot be underestimated as a factor in an individual's spiritual growth and development. Illness confronts the Christian believer with the most fundamental questions about human mortality, the meaning of suffering, and the source and nature of true healing. Over the centuries the church has met the reality of human illness with a range of ministries to the sick, some of the most significant of which are set in the context of a service of Christian worship.

In recent years a number of factors have led to a renewal of interest in the Christian healing ministry, and various initiatives have aimed at moving healing more toward the center of the church's life. The pentecostal and charismatic movements have seen healing as one of the marks of a Spirit-filled community, and the documents of the Second Vatican Council speak of the need to place anointing of the sick in the context of the total ministry of pastoral care to the sick and dying. In addition, both biblical and historical research have highlighted the importance of the healing ministry to the earliest Christian communities, and theologians have sought to undergird Christian healing with a deeper understanding of its relationship to the essential nature of God and the reign of God. All of this is set in the context of a medical profession that is currently seeking a more holistic view of health and sickness.

The diversity of approaches to the Christian healing ministry is indicated by the number of terms used to describe it: anointing of the sick, healing, visitation of the sick, extreme unction, and sometimes the "Last Rites." But whatever the terminology, the basic action we will be discussing here is the same: a rite that consists of the anointing of a sick person with oil (which itself is often, but not always, given a special blessing) accompanied by prayers for healing. The service may also be expanded by readings from Scripture, Holy Communion, confessions of sin, and other prayers and affirmations of faith.

From the very beginning, the church has made a clear theological connection between the rites of anointing of the sick and Jesus' own healing ministry. Healing was a sign of God's blessing and a foretaste of the New Age inaugurated in Jesus Christ (Matt. 11:4, 5), and it was a part of the disciples' own missionary activity (Mark 6:13). Healing in the earliest Christian communities took two forms. Not only were the charismatic gifts of healing given to individuals, but healing was also seen as an apostolic ministry of the whole church. In the Letter of James, for example, Christians are admonished: "Is any of you sick? He should send for the elders of the congregation to pray over him and anoint him with oil in the name of the Lord" (James 5:14–15).

In the *Apostolic Tradition*, attributed to Hippolytus of Rome (from around 215), we see the way in which the anointing of the sick is integrated with the ordinary life and worship of the Christian community as a whole. On occasion, individuals would offer olive oil with the other foods at the eucharistic feast. It would be set on the altar and blessed by the bishop with the following words:

> O God, who sanctifies this oil, as you grant to all who are anointed and receive of it the blessing with which you anointed kings and prophets, so grant that it may give strength to all who taste of it and all who use it.[3]

After the service, the blessed oil was returned to the donor for medicinal use at home. It is important to remember that olive oil in the ancient Mediterranean world was a standard medicine, used as an ointment, a tonic, and a food additive, and its curative powers were well-attested. So this particular blessing of olive oil could simply have been the blessing of an ordinary medicine, with no ecclesiastical or symbolic use anticipated. But the symbolic value of oil for healing is obvious. Oil penetrates and covers and spreads, it lubricates and protects, and the Old Testament image of oil as a symbol of national and personal well-being is often carried into the church's prayers for the blessing of healing oils.

It is difficult to say how widespread the practice of anointing of the sick was in the earliest centuries of Christianity. It was probably the custom in some places and not in others. In all the works of Augustine, for example, the practice is never once mentioned as occurring in North Africa, but in precisely the same period Pope Innocent I says that Christians in Rome who are sick "can be anointed with holy oil which has been prepared by the bishop." In any case, all the early references to healing indicate that proper ministers of the anointing of the sick were not only clergy and those with charismatic gifts of healing, but also ordinary lay people, and this situation prevailed up until about the year 800.

But the reformation and reorganization of the church undertaken by Charlemagne in the ninth century had a profound effect on the rites of healing. In the interest of enforcing discipline among the clergy, Charlemagne decreed that priests ought to be more serious about their ministry to the sick. At the very least, the parish priest should attend those Christians who were dying, insuring that they were anointed with oil (previously blessed by the bishop) and given Holy Communion before their death. This had two important effects on the healing ministry. Within a very short time, all anointing of the sick was performed by the clergy, and such things as charismatic gifts of healing and lay ministries of healing had virtually disappeared. In addition, certainly by the late-eleventh century, anointing became unambiguously a rite for the dying, and prayers for physical healing dropped out of the rite altogether.

Debate over the anointing of the sick became part of the larger Reformation debate on the sacraments of the church. Because anointing had degenerated into simply a deathbed ritual, none of the reformers could see how it was connected with the text from the Letter of James or other New Testament teaching. Martin Luther did indicate that a pastor's ministry to sick parishioners might stimulate their faith in the promises of God, and gave a set of instructions that he should go "with two or three others" to the sick person's house to lay hands on the person and pray in common for recovery. This was always to be accompanied by the public prayers of the church for healing. John Calvin was more sharp with his criticism of current practice, saying that it was foolish to think that smearing oil on half-dead carcasses would do any good at all, and that it was nothing but "hypocritical stage-play."

In the first Book of Common Prayer (1549), a service for the "Visitation of the Sick" was provided, with prayers and psalms, and "if the sick person desire to be anointed then shall the priest anoint him upon the forehead and breast only, making the sign of the cross." Communion for the sick person follows as a separate rite. But much of the language suggests that sickness is God's visitation upon sinners, and this relationship between sickness and sinfulness gives the whole rite a fairly penitential tone. John Wesley was deeply concerned with the circumstances of human health and sickness, and gave careful instructions to his Methodist followers on visiting the sick.[4] He objected, however, to prayers of absolution from sin at the deathbed, since there was no hope that the dying person would be able to undertake any meaningful "amendment of life." Among pentecostal and charismatic groups, healing as a gift of the Spirit is given liberally as one of the manifestations of the "second blessing," and ecstatic healing services have attested to the power of God whose healing miracles did not stop with the close of the apostolic period.

Contemporary services of healing in the mainline denominations take a variety of forms. Many are simply extempore prayers for healing and endurance at the bedside of a sick person. Some churches include the laying-on-of-hands and prayer as a normal part of the Communion service, with people remaining at the rail or moving to another part of the building after receiving the sacrament. Many other Christian communities are recovering the value of the ancient symbol of anointing with oil as a sign of God's will for healing, and of the larger process by which we are moving toward wholeness in Christ Jesus.

In making choices among the various possibilities for ministry to the sick, a number of things must be considered. First, any form of the Christian healing ministry must be rooted in and motivated by confidence in God's radical commitment to the world of flesh and blood (as manifested in the incarnation), rather than by a fear of death. In addition, it is probably unwise to engage in any form of ritual healing ministry without at least some sense that God is the ultimate source of healing, and that healing encompasses both physical and spiritual aspects of the human person. Like all prayer, prayer for healing is never a magic formula to coerce God into doing what we want, but is a way of affirming that health is a part of God's future for all people. But the faith of the sick person must always be taken into account and respected as well. Sick people can be in a particularly vulnerable state, and their dignity and sense of comfort is always the baseline from which we begin. To promote false hope, to suggest that we have some control over or special knowledge of God's will, or that the illness is a divine judgment on specific sinful behaviors is never a part of the liturgical ministry to the sick. It is also important to recognize that, because we are mortal, "dust and returning to dust," healing in this life will always be partial and incomplete.

## CHRISTIAN BURIAL

Although fewer people are coming to church for marriage at the turn of the twenty-first century, most still come for funerals since (despite the efforts of humanist societies) there is very little awareness of nonreligious alternatives to burial rites. In the Christian funeral the relationship between worship and pastoral care is most clearly visible, and for this reason most Christian pastors find presiding over the rites of death both immensely challenging and immensely satisfying. It is certainly true that every funeral is different. But whether it is the funeral of a person of uncertain Christian allegiance or a close companion in the faith, someone who has died quietly after a long and fruitful life or a young parent, all services of Christian burial are proclamations of our trust in a God whose love for us extends to the grave and beyond.

Like the other rites we have been discussing in this section, the earliest Christian burial practices grew up in two worlds, the world of Judaism and of the hellenized Roman Empire. In both contexts, the rites of death were a composite unity, consisting of rituals at the point of dying, ceremonies at the burial of the corpse, and various elements of formalized mourning during the period that followed the death. Some of these originated as delaying tactics between death and burial, to ensure that the dead person was actually dead (not simply unconscious or in a coma) and would remain dead. But they also served to express trust in the benevolence of the deity, to manage grief, and to reintegrate the bereaved into the community.

Greco-Roman funerary practice was ritually and philosophically complex. Undergirding it all was a deep apprehension over death; not only concern over the fate of the soul, but also concern that the dead might return to seek revenge. The rites of death and burial, then, were intended as both reassurance for the living and appeasement of the dead. Burial guaranteed a certain peace for the departed, preventing the "shade" from wandering ceaselessly. Because of this, even strangers were accorded a dignified funeral at the public expense.

The Roman rites of death began at the point of dying, when friends and family members gathered around the bed and gave the person a farewell kiss (preferably as the final breath was being drawn in order to catch the soul as it was breathed out). The nearest relative closed the eyes of the deceased and, after a period of formalized wailing and calling the person by name, the body was washed, anointed with olive oil, and dressed for burial. In most cases, a coin was placed in the mouth of the dead person, with the intention that it would pay for the mythical ferry trip across the river Styx into the abode of the dead. (This coin was called the *viaticum*, meaning "that which goes with you on your way.")

The funeral took place on the first night after the death—the climate discouraging a long delay between death and burial—and family and friends, musicians, and a number of corpse-bearers, all wearing black garments (the *lugubria*) processed to the burial site. The eyes of the deceased were opened, and the body was placed on the funeral pyre for cremation; later the cremated remains were mixed with wine and buried or entombed. After thoroughly cleaning the house where the person died, the mourners held a feast at the grave and then again nine days later to mark end of the official mourning period.

Broadly similar patterns prevailed in pre-Christian Judaism. Although we have no full written liturgy of burial until the ninth century, there is sufficient information in both the Old Testament and the writings of early rabbis to reconstruct the likely shape of rituals at the deathbed, for mourning, and surrounding the disposal of the body. When a member of the family died, those in attendance closed the eyes of the deceased and then proceeded to overturn all the couches in the house (so that the soul would find no comfortable resting place in the proximity of the living), and to discard any standing water. Open vessels which had been in the house at the time of the death were considered ritually unclean and placed outside, where they remained for seven days.[5] The body was then washed, wrapped in a linen shroud, and laid on a bed of sand, which helped to preserve it in the Mediterranean climate.

As in its Roman counterpart, burial took place as soon as possible, usually within twenty-four hours. During the procession to the burial site, friends and family members recited prayers and psalms (especially Ps. 16:10: "For you do not give me up to Sheol, or let your faithful one see the Pit.") and read appropriate passages from Job, Jeremiah, and Deuteronomy. As the coffin was lowered into the ground or placed in the tomb, mourners sang repeatedly, "May she (he) come to her (his) place in peace!" On the return journey from the burial site, the whole company of mourners made seven stops, sitting down on the ground, wailing and rending their garments, and allowing themselves to be comforted by those in surrounding houses. The following three days were days of high mourning, consisting of weeping, with total abstention from work until the seventh day as a recapitulation of the seven days during which Joseph mourned for Jacob (Gen. 50:10). Then there was a period of lesser mourning until the thirtieth day after the death, recalling the thirty days of mourning for Moses (Deut. 34:8).

Despite the wailing and rending of garments, which served to formalize and channel the grieving process and to allow for the provision of comfort to the bereaved, there was a generally optimistic tone to both pagan and Jewish funerals. The belief in the survival of personal identity after death, and the overall sense that the dead had been released from life and were destined for a happier place beyond the grave contributed to this confident approach to the rites of death, as did the conviction that the event of death was part of a larger pattern of meaning. This is not to say that funerals in late-antiquity were joyful occasions. Rather they were occasions for expressing a sense of resignation to what was variously described as fortune, fate, or divine providence.

In a reconstruction of the likely form of an early Jewish funeral prayer (The *Tzidduk-ha-din* or "Justification of Judgment") this submission to God's will for the dead is expressed:

> Thou art great in counsel and mighty in deed; thine eyes are open upon all the ways of the children of men, to give unto everyone according to the fruit of his doing. To declare that the Lord is upright; he is my Rock, and there is no unfaithfulness in him.
>
> The Lord gave, and the Lord has taken away: blessed be the name of the Lord. And he being merciful, forgiveth iniquity and destroyeth not: yea many a time he turneth his anger away, and doth stir up all his wrath.

Many of these pagan and Jewish funerary customs were retained or adapted by the first Christians, and only those who directly contradicted the faith were abandoned. Pagans and Christians were buried side-by-side in public cemeteries, and only differences in tombstone decorations indicated which graves contained the remains of Christian believers. Christians also attended pagan funerals, but were cautioned about being circumspect in their behavior. A third century document put it this way:

> Now when you are invited to their memorials, do you feast with good order, and the fear of God, as disposed to intercede for those that are departed? For since you are presbyters and deacons of Christ, you ought always to be sober, both among yourselves and among others, that you may be able to warn the unruly. . . . We say this, not that they are not to drink at all, otherwise it would be to the reproach of what God has made for cheerfulness, but that they be not disordered with wine . . . Nor do we say this only to those of the clergy, but also to every lay Christian, upon whom the name of the Lord Jesus Christ is called.

But because of the centrality of resurrection hope in early Christian theology, several things distinguished Christian funerals from those of their pagan and Jewish neighbors. The most significant difference was the overwhelming sense of joy with which the death of a Christian was met. The day of death was called the "Heavenly Birthday" (*dies natalis*) of the Christian believer, the day on which he or she took up the place in heaven that had already been prepared by Jesus Christ (John 14:1–4). Instead of the Roman-style *lugubria*, Christian mourners wore white garments as an expression of resurrection hope, and carried candles and sang hymns and psalms of victory as they accompanied the corpse to the burial site.

At the grave, a short service of prayers and readings was held, and additional hymns and psalms were sung, all expressing faith in Christ's triumph over death. The Roman funeral feast was supplanted by a celebration of the Lord's

Supper, and the kiss of peace was shared with the departed for the last time as a sign of the ongoing communion between the living and the dead. Because the funeral was an occasion for praise and not for lament, mourners were encouraged neither to wail nor rend their garments. In the *Confessions* (Book IX) Augustine describes the funeral of his beloved mother, Monica, and communicates the sense of joy that pervaded the occasion:

> So when the body was carried forth, we both went and returned without tears. For neither in those prayers we poured forth to thee, when the sacrifice of our redemption was offered up to thee for her—with the body placed by the side of the grave as is the custom there, before it is lowered down into it—neither in those prayers did I weep.

A feast (or perhaps an Agape meal) followed the funeral, and on the third, ninth, and fortieth day after the death, relatives gathered for a brief service of prayers and psalms. But by the end of the fourth century, the funeral feast was banned, since it had become detached from the celebration of hope in the resurrection of the dead and had begun to be an occasion for intemperance.

The general uncertainty of life in the Middle Ages, compounded by successive waves of deadly plague (which, at its height in the fourteenth century carried off nearly one-third of the population of Europe), made the preoccupation with death an inevitable feature of medieval thought. Indeed, the figure of Death became as much a character in medieval life and society as Mary, Christ, or the saints. The omnipresence of death not only left an indelible mark on theology in this period, which was marked by a deep concern with such issues as the fate of the soul, the intercession and intervention of the saints on behalf of the living, and the grades of eternal punishment, but also shaped the rites of death as well.

Like the services that attended the death of a Christian in the early period, the medieval rites also consisted of a number of components, with individual elements for use at the home, in the church, and at the grave. The domestic ritual was the longest and most complex of these. Prayers and psalms were said at the bedside of the dying person, who shared in a service of Holy Communion with family and friends. (The eucharistic bread, placed in the mouth at the point of death was given the same name as the coin placed in the mouth of the dying pagan, *viaticum*: "that which goes with you on your way.") The passion story in the Gospel according to John was read while the person was anointed for death (*unctio in extremis*), and this was concluded by prayers which commended the soul to God. Once the death had occurred, the body was prepared for burial to the chanting of psalms interwoven with the antiphon: "You formed me from the earth, you clothed me with flesh; Lord, my Redeemer, raise me up at the last day."

The body was then taken in procession to the church, where special prayers were said and psalms and anthems sung, followed by a second celebration of the Eucharist. The overall tone of the service was penitential, and the liturgical color had turned from white to black. The famous thirteenth-century funeral anthem attributed to Thomas of Celano ca. 1190–1260), the *Dies irae*, suggests something of the flavor of the occasion:

> Day of wrath. O! day of mourning
> See fulfilled the prophets' warning
> Heav'n and earth in ashes burning
>
> O! what fear man's bosom rendeth
> When from heav'n the Judge descendeth
> On whose sentence all dependeth!
> . . . . . . . . . . . . . . . . . . . . . . . . . . . . .
> Ah that day of tears and mourning!
> From the dust of earth returning,
> Man for judgment must prepare him.

By the fifteenth century, judgment themes had almost entirely replaced themes of hope and reassurance in the Christian funeral, and in various ways the rites of death were used to allay some of the existential anxiety that was a part of the Christian consciousness. Because the celebration of the Eucharist was seen to be of benefit not only to the living but to the dead as well, endowments and trust funds provided for Masses to be said in the name of a dead person, so that the soul might be released early from its justly deserved torment. The religious literature of the period is replete with hymns of lament, cautionary tales, and poems about the fate of the dead. One epitaph of this period reads:

> I was full fair now am I foul
> My fair flesh begins to stink.
> The worm finds my great brow
> I am her meat, I am her drink.
>
> I beg every man that wise will be
> Take heed hereof what I have said.
> Then may he sure of heaven be
> When he shall in earth be laid.

All of the continental Reformers urged simplification of the rites of death and burial, sought to reduce the potential for abuse and to return to the Christian funeral a sense of hopefulness and joy in the resurrection. In his *Preface to the Burial Hymns* (1542), Martin Luther urged his followers to refrain from singing "dirges and doleful songs" at the funeral, "so that the article of the resurrection may be firmly implanted in us." But of all the difficulties with the rites surrounding the death of a Christian, it was praying for the dead that caused the most distress to the reformers. They were unanimous in condemning the practice and equally unanimous in eliminating such prayers from proposed funeral rites. In the Book of Homilies issued by Elizabeth I in 1562, it says:

> Neither let us dream any more, that the souls of the dead are any thing at all holpen by our prayers; but, as the scripture teacheth us, let us think that the soul of man . . . goeth straightways either to heaven, or else to hell, whereof the one needeth no prayer, and the other is without redemption.

In every case, the Protestant funeral service was designed more for the edification and solace of mourners than as a method for insuring the eternal comfort of the deceased. Despite Luther's admonitions, however, the penitential character of the funeral was largely retained, and prayers warned mourners that amendment of life was the necessary prerequisite to everlasting joy. To some, however, no amount of reformation would remove the burial rites' tendency toward superstition, and in 1644 the Westminster Directory of Public Worship declared that the dead body should be "decently attended from the house to the appointed place of public burial, and there be immediately interred, without any ceremony."

When John Wesley prepared a funeral service for Methodists in North America, he followed almost exactly the rite of burial of the dead in the Book of Common Prayer (1662). But in his hymns and journal entries the note of hope in the resurrection is strong:

> Seeing the father [of the dead boy] (a plain man, a tailor by trade) looking at the grave, I asked, "How do you find yourself." He said, "Praised be the Lord, never better. He has taken the soul of my child to himself. I have seen, according to my desire, his body committed to holy ground. And I know that when it is raised again, both he I shall ever be with the Lord."[6]

In England and North America until the late 1700s, the graveyard surrounding the church was the presumed place for burial for everyone in the congregation. But within a short time the situation underwent a radical change. By 1825, the burgeoning Industrial Revolution had caused a massive population explosion in nearly all cities and towns, putting intense pressure on urban infrastructures. Soon the capacity of churchyard cemeteries was seriously overstretched, especially after successive waves of epidemics (most notably cholera); in some cases the outer walls of graveyards collapsed entirely, spilling corpses onto the city streets. Fearing further epidemic, boards of health began to demand legislation to prohibit burials within the city limits, and in response park-like cemeteries located well away from centers of population were developed. Each one boasted a well-appointed mortuary chapel from which funerals might be conducted. Although clergy still presided over the service itself, for the first time the rites of death were removed from the area in and around the church building, and within a few decades, the "fashionable funeral" became the aspiration of all. Firms of funeral directors were hired to stage-manage the event, and to provide all the necessary accoutrements. Finally, of course, funeral directors began to provide their own chapels.

At the same time, rituals that were a part of the domestic side of death were also lost. Practices such as dressing and laying out the body, wrapping the deceased in a shroud (possibly itself woven at home), and preparing the meal for the wake, all of which had been an important part of the domestic ministry of women and had helped the bereaved come to terms with the death that had taken place, were now assumed by paid undertakers who embalmed, clothed and arranged the body in order to make the dead look "life-like." This legacy of professionalization and removal of Christian burial from the ordinary life of the community of faith continues to affect the shape of funerals today.

In the last few decades, there have been a number of significant reforms of the rites of death. Because all denominations have relied on research by liturgical scholars on the theology and practice of burial in the early church, many modern rites show a common purpose and structure, and there is also a genuine consensus on what a funeral is designed to accomplish. Of these, five are of particular significance.

First, the funeral is a way of securing the reverent disposal of the corpse. The feelings that surround a dead body are subtle and complex, but Christians recognize that the body was the earthly expression of the person, the "temple of the Holy Spirit" (1 Cor. 6:19), and therefore deserves a dignified treatment after death. We bury or cremate a body with reverence not because we confuse the body with the essence of the person. It is rather because we acknowledge that it is through the medium of "bodiliness" that we have known and been known by the deceased.

The funeral is also intended to commend the deceased to God, in faith and hope. This is a singularly important stage in the grieving process, since there is a certain confrontation with the reality of death which takes place when mourners entrust the dead to the love of God that "never fails." This is also the occasion for those left behind to recommit themselves to God, to offer their lives as an affirmation that life (and God's purposes for life) continues

despite grief and anxiety. Both life and death are in God's hands. It is therefore important that those prayers in the service that are focused on commen-
dation (also called committal) be said by the mourners themselves rather than
for them as a way releasing the dead to death and of returning the living to life.
Because of the recognition of this deep psychological need, many denominations believe that the time has come to reconsider the question of prayers for
the dead. Abuses in the past should not prevent us from seeing that to pray for
a departed loved one is an expression of faith in a God who is the God of both
the living and the dead, that we are all a part of one holy communion of saints,
and that prayer continues to bind us together in love even beyond the grave.

The third function of the Christian funeral is to proclaim the resurrection
hope. The Bible is filled with stories of death and rebirth, stories in which,
inexplicably, despair turns to joy, fear turns to hope, slavery to liberation, death
to life. Dry bones come together, clothed with flesh and given breath by the
power of God, barren women become pregnant, dissolute children are welcomed home with open arms. And the resurrection of Jesus of Nazareth is
understood as the culmination, the final seal on all of God's redeeming and
life-giving activity. In baptism, the Christian is said to be "buried with Christ"
that in death he or she may be "raised with Christ at the last day." The proclamation that God's will for life will not ultimately be defeated, and that the time
is coming when God "will wipe every tear from their eyes. Death will be no
more; mourning and crying and pain will be no more, for the first things have
passed away" (Rev. 21:4). This, of course, is the essential message of each and
every service of Christian worship, but it is perhaps most powerfully spoken
in the context of death, and the grief, pain, and brokenness that can accompany it.

Because of this assurance, the funeral can state with confidence that the living and the dead are a part of one holy communion, and that the company of
believers is united in Christ across the chasm between life and death. This is
not to deny the reality of death, but to affirm that love in Christ Jesus is
stronger even than death. This is the reason that many funerals, particularly
those of committed Christians, now include a celebration of the Lord's Supper, as an affirmation that "neither life nor death . . . can separate us from the
love of God." To share our eucharistic thanksgivings with "the whole company
of heaven" is to receive a foretaste of that great banquet in heaven in which we
all will share.

In the midst of this, however, is the fact of human mortality, and the fourth
purpose of the Christian funeral is to remind the living of that fact. The death
of a fellow Christian can bring us face to face with the meaning of our life, and
can drive us to confront questions about the ultimate source of our security.
At times, the funeral can also be the beginning of a release of our feelings of

guilt and failure, a safe place for us to express our sense not only of loss, but of rejection and anger. While it is inappropriate to use the funeral either to manipulate or to deny these feelings, it is important to see it as a key moment in the bereavement process.

All of these elements blend together to accomplish the fifth purpose for the Christian funeral: to console the mourners and to inaugurate the process of reintegration and healing. When we hear the gospel of new life proclaimed and commend the one we have loved and lost to the God of all mercies, when we commit our own lives anew to God's future, thank God for the life of the deceased, and have feelings of guilt met by the assurance of forgiveness: all of these are deep resources for consolation and comfort. The funeral is also the context within which the congregation can commit itself to its own ministry to the bereaved, and to pray and work for the wholeness that God intends for all people.

The latest generation of official burial rites in many of the mainline denominations' rites acknowledge that there is a wide variation in rituals surrounding death, both regional and cultural differences, and that it is imperative that the funeral service allows for a diversity of patterns. The contemporary funeral also makes a more definite link between Christian death and Christian baptism, and expresses the "Easter" quality of all Christian existence. As the Constitution on the Sacred Liturgy of the Second Vatican Council says,

> The rite for the burial of the dead should express more clearly the paschal character of Christian death, and should correspond more closely to the circumstances and traditions found in various regions.[7]

The funeral service according to all the new rites is much more clearly a service of Christian worship than its predecessors, a service that makes a clear connection between death, the resurrection of Jesus Christ, baptism, and the Christian life. Because of this there has been a significant shift away from the use of non-Christian symbols in funeral services. Flags, civic emblems, the insignia of various fraternal and paramilitary organizations are all seen to be inappropriate for the proclamation of the gospel. In their place are more explicitly Christian symbols—the paschal candle, incense, the funeral pall emblazoned with images of the resurrection life (the cross, the shell, the dove) to be placed over the coffin, the color white as a symbol of victory. This very explicit link between death and baptism does cause significant problems with funerals for those with no definite Christian adherence, or for those who have never "owned" their baptism, and pastoral sensitivity is required to avoid any embarrassment or dishonesty.

There is a strong encouragement for members of the congregation to participate in the service, to add their own thanksgivings for the life of the deceased, to read from the scriptures, to pray and to lead appropriate parts of the service. It is hoped that people might be encouraged to see the old-style "eulogy," which did little but extol the virtues of the deceased, as a thing of the past, replaced by a sermon or homily which thanks God for the life and witness of the person who has died and proclaims the resurrection hope on the occasion of his or her passing. The inclusion of prayers of intercession, which ask not only God's blessing on the bereaved but also turns the hearts of the whole congregation toward the needs of the world, is also encouraged. There is also an acknowledgment that a wide variety of local funeral practices exists and should be accommodated in the official services, and so flexibility has been a hallmark in recent thinking about funerals. Most give positive encouragement to the practice of holding separate services in the home, the church, and at the burial site.

Special provisions are made in the contemporary rites for the funeral of a child or for an untimely death, but there has been a general unwillingness to view a suicide as a special case needing a separate rite. There are also rites being developed and circulated for use in the case of miscarriage and stillbirth, many of which include naming rites for the fetus. Certainly in such cases, the needs and desires of the bereaved parents are always to be respected. The anniversary of the death of a beloved partner, child, or parent is also an appropriate occasion for common prayer, either in a brief worship service (at home or in church), or as an element in the prayers of intercession at the main Sunday service nearest the date of the death.

Those who argue that the funeral is primarily an evangelistic opportunity, a chance to warn unrepentant sinners about the judgment that awaits them, will not find any real support in the most recent generation of Christian burial rites. If there is evangelism in the Christian funeral it is to be found in the confident proclamation of the gospel in the face of death.

## OTHER OCCASIONS IN THE LIFE CYCLE

Many Christians believe that other significant moments in the human life cycle deserve to be marked with services of Christian worship, and have drawn up concrete proposals for such services. The most controversial of these are rites for the making and dissolution of exclusive relationships. In many cases, for example, persons in the process of divorce find that this major event in their lives is somehow seen to be outside of the church's pastoral liturgical ministry. They express the need to offer prayers of confession and to seek reconciliation with their partner, their children, and the Christian community as a whole in the presence of God who is the source of all reconciliation and peace. Few churches have produced official services for this purpose, but a variety of independent efforts have been circulated. They are not intended as "divorce rites," but as opportunities to bring the pain of marital breakdown before God, and to encourage the healing process to begin. In this way, it is argued, life and hope can be reborn from the ashes of disappointment and loss.

Another issue that is increasingly the subject of discussion among those with responsibility for the church's liturgy is the desire of gay men, lesbians, bisexual, and transgender people to seal their relationships with a service of Christian worship. Although it is most often described as "gay marriage," most advocates of this kind of service insist that traditional nuptial categories are not necessarily appropriate for the kind of celebration of commitment desired by homosexual couples. But like marriage rites in general, all the liturgical proposals that have been made rest on the deep conviction that God is the author of all love and the guarantor of all fidelity, and that any commitment which is entered into with the intention that it be exclusive and lifelong is upheld by the grace of God from its inception.

The celebration of other forms of committed human relationships may also be appropriate occasions for a service of Christian worship: the establishment of a foster family, the anniversary of the beginning of a deep and lasting friendship, the merger of two step-families, or of two or more congregations. In addition, there may at times be a call for the liturgical expression of reconciliation and of a renewal of commitment after a serious breakdown of one of these types of relationships. Rites that signify a change in status of persons also fall within this category. Rites of passage can be important not only in helping individuals manage a change in their own state of life, but also to help the community to recognize that such a change has taken place and to reassimilate the person in his or her new role. A significant birthday, a betrothal, the departure of a child who is leaving home to set up housekeeping for herself, a new job, an unexpected recovery from illness or escape from imminent danger, or the receipt of a degree or achievement award are all examples of occasions which might be marked with a service of prayers, hymns, and Scripture readings. These will be especially appropriate in closely-knit Christian congregations, where the welfare of each individual is of vital interest to the whole community.

Christian worship is an indispensable part of the total pastoral care of men, women, and children at significant moments in their lives. To ritualize joy and grief, to celebrate and renew commitment, to pray for those embarking on a new course in life are not only critical factors in the well-being and psychosocial integration of individuals, but also necessary for the health of the Christian community as a whole. In all cases, the longing of human beings to see their lives as having real meaning is met by the proclamation of the gospel of God's love for us all, and by a vision of the Christian vocation that embraces all states of life. The services of Christian worship we have been discussing in this chapter all rest on the same foundation. They all take the human life cycle seriously as a locus of God's redeeming work, and they all create occasions for the church to work out its calling to pray, work, and love in the name of Christ for the sake of the world.

# 6

# Contemporary Challenges
# to Christian Worship

In every age, those with responsibility for Christian worship have had to confront questions that are specific to the particular time in which they live. The situation today is no different. Not only are we having to respond to the perennial questions which have faced Christians in the past, but we are also dealing with a number of new questions, for which new solutions are needed. In this chapter we will look at five of the most significant of these contemporary questions, and will discover how the theology and practice of Christian worship is responding to them. This chapter will begin by discussing the place of worship within both ecumenical conversations and encounters with people of other faith traditions. It will continue by exploring the issues which arise from the recognition that worship needs to be adapted to the various cultural situations in which it finds itself, and then will turn to the challenges minority groups have raised to the hegemony of traditional liturgical language. Finally, we shall consider the ways in which the growing crisis of authority in both the churches and the world affects Christian worship.

## WORSHIP AND ECUMENISM

It has been observed that the age in which we live may be known to those who come after us as the "ecumenical century." Clearly, the attempts by the various Christian churches to come to agreement about those matters that historically have divided them have made significant impact both on the shape of the church as a whole and on Christian worship, especially in the past fifty years. Church mergers and reunions, bilateral conversations, and ecumenical councils of churches committed to working together on contemporary religious and social issues all have been occasions for the creative exploration of new forms of worship. In each of these different contexts, worship has been seen as a source of both frustration and hope. Many have found Christian worship to be the principal barrier to church unity, that activity which most fully exposes our deep divisions; others have found in common worship a sign that barriers can be overcome when people are willing to pray together. The place of worship in ecumenical discussions often becomes a "chicken-and-egg" problem. Must we come to full doctrinal agreement with one another before we can pray together? Or is it only by actually praying together that we will be able to reach agreement?

We must not be naive about this matter: there are points at which the churches are still deeply divided over questions of Christian worship. The appropriate form and content of the Lord's Supper, the necessity of ordained ministers for certain key liturgical functions, the recognition of the ordination of women and homosexual persons, questions surrounding the baptism of infants, and the precise wording of the Nicene Creed all remain matters of intense disagreement between and among certain Christian churches. (And unfortunately, this does not exhaust the list of controversial issues.) But at the same time, actual experiences of Christians worshiping together across denominational boundaries have led, in many cases, to the softening of those boundaries, and to changes in both pastoral practice and canon law.

The history of division in the Christian church over matters of worship is a long and unfortunate one. As we have seen, the word "orthodox" had as its original meaning "right praise,"[1] and anxiety about the proper interpretation and conduct of Christian common prayer was a part of many heated debates about the limits of authentic Christian belief in the early centuries. Could a valid Christian baptism be presided over by someone who had renounced his faith under threat of torture? Could those who failed to subscribe to the doctrinal formula worked out at the Council of Nicaea (325 CE) preside over the Lord's Supper? Were women allowed to preach and to teach in services of worship? On what date should Easter be celebrated? Could one group of Christians worship together with another group that happened to have different beliefs about the Trinity or the nature of salvation or the work of the Holy Spirit? These kinds of questions not only describe early controversies about worship, but have also set the agenda for contemporary ecumenical discussions as well.

The notion of barring certain individuals or groups from continued fellowship around the Communion Table because of doctrinal divergence has a long history, but was consolidated by the Protestant and Catholic Reformations of the sixteenth century. Although the Catholic Church's Council of Trent

(1545–1563) did not condemn specific persons or groups, but only doctrinal errors, those (mainly Protestants) who persisted in those errors were clearly part of a dissident community and were, as such, excommunicated. As divisions between and among the Protestant churches increased in the period after the Reformation, restrictions on worshiping in common became a sign of mutual unwillingness to recognize separated brothers and sisters as a part of the one body of Christ. Many of these restrictions on worship in common became a part of denominational canon law.

Beginning in the early decades of the twentieth century, momentum grew in the process of union and reunion of separated churches. Much of this energy for Christian union came as a result of questions raised on the various mission fields of the world, where division among Christian denominations was a most serious barrier to the spreading of the gospel. As actual church mergers began to occur, both those uniting within the same confessional family (such as those churches forming the United Methodist Church), and those coming together from different confessional families (such as those which make up the Church of South India or the United Church of Canada) found that the problems of common worship were among the most difficult to negotiate. As the 1952 World Council of Churches' Faith and Order Conference (held in Lund, Sweden) said, in worship "disunity becomes explicit and the sense of separation most acute." In some cases (such as in the Anglican-Methodist Unity Scheme in Great Britain in the 1970s) worship issues were a key factor in the failure of proposed institutional unions.

Despite the difficulties, forms of common prayer are (in nearly all cases) the most eloquent testimonies to the efforts of separated churches to unite or reunite. These rites tend to fall into two categories. There are some who have used the current worship materials of the churches participating in the merger as the basis for new united services, by careful adaptation and amalgamation. Others have taken the opportunity presented by church union to forge a completely new set of rites, as a symbol of the new church that is being born. In 1947, the formation of the Church of South India from Methodist, Anglican, Reformed, and Congregationalist churches provided a model to other uniting churches for what a completely new set of services might look like. The framers of the rites of the Church of South India attempted to reach back behind the liturgical divisions in the denominations represented by reclaiming common forms of worship from the early centuries of the church.

But not all ecumenical activity in the area of Christian worship has been the result of institutional mergers of separated churches. Some are the result of discussions among denominations which are not seeking institutional union but which nevertheless wish to find ways of praying together. In Lima, Peru, at the January 1982 meeting of the Faith and Order Commission, one hundred theologians from the WCC member churches voted unanimously to produce a set of ecumenical rites for baptism and the Lord's Supper. The eucharistic rite that had been produced as a discussion document for that meeting (called the "Lima Liturgy") was used for the first time at that meeting, and then at subsequent World Council gatherings. The liturgy itself embodies the doctrinal agreement reached up to that point by the member churches of the WCC (although not all of the representatives of those churches have felt able to receive Communion because of their canonical obligations). Quite soon, as the ecumenical excitement felt in Lima was transmitted to local and regional churches, the Lima liturgy began to have wide use in smaller ecumenical gatherings, and the service was adapted to a variety of circumstances.

Local ecumenism has also been expressed in new services specifically designed for use by two or more separate liturgical traditions. Covenanting churches, such as the Evangelical Lutheran Church of America and the Episcopal Church (USA), Local Ecumenical Projects (LEPs), and community churches of various kinds have all devised services in which all parties can worship together. The Consultation on Church Union (now Churches in Covenant Communion) and the Consultation on Common Texts have provided worship materials for local ecumenical use. Other such organizations around the world are working on similar projects in order to respond liturgically to the very important local initiatives at cooperation and unity between the denominations.

## Ecumenism and the Eastern Churches

One of the most pressing of contemporary ecumenical problems is the continued division of the Christian Church into Eastern and Western branches, and worship has been a significant point of contention in bilateral dialogues between East and West. Although the date 1054 is usually cited as the date of the schism (because that was the year the bishop of Rome and the bishop of Constantinople mutually excommunicated one another), the full story of the separation is a long and complex one. Various proposals for reunion have been suggested, and significant steps in that direction have been made, but the persistence of disunity is symbolized by the unwillingness of the Eastern Orthodox delegates to the WCC assembly at Lima to partake of Communion using the Lima liturgy.

One of the main difficulties in the area of ecumenical consensus in the area of worship is that within the Eastern churches are several distinct liturgical traditions grouped in families (the Byzantine, Syrian, and Alexandrian[2]). Most of the rites used by these churches are very ancient, some reaching back to the fourth century, and so changes in worship, even for important ecumenical reasons, are not often welcomed by Eastern Christians. Liturgical change among the Eastern churches happens not by authorities devising new rites to reflect changing theological agenda, or even by local congregations seeking to meet local religious needs, but occurs slowly and gradually over the centuries. Worship in Eastern Christianity is a rich tapestry of color, sound, smell, and imagery, emphasizing the transcendent experience of coming into the presence of God. To most Eastern Christians, Western Christian rites are perceived to be overly plain, direct, and cerebral. There is some sense in the ecumenical movement that Eastern Christians are unwilling to allow their worship to respond to the pressures of modernity, and this basic incompatibility of approach between East and West means that many conversations on questions of worship are sometimes quite painful and difficult.

Where and how worship will come into play in the continued efforts toward reunion of the Christian East and West is uncertain. Not only is there a wide variety of practices and rites to be reconciled, but there are also very different theologies of worship at work. Most Eastern Christians are highly committed to Christian unity, but believe that full Communion can only come with confessional and liturgical agreement. Eucharistic sharing between East and West is unlikely to be seen as a means to full doctrinal accord, but rather as a symbol of its completion. More recently, the willingness of Western Christians to consider dropping the words "and the Son" (the *filioque* clause) from the Nicene Creed has been an important step toward the day when Christians from the East and West will gather around the Communion Table, but the future direction of this journey toward reunification is unclear.

## CHRISTIAN WORSHIP IN A WORLD
## OF MANY FAITH TRADITIONS

Increasingly, the impact of religious pluralism is being felt by those with responsibility for Christian worship. Because of the mobility of populations and individuals, the leaders of Christian churches often now share a responsibility for the religious life of any particular location with their Hindu, Sikh, Muslim, and Jewish counterparts, as well as with the representatives of smaller religious groups. As we have begun to know our brothers and sisters from other faith traditions better, and to work with them toward the building of a more just, humane, and peaceful society, questions surrounding worship inevitably arise. Very often, true dialogue between members of different traditions arises from witnessing firsthand the devotion and seriousness with which others approach their own public worship or private prayer, even when the form of that worship may seem quite strange. The simple question asked of a person of another faith tradition such as, "Why did you do this in your worship?" or "What is the meaning of that act?" can be a significant first step in building a relationship of real depth and mutual enrichment.

To be invited to a service of worship in another faith tradition is a great privilege, and needs to be approached seriously and thoughtfully. Whether it is the wedding of a Sikh business colleague, the funeral of a Jewish friend, or the ordinary gathering of the Muslim community to which a future son or daughter-in-law belongs, there are certain rules of ordinary courtesy which should be observed. Sometimes, the Christian guest will be expected to do things which seem odd, such as removing shoes or covering the head. At other times, there will be things which should be said or done only by those within the faith community itself. This may include the recitation of certain prayers, affirmations, or physical acts of worship and devotion. If possible, Christian guests attending the worship services of people of other faith traditions should always learn as much as they can before the service about both the tradition as a whole and a particular act of worship, in order that neither they nor their hosts will be embarrassed.

Some people find that they cannot, for reasons of conscience, attend a service of worship of another religious tradition. In this case, they should decline politely and without elaborate explanations. If the invitation is for a special occasion, such as a wedding, a funeral, or an initiation ceremony, the Christian may wish to say that he or she will offer informal private prayers at the time of the service, or at some other time together with the person who has tendered the invitation. To witness in this way to the charity, hospitality, and generosity of spirit that the gospel message engenders, rather than using the occasion for dogmatic pronouncements or testimonies, is the warmest possible invitation to genuine dialogue with a person of another faith tradition.

There are times, especially on civic occasions or in periods of national calamity, when a service of worship shared by two or more faith traditions is desired. Services for peace, at times of national thanksgiving, or of public mourning or celebration can be moving tributes to the common striving of the human spirit toward wholeness. Often, though, such services present extraordinary challenges to those involved in planning, and a multitude of opportunities for offense or misunderstanding.

There are four distinct possibilities for such an interfaith service of worship. The first possibility is that one religious group hosts an ordinary worship service in their own tradition and extends an invitation to others who share the particular concern being addressed in prayer. While some will feel unable to attend, there is in this approach a clarity of purpose which leaves little room for misunderstanding. A second way of constructing such a service is to follow the basic format of the worship of one particular tradition, but to adapt it so that as much of the content as possible can be shared by others. For example, if a service of Christian worship forms the basis for the service, then this approach would call for the reading of lessons which do not speak of God in explicitly Trinitarian terms, or of Israel as God's chosen, or of the nature of salvation in Jesus Christ. This is the most difficult type of service to plan, and the most likely to cause distress and misunderstanding, both for the community whose worship is being adapted and for those of other traditions whose religious "sensitivities" are being accommodated.

In interfaith services of the third type there is an agreed order of service and participants of each faith group make a contribution from their own worship tradition that they feel is most appropriate for the occasion. These can be very effective ways for people from different traditions to pray together. If a unifying theme and order of service can be agreed upon by all parties, there is less likelihood of giving serious offense in this form of service than in the previous type. But it can begin to look much like a religious "variety show," and the length of a multi-faith service of this type can be difficult to manage.

The fourth option for an interfaith gathering for worship, one that is particularly effective in times of national emergency, mourning, or thanksgiving, is a service in which the intention of the service is introduced at the beginning and then silent prayer is offered by all participants. To invite the presence of God in such a gathering, to meet God in silence in the company of others, can be the simplest, most moving testimony to a shared confidence in one another and in God. Certainly, even if the entire service is not silent, silence has an important place in every act of multi-faith worship. The recent example of the very moving services held on the site of the events of September 11, 2001, provides a model for multi-faith services of this type, and shows how a shared human experience can become a bridge between and among those who are divided by their religious commitments.

For most situations in which a multi-faith service is demanded, the first or final option above will be the most effective and the least likely to cause misunderstanding or offense. Such occasions, however, are probably rarer than we would like to suppose, and the appropriateness of any sort of multi-faith service of worship should be considered very carefully. There is a high degree of risk in such services, since a misguided form of words, a thoughtless or ill-informed act, an imprudent gesture may have high symbolic value, and could cause serious damage to the delicate balance of interfaith relations in a particular place. In other words, the decision to hold a multi-faith act of worship should never be taken lightly.[3]

Of course pastoral occasions, such as weddings or funerals, present their own special challenges. To share joy or grief with people of other faith traditions offers a particular opportunity for the formation of strong and lasting bonds. At the same time, it is often the case that the very presence of the interfaith dimension is the source of some tension, and the need for care and attention is heightened in such circumstances. The early involvement of representatives of the faith communities concerned is absolutely necessary in planning this type of service. It would be hoped that interfaith relations are sufficiently healthy in every place so that conversations among clergy and other leaders of the various faith communities involved in weddings and funerals will be natural and congenial. In the case of the marriage of people from different faith traditions, the problems and challenges of interfaith worship will continue throughout their married life, and those with responsibility for Christian worship need to have sufficient information and insight to provide adequate advice and counsel.

## THE INCULTURATION OF CHRISTIAN WORSHIP

In the past half century, pastoral liturgists have given a high priority to creating the conditions for the fullest possible participation of all people in Christian worship. Because of this commitment, the adaptation of Christian worship to local cultures, customs, and interpretations of the gospel message has been given a great deal of serious attention. The process by which these adaptations occur is called variously "inculturation," "indigenization," or "assimilation," and for much of the history of Christian worship this has referred to the ways in which authoritative Western rites were adjusted to meet local circumstances, especially on the mission fields. More recently, however, inculturation has been a process by which the insights, attitudes, and practices of indigenous cultures and traditional patterns of worship are creatively combined to give birth to new forms of Christian liturgical expression.

The relationship between Christian worship and culture has always been a complex and problematic one, and underlying it are serious issues concerning the theology of both the church and the liturgy. Why should Christian worship not be exactly the same everywhere? We believe, after all, that every Christian community is imbued with the Holy Spirit, which is the Spirit of unity, and also that we all worship the One God. Why, then, have some Christians been led to worship God in different ways from others? Are some ways of worship "wrong" and others "right"?

For many theologians, the answers to these questions lie in an understanding of the nature of the Holy Spirit itself. It has been argued the Spirit is not only the Spirit of truth, but the Spirit of creativity and flexibility as well, and that through this Spirit Christians and Christian communities are able to respond creatively to the situations in which they find themselves. Insofar as situations are different, then the church's responses to those situations will be different as well. There is, then, legitimate diversity in the body of Christ, including diversity in forms of Christian worship. This is the theological conviction that underlies all of the efforts toward liturgical inculturation.

We can see this idea at work even in the worship of the earliest Christian communities. Nowhere does the New Testament give any sort of "blueprint" for how worship is to be conducted, and Christian worship has always been inculturated for local conditions and forms of expression. As we have seen, worship in the early church represented a wide variety of local rites and practices, each one reflecting the heritage and religious situation of a particular worshiping community. The various components of the Passover Seder, for example, which formed the thematic core of the Lord's Supper, were undoubtedly handled differently in communities of Gentile Christians than in communities of former Jews, handled differently in a sophisticated place like Corinth than in a backwater village in West Syria. As the gospel message took root in the various parts of the Roman Empire, new challenges arose, but Christians readily adapted the worship of God to their various local circumstances, religious, linguistic, and cultural.

This process of inculturation continued for at least the first four centuries of the church's existence. But gradually, with the growing desire on the part of political leaders to use Christian worship as part of a strategy for unifying the empire, the original liturgical diversity began to be restricted. In the fourth and fifth centuries, increasing concern about worship as a potential vehicle for the expression and celebration of heretical views further reduced the creativity of liturgical practice, until by about the year 600, total uniformity of Christian common prayer was the desired goal. Eventually, even the native languages people used for common prayer were deemed to be unacceptable deviations from the uniformity of public worship, and Latin was everywhere promoted as the only appropriate language of Christian liturgy.

But despite these efforts at centralization and uniformity, wherever the missionary expansion of the church occurred, pressure to accommodate worship to local customs and religious sensibilities was felt. When in the year 601 Mellitus was sent to join Augustine in order to spread the gospel in Britain, Pope Gregory wrote the following words of advice:

> We have been giving careful thought to the affairs of the English, and have come to the conclusion that . . . since they have the custom of sacrificing many oxen to devils, let some other solemnity be substituted in its place, such as a day of Dedication. . . . On such occasions

they might well construct shelters of boughs for themselves around the churches that were once temples, and celebrate the solemnity with devout feasting. . . . If the people are allowed to continue celebrating with worldly pleasures in this way, they will more readily come to desire the joys of the spirit.

This sort of pragmatic approach on the part of church leaders to the creative adaptation of local worship practices for the sake of spreading the gospel became rarer and rarer as the centuries went on, however. Official investment in a standardized Christian worship was growing. It soon was believed by all those in authority that a stable form of worship would result in a stable church, stable doctrine, and a stable social and political order.

## Liturgical Inculturation and the Modern Missionary Expansion of the Church

Although some of the original diversity in worship practices was restored with the sixteenth century Reformation, it was not until the twentieth century that people began to consider local culture and value systems a decisive factor in the shaping of Christian worship. Much of this new awareness came as missionaries strove to understand the dynamics of faith development and the relationship between the timeless truth of the gospel and the particular circumstances of those they sought to evangelize. This reflection resulted in an emphasis on the development of grassroots initiatives in worship planning, the incorporation of local artistic, architectural, and musical resources, and the search for ways to adapt indigenous forms of expression and values into common prayer. In the Christian worship inculturated for many parts of Africa, for example, the veneration of ancestors and deep reverence for the land were given a central place in worship, and the traditional "call and response" form of ritual expression was often appropriated.

Often, however, recently evangelized people have been unwilling to allow their native culture to be incorporated into the practice of their new-found faith. They wish to put away all vestiges of their pre-Christian past, and embark upon a fresh course; they wish to practice a form of Christianity that is "untainted" by elements of their culture. In many parts of Asia, Africa, and the Indian subcontinent, Western-style worship has been eloquent testimony not so much to the cultural imperialism of the missionaries, but to a desire on the part of those embracing Christianity to adopt the trappings of Western culture as a part of the Christian "package." Unfortunately, for these reasons traditional cultures have all too often been casualties of the missionary expansion of the church. But increasingly, as people began to recognize that the strength of the gospel lies precisely in the fact that it is able to be expressed through the countless particularities of human culture, the creative amalgamation of Christian worship and local forms of religious expression has come to be the goal.

## Local Forms of Liturgical Inculturation

Of course issues of inculturation affect not only Christian communities on the mission field, but increasingly those at home as well. Like religious pluralism, cultural pluralism is a social reality that must be taken into account by all those concerned with Christian worship. Sometimes Christians in the dominant culture have failed to recognize the growing diversity in their local communities, or have been reluctant to tailor their Sunday worship to meet the religious needs of the population. However, those congregations who have widened their horizons to include the liturgical contributions of other cultures have often found their worship lives deepened and enriched, and their congregations filled with new energy. In any case, the era of homogeneous congregations is quickly fading; all communities are becoming more racially, ethnically, and culturally plural, and it is irresponsible to fail to address the issues that this situation raises for Christian worship.

We have seen the ways in which new Christians on the mission field are often initially resistant to including elements from their culture within services of Christian worship. The same is sometimes true for members of immigrant communities, who see assimilation into the dominant culture as a primary goal. For these people, worshiping in a thoroughly "Western" style will be a mark of their acceptance into their adopted culture. At the same time, however, many people coming to a new country wish to retain their linguistic and cultural identity and the sense of connection to their native heritage. This need can be expressed as a desire to feel "at home" in Christian worship, to find a form of worship that reflects their national, tribal, or ethnic origins. The style and tempo of music, the amount of congregational response and movement, the choice of images and analogies, and the use of visual materials and instruments can all provide significant cultural cues in worship. Real care is necessary, therefore, to balance the different social needs of participants in a given service of worship, and to be sensitive to the degree of assimilation people are seeking.

Many relatively homogeneous local communities have also sought to include worship resources from the world church as a way of experiencing the richness of global Christianity. Prayers, hymns, chants, songs, visual materials, native instruments, and stories from other cultures have given congregations a sense that they are part of a wider world of Christian faith and practice. Several collections of these kinds of worship resources are available, and when their use is closely tied to, for example, intercessory prayer or offerings of money for the needs of a particular part of the world, it can be a highly effective form of worship. More recently, however, some serious questions are being raised about artificially constructed cultural diversity in worship. Musicians especially, and in particular those from the developing world, increasingly have been speaking out against the practice of incorporating elements of another culture into the common prayer of Western Christians. They are calling it a new form of cultural imperialism, in which the "natural religious resources" of another place are exploited for the spiritual nourishment of the dominant culture. Continued reflection on this issue is needed by pastors and theologians from both sides, and sensitivity to the cultural integrity of all people is an absolute necessity in making decisions about the use of materials from the world church.

## New Forms of Inculturation

Culture is a complex and subtle thing. We are often more aware of the cultures of others than we are of our own. So when we speak of the inculturation of worship we tend almost automatically to focus on the ways in which our "normal" worship is changed to meet the needs of those from a "foreign" culture. But the speed with which our own culture is changing means that often we worship using forms from a culture that we have moved beyond. For example, most of us now live in a highly urbanized, technological culture that has profoundly shaped our worldview, values, and attitudes. But our worship tends to rely on images from an idealized, rural past, where green fields, grazing sheep, and starry skies were commonplace experiences. Should we not think about the ways in which we might inculturate our worship to the technological culture of which we are a part?

Many people resist the idea that our God is as much the God of concrete and steel as of still waters and verdant pastures. Some wish their Christian worship to evoke images of a bygone era, of a time when the pace of life was slower and people remained connected to one another and to the land. For others, the beauties of nature speak to them powerfully of the beauty of God and of holiness. Still others believe that biblical language is normative, and no evidence of "technological" imagery is found in the pages of Scripture. All of these responses need to be handled with pastoral sensitivity by those with responsibility for Christian worship. Whether the adaptation of worship being considered is the inclusion of a hymn that mentions the city or the workplace as a locus of divine revelation, or the introduction of "high-tech" equipment such as sound amplifiers or projection screens, the question of the relationship between gospel and culture is raised.

## THE LANGUAGE OF WORSHIP

Questions of the most appropriate language for Christian common prayer are certainly not new. In the sixteenth century, those who sought a reformation of the church sought also a reformation of liturgical language, in order to allow Christians to pray, sing, and proclaim their faith in God in their own language. The move to vernacular liturgy as the norm was finally completed with the permissive stance of the Second Vatican Council which stated that "since the use of the mother tongue . . . may frequently be of great advantage to the people, the limits of its employment may be extended."[4] The problems of vernacular liturgy were sharpened as Christian missions expanded into territories where the Bible had not yet been translated into the local language. In some cases, unfortunately, Christian worship was left in the language of the missionaries, and worship became a teaching tool for the "civilization" of native peoples. But in many other instances, creative translations of both Bible and liturgy gave a vibrancy to the language of Christian worship which was indispensable to the process of evangelization.

To speak of a "vernacular liturgy" traditionally has referred to forms of worship expressed in the native language of the people who use them, rather than in a foreign or "esoteric" language (such as Latin or Old Church Slavonic). More recently, however, questions have been raised about the adequacy of Elizabethan English as a useful language for Christian common prayer. The earliest full English translation for the various services of public worship is found in the 1549 Book of Common Prayer, attributed to Thomas Cranmer, Archbishop of Canterbury from 1533 to 1556. Although it was slightly modified during the next century, Cranmer's masterful use of the language for devotional purposes became the standard measure for the suitability of any public worship in English, not only for Anglicans, but for all English-speaking Christians. Indeed, the rhythm, dignity, and restraint, as well as the memorable imagery ("we have erred and strayed like lost sheep," "for better, for worse, in sickness and in health," for example) of Cranmer's prayers have given them pride of place among the greatest examples of liturgical prose.

However, these words are nearly four and a half centuries old, and language, like any living system, changes and evolves over time. The meanings of many of the words in Cranmer's prayers have shifted. For example, "Prevent us, O Lord, in all our doings" originally meant "Go before us, O Lord, in all that we do." But in contemporary usage "prevent" means to impede or prohibit, and "doings" has fallen out of common use altogether. Certain words are now employed exclusively in liturgical or devotional settings: the pronoun forms "Thee," "Thy," and "Thine," the second person verb forms ending in "st" or "est" ("hast" or "wouldest") and third person forms ending in "eth" ("desireth," "goeth"). Beginning in the 1950s, many with responsibility for Christian worship began to demand a "revernacularization" of the language of common prayer, and encouraged efforts to bring liturgical prose in line with contemporary English usage.

In many quarters these modernizing efforts were (and continue to be) strenuously resisted. It has been argued that when human beings were addressing the Deity, common street language was inherently disrespectful, and a special, more deferential language was a necessity for maintaining a proper creature/Creator relationship. Others worked from an anthropological perspective, arguing that in most tribal religions a technical or "esoteric" language for worship was invariably used, in order to heighten the sense of an encounter with mystery and Divine transcendence. Others believed that the beauty of Elizabethan language was unsurpassable, and should not be tampered with; it was a great "national treasure," and to abandon or change it was to desecrate a part of our living heritage. Nothing could be written today which would meet the standard set by Elizabethan prayer language.

Unfortunately, the earliest efforts at finding a contemporary liturgical language did little to dispel this anxiety. Many liturgists were concentrating more heavily on articulating and incorporating the major changes in theology that had occurred in the previous twenty-five years than on crafting a beautiful form of expression. After the Second Vatican Council, an international commission was established to devise common translations of the official Latin texts for all English-speaking Roman Catholics, and the work of finding agreed English liturgical texts is carried on ecumenically by the English Language Liturgical Consultation (ELLC). Gradually, by the mid-1970s, a richer and more elegant style of contemporary prayer language began to emerge, one which incorporated both biblical imagery, traditional prayer motifs from many centuries, reworkings of Cramner's prose. But this transformation was not yet complete when the first generation of revised services were introduced (for example, the *Lutheran Book of Worship* in 1978, *The Book of Common Prayer* in 1979, and the *United Methodist Hymnal* and *Book of Worship* in 1984 and 1989), and within two decades calls for new forms of service were being voiced in many of the English-speaking churches. In all of this, there is recognition that it is not only theologians and liturgical scholars who are needed for the drafting of prayers, hymns, and affirmations for Christian worship, but that poets and other skilled crafters of the English language are indispensable to the task as well. Those with no official orders of service also need to give due attention to this matter of liturgical language, since it is all too easy to fall into slangy or jargon-laden speech in such situations. If anything, the work of finding a language that has the qualities of both accessibility and dignity is perhaps even more demanding when praying and speaking extemporaneously. Perhaps it is worth reconsidering the notion that the Holy Spirit only works when we speak "off-the-cuff," and not when sitting prayerfully during the week, pondering deeply the pastoral-theological needs of our congregation, and carefully preparing for Sunday worship with a pen in our hand or at the computer.

## Inclusive Language for Christian Worship

One of the most significant challenges to this process of contemporary language for worship has been the challenge of a growing awareness of the ways in which our use of language can hurt or demean or marginalize others. The quest for an "inclusive language" began in the tumultuous 1960s, when there arose a number of groups in society that sought an end to social, political, and economic discrimination. Virtually all of these groups made language issues a part of their respective platforms, believing that the existing language and imagery had been shaped by those in power and was instrumental in maintaining the status quo. These marginalized people knew that if they were ever to establish equality for themselves, they would have to break up the monopoly on the control of images. Soon, the media picked up on this matter of inclusive language, and publishers began to issue guidelines for authors in order to avoid words and images which seemed to be causing offense to certain groups of people; these changes in the secular media's use of language quickly became part of the public conversation.

But it is only relatively recently that religious language and liturgical language has been subjected to a systematic critique on grounds of inclusiveness. Beginning in the early 1980s, several studies and reports were issued on the various liturgical implications of the inclusive language question.[5] Complicating matters was the fact that the term "inclusive language," has a variety of different meanings. For some, it refers to language about human beings, and seeks to eliminate words like "man" and "mankind" as synonyms for "human" in standard English and to remove literary and liturgical stereotypes of women and men, women's roles and men's roles. For still others, though, it can mean finding new ways of speaking about God, although for some of the more radical feminist theologians even the word "God" is too overlaid with patriarchal associations to be retained. In addition there are those who use the term "inclusive language" to describe a process which is designed to erase ageism, handicap-ism, racism, and species-ism from the language of common worship. But generally, the most common meaning of the term "inclusive language" is a form of words and images that reflects and reinforces the full equality of women in church and society.

A number of specific proposals are being made by those seeking to make the language of Christian worship more gender-inclusive. The most conservative voices in this matter argue that there is no need for any change at all on any level, and that to deprive our liturgical language of words like "man" and "mankind" (in their generic sense) will eventually deprive the church of a whole body of the most meaningful and poignant Christian poetry, hymnody, psalmody, devotional prose, and prayer language. Others believe that late twentieth century English is indeed in a state of flux, and that words such as "mankind" are no longer understood in this society to be inclusive of both men and women alike. Other words included within this category are "brother-hood" and "sons of God," "fathers" (meaning ancestors), and some would also eliminate the word "fellowship." But in any case, many people are only will-ing to discuss gender-inclusive language that refers to human beings and human communities.

Those who wish to take the matter of gender-inclusive language for wor-ship one step further raise the question of pronouns for God, and more specif-ically, whether or not we are going to refer to God as "He." In terms of liturgical language this problem is alleviated somewhat by the fact that most liturgical references to God are a part of direct address, and so in the second person (for example, "O God, we worship and praise you"). But on the whole most advocates of gender-inclusive worship would support the elimination of male pronouns for God wherever they appear. There are also those who would argue that the pronoun "he" should not be used for Christ either. Although Jesus of Nazareth was biologically male and can be referred to by the male pro-noun, the risen and ascended Christ is beyond human gender.

Various solutions to the problem of pronouns for God have been proposed. Some routinely refer to God as "she," although most would agree that this does nothing to encourage the idea of God's essential genderlessness. Others suggest alternating references to God between "he" and "she," balancing them equally, but this creates serious problems in clearly identifying the antecedent of the pronoun. Most people, though, believe that it is entirely possible within the bounds of elegant English prose to eliminate the need for pronouns for God altogether.[6]

Those wishing an even more radical revision of liturgical language have called for the elimination or reworking of a whole class of words with very strong roots in Scripture and in the Christian tradition: words like "Lord" and "King" and "kingdom." They say that words like "Sovereign" and the "reign of God" (in place of the "kingdom of God"), are perfectly acceptable gender-inclusive substitutes.[7] At the same time, many people who are working for the elimination of certain images which they find exclusive and sexist, are also call-ing for a complementary expansion of images, so that our prayer language includes feminine images of God as well as masculine. Many look to the Scrip-tures to uncover certain images that have been lost in liturgical history, many from the parables of Jesus, (for example, the woman with the lost coin, the mother hen gathering her chicks under her wing) others from the psalms, such as the idea that we are brought to birth by God. The biblical image of Holy Wisdom, *sophia* (a word which is in the feminine gender in Greek) is also gaining in currency as a divine name.

More serious theological and pastoral difficulties arise when changes are proposed for language about the Trinity (traditionally Father, Son, and Holy Spirit). Many of those concerned with gender-inclusive liturgical language allege that Father and Son, certainly, and Holy Spirit to a lesser degree, can only be interpreted as connoting the maleness of God. A whole range of Trinitarian alternatives has been proposed, the most widely used is "Creator, Redeemer, Sustainer" (or "Creator, Redeemer, Sanctifier"). Occasionally the first person of the Trinity is referred to as "Father and Mother" or simply as "Mother," highlighting the creative, nurturing side of God.

There are serious and substantive objections to these proposals for alternative Trinitarian formulas for use in Christian worship. People opposed to changes in Trinitarian language say that there are certain crucial liturgical moments at which invocation of the traditional triune name of God is seen to be absolutely essential, and that failure to use it at those moments puts one outside of the Nicene faith, and hence outside of orthodox Christianity, outside of "right praise." (These "crucial moments" are considered to be in the rites of baptism, ordinations, and the Lord's Supper.) Moreover, it is argued that to make such important changes unilaterally, without substantial ecumenical agreement, is dangerous, and that to use alternative Trinitarian formulas will have serious interdenominational implications. There are also serious objections on systematic-theological grounds. First, there is the argument that "Creator, Redeemer, Sustainer" refers only to the action of God and not to the person of God, and that since our relationship with God is personal, one-on-one job descriptions simply will not do. The second objection is that the way we refer to persons within the Trinity highlights not only God's interaction with us, but also points to a relationship within the Godhead, which is a relationship of persons to one another: Father to Son and Son to Father, with the Spirit as the expression of their mutual love and the bond of their unity. A "functionalist" approach to the Triune name of God poses difficulties in this area as well.

All of us struggle to find adequate words to convey the most significant things in our lives: the mystery of ourselves, our experience of the world, of love, hope, honor, and joy. In many ways, the Christian church is engaged in that very same struggle. Like the Christians in every age before us, we face the challenge of trying to find the words, the images, and the language to convey the experience of walking with God as faithful Christian people in the world. Because of the natural limitations of our language and our ability to use that language, we must always view the words we use to worship God as provisional. But at the same time, we must recognize that the words of our worship are an indispensable part of our relationship with God, the common currency of the shared world which God graciously sets up with us. This gives the search for a suitable liturgical language a particular urgency. Christian worship is always the primary setting in which the church's search for a living language thrashes itself out, and where the outcome is most keenly felt.

## WORSHIP AND THE CRISIS OF AUTHORITY

Many commentators have remarked that the contemporary world is qualitatively different from the world of the past. The pervasiveness of electronic media, the experience of the power of weapons of mass destruction, the speed with which knowledge and information are increasing in every area of intellectual inquiry, all these combine to forge a situation which many have labeled "postmodernity." Postmodernity is often said to present, for a number of different reasons, a "crisis of authority" within societies and institutions, including the Christian church. In premodern times, structures of church, kinship, and community provided a single, coherent system of authoritative norms for behavior, thought, and values. But this system is in the process of breaking down. Increasingly we are confronted with not just one or two legitimate claimants to authority, but by a whole variety of allegedly "authoritative" sources of information and interpretation, advice, expertise, and commentary. Such things as the news media, online services, video resources, self-help books, and advertising compete not only for our money but for our loyalty. At the beginning of a new millennium, religion has become for most people but one authority among many.

This situation has caused a degree of generalized uncertainty and, according to some social commentators, anxiety. There is a high premium placed upon individual responsibility in decision-making in such a situation, and doubt is not easily overcome. In order to cope with the pervasive sense of uncertainty, many people fall back upon types of religious belief and practice that recall a more stable and consistent world. Highly structured and rigidly enforced patterns of authority (described by many as "authoritarianism") and ritual are often very attractive to those who wish to retain a sense that there remains one, single, unassailable source of truth. There is also a resurgence of interest in "tradition," both in worship and in doctrine, and a desire to return to Christian roots.

Others, however, see this situation as a liberating one, allowing for the exercise of freedom and creativity in worship and theology. As a result, new forms of worship, music, proclamation, and liturgical space have flowered. In addition, and especially with the social revolutions in the 1960s, the Christian liturgy has been increasingly responsive to the needs and desires of those at the church's grass roots. This has resulted in services which are open, user-friendly, and nonhierarchical, and which call for a high degree of participation on the part of the congregation. In other words, the democratization of worship, a form of shared liturgical authority, is a hallmark of contemporary Christian worship in many denominations.

## The Bureaucratization of Christian Worship

Another form of power-sharing in the area of worship is the growth and development of the various forms of "worship bureaucracies." Many social commentators have remarked on the growth of bureaucratic systems in the past fifty years, and on their increasing impact on many areas of our life, including our religious life. Like all bureaucracy, denominational and local worship boards and committees are intended to manage the process of change and to make it orderly and predictable. Under the direction of a central body (such as the Annual Conference or General Assembly), a mandate is given to a group of people responsible for worship to accomplish a particular liturgical task, the development of a new hymnal or baptismal rite, for example, or the revision of a lectionary. The project enters the bureaucratic system and is immediately conformed to its processes and procedures. Sub-committees, task forces, procedural flowcharts begin to break the work down into its component parts, specific needs are categorized, and consultants brought in to tackle the various aspects of the project. Worship becomes a "product" which is "processed" through the bureaucratic system and conformed to that system's characteristics and limitations.

If the worship "product" is conformed to the bureaucratic mould, so too are those for whom this product is intended. The bureaucracy is designed to meet the needs of the "typical client," (in this case, the "average worshiper") and for the worship bureaucracy each individual worshiper or worshiping congregation is reduced to a "case" or a "category." Although bureaucratization is designed effectively to spread the authority base in the process of making official changes in worship, it tends to limit the degree to which liturgical creativity can flourish. Creative ideas often fall outside the categories set up to manage the task of worship reform, and are thus lost to the church through the bureaucratic process.

Because of these limitations, many worshipers feel quite alienated from both the process and the products of bureaucratically driven revisions to official liturgical texts, hymnals, and procedures. Often this alienation causes serious pastoral difficulties for those with local responsibility for worship. This is not to say, however, that bureaucracy is always harmful to Christian worship. Bureaucracy can ensure fairness, diversity, and the appropriate use of expertise as necessary reforms in worship are being undertaken. But care must be taken to see that the board or committee is highly representative and that all points of view are heard. It is also important that the boundaries of the committee are quite permeable, so that creative ideas from the outside can penetrate and interaction with the actual (rather than the "theoretical") clientele is maintained.

## Computers, Worship, and Authority

The presence of computers has also raised important issues in the area of authority in Christian worship. The number and kind of materials available to those planning Christian worship is growing: bibliographies, ancient and modern liturgical texts, hymns and other worship resources, visual aids. These are available to anyone with access to certain types of software or to online services, and with desktop publishing capabilities, anyone can produce his or her own texts and compilations of texts for use in congregational worship. The worship planner can choose from a vast array of worship resources, from many centuries, theological and liturgical traditions, and parts of the world and create a unique product for a particular occasion in the life of the church.

But again, in this sort of situation the question of authority arises. Under whose authority does one undertake to provide congregational worship materials? Many would argue that the presence of computers threatens further to diminish the authority of ecclesiastical institutions and leaders, and reduces the worship of the church to a collection of local flavors-of-the-month. Others say that the continuity of liturgical tradition will be seriously weakened within denominations, as each congregation devises its own worship materials, unrelated (theologically or ritually) to any larger church structures. Indeed, the difficulty with some of these computer-generated composite rites is that they are theologically inconsistent, since the materials have come from sources that are doctrinally incompatible with one another (or incompatible with the theological tradition of the congregation). As a result, many denominational leaders are anxious about the presence of computers as tools for the planning of congregational worship, and are asking those with responsibility for congregational worship to exercise special care in this matter.

## Charismatic Worship and the Authority of the Holy Spirit

The neo-charismatic revival in Christian worship has caused a great deal of controversy in the past several years, and again the debate is a facet of the larger debate over the nature of authority in worship. In some Christian traditions, and especially the Reformed, Lutheran, Methodist, Roman Catholic, and Anglican traditions, order and stability in worship are valued. Official hymnals, prayer books, and orders of service are seen as guides to the boundaries of a particular worship tradition and sources of both devotion and theological reflection in their own right. The authority of church institutions to establish forms for worship is deemed to be good and proper, and an exercise of legitimate pastoral care over the denomination as a whole.

But many congregations are looking to another and (in the minds of many), a higher, source of authority in worship: namely, the Holy Spirit. Among those who would identify themselves as "charismatic," the Holy Spirit, present and active in the worshiping community, is the principal guide to what is said and done in Christian worship. In this form of common worship, worshipers seek to open themselves to the movement of the Spirit, and to speak, sing, pray, and preach "as the Spirit gives utterance." Many would say that officially produced rites and text inhibit the ability to respond to the Spirit's prompting. Because charismatic worship is now found in all denominations, lively debates about the relative authority of text and Spirit are quite common in many congregations.

As we saw was the case in the question of liturgical inculturation,[8] these debates about charismatic worship hinge on a debate about the nature of the Holy Spirit itself. Is the Spirit a Spirit of chaos, or of order? Can the Spirit be given voice in bureaucratically produced rites and texts, or must it always work through extempore prayer and praise? Is there room for both forms of worship in a given service, or in a given congregation, or will set forms of worship always drive out pneumatic activity? Is one form of worship more or less "legitimate" or "godly" than another? Who is to judge whether the various verbal and physical manifestations of the Spirit in worship are genuine? All of these questions will be a part of the future of Christian worship, and of each tradition and congregation as well.

The whole issue of the nature of authority in our worship is a complex and difficult one, and is connected to issues of what has been called life politics. In life politics, decisions made in one area have an impact on other areas of life, since all aspects of our existence are seen to be interconnected and interdependent. Because of this, many are asking the deeper human question, What is really at stake here? as we make decisions about the relationship between authority and freedom in our worship lives. This is a dilemma as old as the New Testament itself, and enshrined as a paradox in the pastoral Epistle 1 Peter

> For the Lord's sake, accept the authority of every human institution . . .
> As servants of God, live as free people, yet do not use your freedom as a
> pretext for evil.[9]

In the end, even if the choice we make is simply to submit to authority in matters of worship, it is our choice, and we must not use the freedom we have to make that choice as a "pretext for evil."

Of course, this is not the first paradox we have seen in the pages of this book. The experience of Christian public worship, in every place and in every age, is filled with such paradoxes. Worship can knit us together or break us apart. Worship can build us up or tear us down. Worship can draw us in or exclude us, release us or imprison us. The decisions we make about what we want from our Sunday services, our baptisms and our funerals, our celebrations of the Lord's Supper have real consequences for real lives. And these decisions are ours to make, as pastors, as lay leaders, as local preachers, as worshipers, as "free people." But to base these decisions on anything less than sound learning, prayerful discernment, and faithful obedience to the law of mutual love is to fail to live as free people who are at the same time "servants of God."

# 7

# Case Studies in Christian Worship

Learning a subject such as Christian worship is not only a matter of absorbing facts and figures; it also consists of the ability to apply what one knows to various situations. Case study work is one way of making creative use of the material in this book in order that your learning may be enhanced. The case studies in this chapter will help you to make vital connections between the historical, theological, and biblical information and certain practical, pastoral situations. A "case" is simply a description of a particular situation. It aims at providing sufficient information for the student to enter into the situation imaginatively as a participant. In other words, the question, What would I do in this situation? is at the heart of each of these exercises. There are no right or wrong answers in case study work, and there are few clear-cut solutions; most of the cases offered here are set out in a quite open-ended way so that the decision you make (and the way that you arrive at it) is your own. But there are certainly more appropriate and less appropriate ways of thinking about the issues presented, and more coherent and less coherent arguments, which take account of the facts, which set the case in its wider context, and which begin to define a specific result or goal. Although case study work is intended to be done collaboratively in small groups, so that the insights and knowledge of all members of the group can be brought to bear on the situation, it can also be used as a springboard for individual study and reflection.

Each of the following twelve case studies in Christian worship attempts to pose questions about such things as

- the place of religious ritual in the life cycles of human beings and human communities

- the relationship between faith, belief, and Christian worship
- the appropriate limits of flexibility within Christian worship
- the pastoral-liturgical role of the minister or worship leader
- the "ownership" of Christian worship—whose rites are these?
- the degree to which the history of worship constrains or empowers the worship of contemporary Christians
- the degree to which denominational polity, theological reflection, and biblical interpretation make an impact on worship.

It will be important to try to attend to all of these elements in a deliberate way as you work. In other words, consider not only what you think about the various issues presented, but why you think about them in the way that you do. Questions for discussion and reflection are provided at the end of each case in order to stimulate your thinking.

## THE PROCEDURE

The first thing to do in case study work is to read the case carefully. Identify the significant factors in the case (that is, factors you will want to take account of when you are thinking about an outcome for the situation). Are there elements included in the case which are distracting, or which should be ignored when planning an outcome for the case? (For example, is the size of the congregation a significant factor, or is it irrelevant? Are such things as the ages of the members of the congregation or their social standing important factors, or are they irrelevant? And so on.) Discover what the various participants in this case have to say for themselves, and what others say or think about them. What presuppositions or misunderstandings are at work? Who wields power? Why is there a difficulty at all? In other words, do a careful "exegesis" of the pastoral situation presented. Try speaking "in character" for yourself as the minister or worship leader, for the various key participants, for members of the congregation, for the extended families. What are they feeling and thinking? Are there important questions left unanswered?

Next, move to the questions at the end of each case. Try to be honest in your assessment of the situation and to answer each question carefully. Try also to look at different points of view, different perspectives on the situation, especially if you are working alone. Ultimately, you should have a good idea of how you would proceed, of what sort of process you would initiate, and finally of course, of what proposal you would offer for a service of Christian worship. In some cases, you are asked to write prayers or select hymns, in others to provide an outline of a service or to select elements within it. Overall, the goal is to understand where a particular service of Christian worship will fit into the situation as it is presented. At the end of your work on each case, you should have gained

- a good sense of the central issues of the case
- some awareness of the biblical, theological, canonical, historical, sociological, psychological and cultural parameters within which solutions to the case situations must be set
- a sense of the desired outcome (or outcomes) of the situation
- a sense of the place of this local event in the wider mission of the church and in the workings of God in the world.

Although all of these cases are fictional, all of the elements within the situations described have happened to women and men with responsibility for worship in local churches.

## THE CASES
## CASE STUDY 1: CHARISMA AND CONTROVERSY
## (CHAPTERS 1 AND 2)

You are the pastor of New Life Community Church in Wiverdale. New Life is the only church in Wiverdale, a town of about 875 people, many of whom work in various businesses related to agriculture. Although some residents drive to churches of their own denominations in Center City (about twenty-five miles away), most Wiverdale residents who are practicing Christians are members of New Life. The three previous ministers have been, successively, a Baptist, a United Methodist, and a Presbyterian; but the minister is always chosen for his or her willingness to work ecumenically with the various denominations and worship traditions represented in the congregation. There is one Sunday service, with an average attendance of about sixty-five. You have been in Wiverdale nearly nine months and have come to know and love the place and its people.

Despite your affection for Wiverdale, you are aware New Life is a Christian community heading towards a crisis. Two years ago a charismatic prayer group was established, and since then the community has become more and more divided. Members of the prayer group have begun to believe themselves to be the "spiritual elite" and they point to the gift of speaking and singing in tongues, and healing as evidence of God's special grace and favor among them. They have begun to ask that admission to Communion be more tightly regulated, and want the leadership of the church to affirm them in various ways.

The charismatic prayer group had been meeting in the home of one of the members, but recently the group has expanded to twenty members, and none of the individual members now has space large enough for their meetings. They have asked you if they can meet in the fellowship hall three times per week. This would mean moving the night of choir practice and also the biweekly meeting of the Social Responsibility Team. Several long-standing members of the church who are not part of the prayer group have seen this as a crucial issue, and have insisted that the prayer group should not be allowed to use the fellowship hall for its meetings. They have been heard to say that the group are "weird" and "New Age," and they want you to exercise discipline in the matter.

You have been in Wiverdale long enough to know the various players in the debate, and you believe that the prayer group is sincerely seeking the will of God for themselves and for their community. But you also think that the "ordinary" church members are devout and faithful Christian people, trying to maintain the life and worship of the church as they have always known it.

At the same time, you have decided that the "separatist" nature of the group is beneficial neither for them nor for the community as a whole. You also are convinced that if the worship needs of both the prayer group and the more conservative members of the congregation could be met within a single Sunday service, the destructive divisiveness might be contained.

In order to begin to discuss the problem, you call a meeting of the Worship Committee. The Worship Committee is a group of four people, all of whom are mature and committed members of the church, but who also represent a diversity of points of view.

The members of the Worship Committee are:

• Joy Jones, a twenty-nine-year-old woman who spent the first eighteen years of her life in churches of the pentecostal tradition. Joy has reacted strongly against her upbringing, and now is most comfortable in a quite formal and well-ordered style of worship. She has been a member of New Life for the past four years, and although she and her husband Lloyd struggle to make ends meet and to support their family of three small children on a meager income, she has tithed each year and contributes her time to many of the church's activities. In addition to the Worship Committee, she is most heavily involved with the church's social outreach work with the homeless in Center City.

• Peter Smith, a seventy-year-old retired university professor. At first Peter was suspicious of the charismatic prayer group, and spoke to you several times when you arrived in Wiverdale about the threat it posed to the life of the church. But quite recently his attitude has softened. Peter's wife Mildred was diagnosed with cancer two years ago, and during the past several months it has looked as if all medical efforts at containing the disease have failed. Mildred's friend Bruce was a founding member of the prayer group and about four months ago he asked if Mildred would allow them to come and pray with her for God's healing. Mildred reluctantly agreed, and the group has visited several times. Two months ago (much to the doctors' surprise) she went into remission, and she is now able to attend church and participate in social activities with her husband.

• Bill Moore, a fifty-one-year old farmer and land owner and a lifelong member of New Life Church. Bill and his wife (Rose) met and married in the church, their four children were baptized in the church, and they are energetic and dedicated contributors to most New Life projects and activities. They also contribute financially, and many of the church's activities (especially the choir, with which both the Moores sing) would be hard-pressed to continue if he withdrew his support. Bill remembers his childhood in the church as its "Golden Age," with worship that was dignified and full of beauty and meaning, and preaching that was powerful.

• Nancy Adams, a single woman forty-five years old who has been in Wiverdale for twelve years. Up until two years ago, Nancy only attended church irregularly, although she came to you occasionally for pastoral counseling. She was invited to join the charismatic prayer group early in its life, and has often found its meetings deeply moving experiences of grace. Estranged from her family at a young age, Nancy has found personal relationships difficult all her life, but has for the first time discovered in the charismatic prayer group people who are accepting and supportive. Since joining the group Nancy has become more and more involved with the church, and seems altogether more in control of her life and happier. She serves on several committees and now hardly ever misses the Sunday service.

The time for the meeting has arrived and you are feeling a bit apprehensive. You realize that this is just the sort of issue that has the power to do irreparable harm to a congregation, and could be the cause of congregational breakdown or schism.

## Questions for Reflection and Discussion

1. What are the various participants feeling and thinking? (Try speaking for each of the members of the Worship Committee.) What are their presuppositions and reactions? How do they inhibit or enhance their effectiveness in this discussion? What do they hope will happen? What do they hope will not happen?
2. What are you feeling and thinking? What are your presuppositions and reactions? How do they inhibit or enhance your effectiveness as a pastor in this situation? What do you hope will happen?
3. What models of worship are at play in this situation?
4. What are the significant problems or issues here? Are they mainly emotional; ecclesiological; theological; liturgical; socioeconomic; other?

5. What role does the Sunday Service itself play in each of the above?
6. Can the Sunday Service function as a source of reconciliation for this community? How?
7. How, precisely, would you order your Sunday Service to accommodate the various needs, anxieties, and desires in this congregation? At what points in the service will stability be important? Which parts of the service can accommodate some freedom of expression? Are there particular rituals which might enable a reconciliation?
8. What will you say to those representing each of the main points-of-view?
    • about gifts of healing?
    • about speaking in tongues?
    • about Communion?
    • about the nature of a Christian community?
    • about the relationship between worship and community?
9. Do any biblical passages come to mind for you as you think about preaching during this time?
10. Would you consider augmenting your weekly worship schedule to include special services? What sort of services would these be? How often would these occur?

## CASE STUDY 2: THE "GOD-SQUAD" (CHAPTER 2)

It is the third Sunday in November and you are preaching at St. Stephen's Church in Longwell. The church is in an affluent suburb of the city of Burbridge, and it has been a key player in the social responsibility work in the city itself. Members of the congregation have been active in setting up and staffing homeless shelters, late-night soup runs, and clothing banks in order to meet some of the real needs of the city. They are a lively, forward-thinking, and self-sufficient (materially and spiritually) congregation, and you have felt fortunate to share in ministry with them.

One of the sources of real pride in the community is the youth group in the church, and especially the young peoples' drama group (called, jokingly, the "God Squad") which is known throughout the region. They too are involved in outreach to the wider community. This past weekend, for example, the fifteen-member drama group was away on tour presenting selections from *Godspell* in a residential nursing home and two rehabilitation centers.

On the way home to Longwell last Sunday night, the minibus in which the young people were traveling turned over on an icy road, and several young people were injured. A week later three remain in the hospital; one boy, Tom, is still in an extremely critical condition with a head injury, and his prognosis is poor. The driver of the bus was Reg Prowse, a member of the congregation and the father of Sarah, one of the less-badly injured children. He was arrested at the scene of the accident for driving above the legal limit of alcohol consumption. He was granted bail and returned to Longwell the following morning.

In your two-and-a-half years in the area you cannot remember when such a tragedy has befallen this community. Although they had been in touch with the difficult parts of life in the nearby city, they had been relatively immune from major trauma in their more immediate world. You are thinking about all of this as you sit down to prepare the Sunday Service for this cold November Sunday, and are asking how this service can contribute to healing and to helping the community to make sense of what has happened.

## Questions for Reflection and Discussion

1. Speak "in character" for yourself as the worship leader, for the parents of the injured children, for the parents of the children who escaped unharmed, for Reg and his family, for other members of the congregation. What are they feeling and thinking? Are there questions left unanswered in your mind?
2. What is the theology with which you are operating? What do you really believe about: answers to prayer; divine providence; sin; good works; divine punishment; forgiveness, both human and divine; and what might the various participants in this situation believe?
3. What do the various players in this situation want from this service? What do they need from this service? What are they able to take in?
4. What texts from Scripture will you use? Will you follow the lectionary readings? What are they saying in this context? Where is the good news for this community?
5. How will you construct the service?
6. Given what has arisen in your reflection and discussion, try to answer the following questions:
   • What is the main focus of the service?
   • How will it progress?
   • How does the liturgical calendar come into play?
   • Who is the service for? How will it balance the needs of the parents of the injured children, the other parents, Reg's family, the regular congregation, and occasional visitors?
7. Are there any symbols or rituals which will help this congregation move toward reconciliation?
8. Write three prayers for this service: a prayer of confession, a prayer of intercession, and a prayer of petition.

## CASE STUDY 3: THE SOUP KITCHEN (CHAPTER 2)

You are the pastor of the Church of the Good Shepherd in Center City. Your church is a lively congregation of about 200 on an average Sunday, set in the middle of the inner city. Good residential housing moved out of the city center long ago, and most members of your congregation come some distance to attend church. But they come because of your passionate concern for matters of justice and in order to participate in ministries of outreach to those left behind by "white flight." With significant volunteer help from members of the congregation, Good Shepherd operates a food pantry, a barbering ministry, and a clothes closet on the church premises, and many of the members of Good Shepherd regularly volunteer at the nearby Soup Kitchen, which serves lunch and dinner to about 300 homeless men and women on weekends.

The mayor of Center City, Elmer Foss, and his staff have become increasingly concerned about the problem of homelessness in Center City, and this concern has increased in the past several months since a new downtown Convention Center was opened. The mayor sold the bond issue for construction of the Convention Center on a promise of the waves of visitors (and their money) that would be drawn to Center City. The presence of so many homeless people, he claims, reduces the city's attractiveness and will reduce the appeal of the Convention Center to organizations and businesses. His case was strengthened, and public fear increased, when a visitor was mugged and stabbed downtown by a street person; the resulting publicity was alarmist and people began demanding that the mayor "Do something about those people."

With the approval of the city council, Mayor Foss has instituted a number of popular measures to alleviate the problem of homelessness. He has declared that the vagrancy laws currently on the books will now begin to be enforced stringently. A new law has been passed which says that any shopping cart that is not on store property will be confiscated immediately and the person in possession of it will be subject to arrest. Worse still, however, he persuaded the owner of the building (who happens to be his brother-in-law) in which the Soup Kitchen is housed to raise the rent, and the Soup Kitchen has announced that it can no longer afford to operate and will have to close.

You and your congregation have watched these initiatives with increasing alarm, knowing the impact it will have on the lives of the people you love and serve. You propose to the congregation that Good Shepherd invite the Soup Kitchen to relocate to the fellowship hall and the congregation agrees by a two-thirds majority vote. Almost immediately "things begin to happen" at the church building (broken windows, noxious substances pushed through the mail slot, vicious graffiti messages spray painted on the walls). In addition, you have received anonymous letters threatening that if you don't give up the idea of hosting the Soup Kitchen, worse things may befall you and your church.

Two weeks ago, you received a letter from the mayor's office expressing the concern that this "nonreligious activity" may be in violation not only of city codes but of your own terms of establishment, and demanding to see a copy of the church's charter. You consult with your board of elders, who say that the charter is somewhere in the archives and that they may not be able to find it immediately. They are certain, however, that a "church supper" in conjunction with a worship service is *not* in violation of any city codes nor of the church's charter, and propose that when the Good Shepherd Soup Kitchen opens that a worship service may be included at the end of the meal for any who wish to attend, and that this become the regular pattern.

Some longtime members of the church, while supportive of ministry to the homeless in principle, are strongly persuaded that since duly-elected officials have weighed in against the plan, the church has no lawful or moral right to move forward. They are feeling alienated from the main body of the congregation, and angry that the church has placed itself (and them) in this position. Several are threatening to leave, taking with them their contributions, which are in some cases substantial.

Despite the best efforts of the mayor and city council, Good Shepherd's new ministry is set to open next Sunday. As you begin to plan the main Sunday Service, an act of dedication for the new ministry, and the service after the meal, several pressing questions are on your mind.

1. How can you design a main Sunday Service that might help to reconcile those who are feeling disaffected by the Soup Kitchen plans?
2. What biblical texts will you choose? What will the theme of your sermon and prayers be?
3. What role will the various constituencies be invited to play in the main service? In the act of dedication? In the service after the meal? Where will the services be held?
4. What kinds of symbols and rituals will be included in the act of dedication?
5. What will you do to make the service after the meal accessible to the congregation that will be present? What components will be necessary to include?
6. Write prayers of all of the types described in chapter 2 for the new ministry, its workers, for Center City, and the church.
7. What hymns would you choose for the main Sunday Service?

## CASE STUDY 4: ADAM'S BAPTISM (CHAPTER 3)

You are the minister of Fairview Church in Plainfield where the Kents are members of your congregation. Sheila and John Kent are in their late thirties and have been married for fifteen years. When they married they agreed that they wanted several children, since they both had come from large, energetic families. But as the years progressed, and one miscarriage followed another, it seemed as if their hopes were not to be fulfilled. You have been serving

Fairview Church for four years, and you know Sheila and John well. Their marriage has been under considerable strain and during the past two years you have seen them periodically for marriage counseling. Frequently they have asked you to pray that a baby would be a part of their lives.

Just when you were beginning to think that more serious medical and psychological intervention was going to be necessary in order to save the marriage, Sheila and John announce that Sheila was pregnant. As the months went by and the fears of miscarriage receded, their interpersonal problems seemed to melt away. It was a difficult pregnancy, and twice Sheila had to be hospitalized; in the last several weeks she was confined to bed. But the image of the baby which would be the answer to their prayers sustained them throughout their ordeal. Many people in the congregation remarked that they had never see the couple so happy. They came to church when Sheila was able, and the congregation was giving them prayerful support.

Two months ago, Sheila gave birth to a son, whom they named Adam. Almost immediately, they realized that something was very wrong and that Adam had severe physical deformities. In addition, his lungs were not well developed and for the first few days the prognosis for survival was unclear. You went to visit as soon as you heard that Sheila had given birth, and the parents were clearly devastated. When you ask if they would like you to baptize Adam there in the hospital though, they begin to get angry. "Our son is going to be just fine!" John shouts at you. "You leave him alone!" Sheila, now crying uncontrollably, tells you that you had better leave.

Adam does survive his early days, and Sheila and John are able to take him home about three-and-a half weeks later. Reports are sketchy since friends of the couple from the congregation say that John and Sheila have not wanted any visitors. What you do know is that early tests indicate that Adam probably has profound hearing loss and other sensory-motor problems, and the doctors are predicting severe developmental delays. But his basic health has stabilized, and he is now considered to be out of danger of dying. Sheila and John have not returned to church, and you have hoped for some word from them. But finally you decide to take the initiative and you phone to see if you can stop by the house for a visit. Sheila hesitates, saying that their days are very busy and tiring, but she finally suggests a time,

When Sheila opens the door you hardly recognize her. She looks exhausted, and there is a great sadness in her eyes and manner. She welcomes you, though, and as you sit down to talk she begins to cry, saying how sorry she is that she and John had behaved so badly when you visited them in the hospital. You ask if you might meet Adam and she looks surprised, but takes you up to his nursery. He is a beautiful child, but very still and when you pick him up to hold him his thin wail is evidence of the problems you have heard about. As Sheila takes Adam from you to put him back in his crib, you notice that she handles him gingerly and does not try to make eye contact with him.

Sheila seems equally reluctant to talk about Adam and the prognosis, but you ask again about baptism. This time she is more receptive, saying finally, "We think we probably should do it. It just wouldn't seem right not to." She looks quite anxious, though, and you ask if there is anything else she is worrying about. After some hesitation, she says, "I suppose it will have to be on a Sunday morning?" You say that there is time to talk about all of that, and you say your goodbyes.

Since your visit with Sheila, you have wrestled with a number of serious questions and all of these come into play as you think about planning this service.

## Questions for Reflection and Discussion:

1. What do you really believe about: answers to prayer; divine providence; disability, weakness, pain and suffering; hope and disappointment; the "ministry of the baptized; the eternal fate of the unbaptized"?
2. If Sheila and John ask for a private baptism, what will you say?
3. What do the various players in this situation *want* to hear in this service? What do they *need* to hear? What are they able to hear on this day? Does it matter that the day you have suggested for the baptism is also Mothers' Day?
4. Which of the New Testament images of baptism discussed in chapter 2 will you highlight?
5. What role should members of the congregation play?
6. Are there particular visual images, symbols, or rituals that will help to convey the love of God to this family?
7. What will you pray for in this service? Write three prayers for Adam's baptism, a prayer of confession, a prayer of intercession, and a prayer of thanksgiving.
8. What hymns would you choose for this service?

## CASE STUDY 5: JANE (CHAPTER 3)

You are the pastor of Springfield Community Church, a congregation with a total membership of about 70 with an average Sunday attendance of 50. Springfield is a small rural town, and most of the people in your church were born and will die there. You have been pastor in Springfield for about four-and-a-half years; your predecessor was the beloved Pastor Brown, who had served the church for nearly 35 years and whose widow still lives in town and attends church when she is able. Although you have felt welcome in the congregation, Pastor Brown still casts a long shadow, and at least once a week someone is likely to say to you "But that's not the way Pastor Brown used to do things!"

Jane Stephens is a 38-year-old single woman in your congregation who has been relatively active in church activities since you arrived. Her family moved to town from New York City when she was 12 years old, and although they had not been churchgoers in the city, they joined the church soon after they arrived. Jane was baptized the next year at the age of 13. Jane's parents are both still living and attend church occasionally, especially at Christmas and Easter. Except for one year away at college, Jane has lived in Springfield since they moved to town.

You have not found it easy to get to know Jane, since she is quite "prickly" and defensive with you. It is very hard to address this with her, since she denies having any problem with you personally. Although it is difficult to prove, you sense that whenever there are church controversies, Jane figures in them somewhere, but again this is difficult to pin down since she never voices her own opinions or opposition to proposals, but rather seems to be in the background, urging others on. Jane is openly hostile to a number of members of the church, including Pastor Brown's widow, and it seems that these animosities began long before you arrived as pastor. Those who are the subject of her hostilities seem to have no idea why they have been singled out. Because Jane has what seem to you to be deep-seated problems which you are unable to confront with her, you are pleased when you hear through the grapevine that Jane is getting outside professional help, although the stories vary: some report that she is seeing a spiritual director, others say it is a pastoral counselor, and still others think it is a psychotherapist.

On Palm Sunday afternoon, about six months after the reports that Jane had sought professional help surfaced, you receive a telephone call from Jane. She has not been around the church for several weeks and you have been concerned, but she has never telephoned you before and you are very surprised to hear from her. She asks if she can have an appointment to see you. She refuses to say what the topic of conversation will be, but says it is "extremely urgent." Because of work commitments, Jane can only meet with you at night, so you arrange a time with her for the following evening (the Monday of Holy Week) at 7:00 p.m. and, with some feelings of anxiety, you hang up the phone.

The next night you wait for Jane in your office, hardly knowing what to expect. Jane arrives and immediately you notice that her demeanor toward you seems different, at the same time friendlier and more nervous; she is dressed and made up more appropriately for a cocktail party than for work, and she moves her chair rather uncomfortably close to yours as she begins to explain what has happened.

For the past nine months she has, indeed, been seeing what she describes as a "counselor." She tells you that this counselor has a rare ability to "truly understand" her, to "know her" in a way she feels she has never been known. She has a radiant look in her eyes as she describes his sensitivity, warmth, and compassion. In the past several weeks, she reports, she has made a breakthrough in her counseling: she has recovered a repressed memory of sexual abuse. She has remembered that when she was 13 and was taking baptism preparation classes with Pastor Brown, he began to touch her in inappropriate ways and eventually he lured her into a sexual relationship. The abuse lasted almost two years, at which time her serious behavioral problems led her parents to send her away to boarding school. Although she was afraid to tell her parents what was happening, she is convinced that several members of the congregation knew what was going on, including Pastor Brown's wife. When she graduated and returned to town at the age of 18, Pastor Brown was no longer interested in her, and she is now certain that he had moved on to another, younger, girl.

Because the memory of abuse is so intimately linked with her baptism, Jane is asking if you will baptize her again next Sunday morning at the Easter Sunday service. She also wants to make a statement before the whole congregation about what Pastor Brown did to her (her "profession of faith" she calls it) and to charge certain members of the congregation with complicity in the act (their own chance to "renounce the devil and all his works.") She uses a strongly theological argument: "Jesus Christ says: 'I am the Way, the Truth and the Life.' Baptism is being united into Jesus Christ and so it should be about the Truth. My whole life has been a lie, and now in my new baptism, I want to tell the truth," she says. "And Easter is the absolutely perfect time, since Easter is about resurrection and that is what I have experienced in recovering this memory of abuse."

Jane says that she knows that you will do as she asks since she is sure that you "will not continue to protect a pedophile from the consequences of his actions." She is very displeased when you say that you would like to have some time to think about your response and that you will phone her later in the week. But as she leaves she asks, "Can I please have a hug?" and, taken aback, you embrace her quickly and then show her out the door.

### Questions for Reflection and Discussion:

1. What concerns do you have with regard to Jane's request? What are your feelings about what Jane says happened to her? What are your feelings about what happened in your office? (The men and the women in the group may want to discuss the differences in how you feel.)
2. What additional information do you need before you respond to Jane?

3. How do you seek advice and information without breaking the rules of confidentiality?
4. What do you think about Jane's baptismal theology? How does her theology relate to the historic baptismal theology of the church?
5. Do you have a way of responding theologically?
6. Will you rebaptize Jane? If not, what are your options? How will you explain your decision to Jane?
7. If you do rebaptize Jane, what conditions will you make?

## CASE STUDY 6: THE OLD GUARD (CHAPTER 3)

You are the pastor of Green Willow Community Church in the small town of Hopeville. The church has been a very stable one, and many of the seventy-five people in worship on a Sunday were baptized and grew up in the church. At the same time, a new automotive plant has just opened about fifteen miles away, employing about a thousand people, and several new members have joined Hopeville and have begun to attend church regularly. This has been difficult for those you have come to call the "old guard," some of whom feel as if their church is being taken over. But it is generally a very friendly congregation, and you feel that things will eventually settle down.

Mark Dawson has relocated to Hopeville from Gotham City and works as a human resources officer at the plant. When Mark first arrived in town last March he came to see you in your office, saying that he was looking for a new church home. He expressed real sadness over having to leave his former church, where he was very active, serving on the worship committee, as a member of the team of Communion servers that assisted at Communion in church and then took it out to the homebound, and in various other outreach ministries. After a time spent talking, Mark tells you that he cannot consider Green Willow unless he has some assurance from you that the church is likely to be welcoming to his partner Steve, who works from home as a computer analyst. Steve and Mark have been together in a committed, monogamous relationship for twelve years, and have an 11-year-old-son, Toby. Toby was born HIV positive and, having been abandoned by his birth mother, was adopted by Mark and Steve when he was two years old. Emotionally and intellectually Toby is thriving, and his health is presently good. Mark asks about the Sunday school for Toby, and about the opportunities for service for Steve and himself. You say that you are certain that the family will be welcome, and Mark leaves saying that they will see you in church on Sunday.

For nearly a year, all goes smoothly. Steve and Mark begin to participate fully in the church's life, Toby enjoys youth activities, and they attend worship together as a family every Sunday. They make some good friends in church, and you know you can always count on them when something needs doing. In November, when one of the Green Willow's Communion stewards died suddenly, you invited Mark to serve Communion which he does now regularly and with a real sense of dignity and joy.

But one Monday morning in January, Penelope Potter and James Gotbucks, two of the most influential members of the "old guard," make an appointment to see you. They have not been especially friendly to Mark and Steve (nor to any of the newcomers for that matter), but neither have they been openly hostile. Now, however, they have learned that Toby is HIV positive. They have circulated a petition to ban Steve from continuing as a Communion steward and Toby, Mark, and Steve from receiving Communion with the congregation. "We believe, for the well-being of this congregation, that we should not be forced to share the common cup and the one loaf with people who carry the scourge of AIDS and homosexuality. If they want Communion, you can just give it to them privately." There are sixteen names on the petition, all of whom are members of the old guard, but Penelope and James claim that many more would have signed it: "The others just didn't want to rock the boat," they say.

You are taken completely by surprise. Clearly this has been in the works for some time, and you are hurt and offended that Penelope and James would have initiated such an action without first speaking to you. You ask them how they think the giving and receiving of Communion, which in your church is done by intinction, each person taking a piece of bread and dipping it into the common cup, could possibly spread the virus. They simply answer with the words, "Better safe than sorry."

You tell Penelope and James that you will take the matter under advisement. "You'd better be quick about it!" Penelope says as she sweeps out of your office. "We'll be watching what happens at Communion on Sunday!"

Once you recover from the shock of the request to excommunicate Mark, Steve, and Toby you decide to call a meeting of those members of the church who have signed the petition. While you want to alleviate their anxieties about the medical situation, more important to you is to talk with them about the theology of Communion, and its importance to the maintenance of the common life of the community.

## Questions for Reflection and Discussion

1. What theological points are you going to make at the meeting?
2. Are there particular biblical texts that will guide you in your argument?

At the meeting, the group acknowledges that they are aware that the risks to Toby's health in receiving Communion is much greater than the risk to their own. But they remain adamant in their demand that you bar Mark, Steve, and Toby from Communion.

You are planning the service for next Sunday morning and a number of pressing questions are in your mind:

3. Will you ask Mark, who is on the Communion steward rotation for this Sunday, not to serve Communion? Will you ask Mark, Steve, and Toby to refrain from receiving Communion? If so, why? If not, why not?
4. Will you make any changes in the procedure for receiving Communion?
5. What will the theme of your sermon be? If not using the lectionary, what biblical texts would you choose?
6. Are there particular symbols and rituals that will be important to employ on this occasion?
7. Write a Great Prayer of Thanksgiving (using the conventions described in chapter 3) or a Communion mediation appropriate for the occasion.
8. What is your long-term strategy for reconciliation in this matter?

## CASE STUDY 7: THE RECONCILIATION (CHAPTER 4)

Catherine Myfield is a member of Christ Church, Diddridge, where you are the pastor. She is a woman of about seventy, and has lived in Diddridge all her life, in the family home Myfield Hall. She never married, and to her knowledge has only one other living relative, a younger brother Claude whom she has not seen in forty years. Lately, Catherine has seemed troubled. She has been ill for some time, and the prognosis is not good. But it is her estrangement from Claude which is causing her the most distress.

As children and young adults, Catherine and Claude had been very close, being only four years apart in age. But upon the death of their father, in the mid-1950s, the siblings had a serious disagreement over the details of the disposition of the estate. Words were exchanged between them, and in the end Claude declared that he would never again enter the house in which he was raised. Catherine had agreed that she would wish to see him again only at his funeral. (Claude had replied that she would not be welcome there under any circumstances.) Claude left Diddridge immediately, taking nothing with him, and brother and sister have made no attempt to contact one another since that day.

Last year, when she discovered that she was ill, Catherine began to come to church more regularly. The congregation has been extremely kind and supportive, and a number of people have made a special effort to befriend her and to look in on her from time to time. You have also made several visits to Myfield Hall, and in the course of your conversations you have sensed that Catherine has begun to take stock of her life. She has realized that her estrangement from her brother has been a most dreadful mistake. She had become quite a lonely woman, and now she is afraid that she will die without seeing again the one person who is dearest to her. She desperately wishes to find Claude, to tell him how much she loves him and to beg his forgiveness.

Two of the members of the congregation, a married couple named Edward and Rosamund, are attorneys with a special, professional interest in missing persons. You ask Catherine if you might speak to them about Claude, and she is very pleased with the idea. Rosamund and Edward visit several times with Catherine through the summer, and although it appears to be quite a difficult case, they set to work to find the whereabouts of Claude Myfield. It seems, however, that time is not on their side, since Catherine has begun to grow weaker. The congregation includes her in their prayers, and members visit her when she is too ill to attend church.

In early October, Edward and Rosamund have had some luck. They have found Claude, who has recently retired and is living in an apartment in Ferris Wood, a village only twenty-five miles away from Diddridge. Claude married the year after he left Diddridge, but his wife divorced him within a few years of their marriage, leaving Claude with the care of a small son, Ragsdale. (Ragsdale is now thirty-seven and lives with his wife and two children in a remote part of the country.) Edward and Rosamund report that Claude is still hurt and angry about his relationship with Catherine, and seems to be unwilling to consider meeting with her. At this point, you decide to intervene. You know the minister of the church at Ferris Wood quite well, and your inquiries lead to the discovery that Claude Myfield has been very active in that church for a number of years. You and Claude's minister go to visit Claude, and after some delicate negotiations, you manage to convince him to see his sister.

Little is known of what transpired at that first meeting between Claude and Catherine, nor of the substance of the several meetings that followed. But by the beginning of December, Claude has decided to move into Myfield Hall with his sister. He has promised to look after her until she dies, and they have both committed themselves to making up for the years they have lost by their estrangement. Both brother and sister have found a new peace, and Claude and Catherine are planning for Christmas, when Claude's son and daughter-in-law and grandchildren will meet their "Auntie Catherine" for the first time.

Claude and Catherine have come to you with a special request. They believe that their reconciliation is something of a miracle, and certainly an act of God. They wish to celebrate it in church. They ask if you would consider holding a special service for them around the turn of the New Year, when they can gather as a renewed and reunited family. With the congregations that have supported them present, they wish to give thanks to God for what has happened. They say that they have never seen or heard of such a service, but deeply desire to make their reconciliation public, before God and the congregation.

## Questions for Reflection and Discussion

1. What do you think of their request? Can you see any serious objections?
2. What day would be most appropriate for this service? (Christmas Day this year falls on a Tuesday.)
3. What themes will be appropriate for such a service? Where do the following fit in to your thinking about this service?
   - repentance and forgiveness
   - God's will
   - human love and commitment
   - the church (and the local congregation)
   - human states and emotions: fear, joy, remorse, love, hatred, anger, pride, gratitude, regret, failure, hope
   - the ultimate reason for and meaning of human reconciliation
4. What readings from the Bible would you choose?
5. What signs and symbols or rituals of the reconciliation might be employed?
6. How, exactly, would you construct the service? What words would you suggest the participants say to one another? Who else besides Claude and Catherine might be directly involved in the service? What part would the congregation play? What would be your role as the presider?
7. Write the following:
   - a prayer of confession to be said by Catherine and Claude
   - a prayer of intercession to be said by the congregation
   - a pastoral prayer to be said by the presider
   - a prayer of thanksgiving to be said by everyone present
   - an exhortation (or "Statement of Intention") for the very beginning of the service, to be said by the presider
8. What hymns would you choose for this service?

## CASE STUDY 8: PETER'S WEDDING (CHAPTER 5)

Peter is a young man about 30 years old. He currently lives in a graded residential complex a short distance from his home. Peter is mentally challenged as a result of Down Syndrome, but otherwise fit and has been living in sheltered accommodation for the past four years. His parents, Geoffrey and Margaret, are in their late 60s and Peter is their only child. They strenuously resisted his move to more independent living, but were ultimately convinced when Margaret was confined to bed after a hip operation and could not care for Peter as she had been doing. They had hoped that the move would be just temporary until Margaret recovered, but Peter's social worker Elaine impressed upon them that Peter's development and future happiness rested on his gaining a certain degree of independence. His parents grudgingly agreed, having become impressed with the need to think about Peter's care after their deaths. Peter works part-time as a cleaner at the local McDonald's and is enormously proud of his ability to live on his own. His parents visit him frequently.

Peter lives in a shared apartment with four other residents and a supervisor. One year ago, 27-year-old Jane moved in and she and Peter soon became good friends. Jane tests slightly higher in mental ability than Peter, but is confined to a wheelchair because of mild cerebral palsy, a result of the same birth trauma which caused her other forms of developmental disability. Jane's father died in an accident thirteen years ago and her mother placed her in residential care since there were four other children in the family and she found the burden of a handicapped daughter more than she could carry alone. Jane has not seen her mother for nearly five years, but her older sister comes to visit every few months. Along with two other apartment residents, Peter and Jane faithfully attend St. Anne's church (where Peter was baptized), and are well-loved and well-integrated members of the community of faith.

Last March, Peter and Jane went to the supervisor of their apartment and said that they were in love and wanted to be married. They also said that they wanted to "make a baby." The supervisor decided that the best thing to do under the circumstances was to call a meeting between Peter and Jane, their parents, and their social workers. You were also asked to be present, not only because you are the vicar of St. Anne's, but also because you serve as chaplain of the complex. At that meeting, tempers flared, since both Peter's parents and Jane's mother were adamant that such a relationship was impossible, that the supervisor should be held responsible for the situation and fired immediately, and Peter removed to his parent's home as soon as possible. (They also threatened legal action to force Jane to be surgically sterilized.) Jane and Peter became very excited and upset and Elaine took them out of the room. You managed to reduce the levels of tension somewhat, and the parents agreed to a moratorium on any action while a complete social work evaluation is made.

Peter's social worker Elaine is of the clear opinion that Peter and Jane are capable of making a home for themselves, with the proper support and supervision, and as adults have a legal and moral right to do so without their parents interference. The independent social work consultant agrees, with certain reservations. After talking at length with the couple, you are inclined to concur with the social work professionals. You begin marriage preparation classes with Jane and Peter with a view to a September wedding. At the same time, you feel a pastoral responsibility to Peter's parents who have been your parishioners for many years, and you work to help them to understand Peter's need for an independent life. They persistently threaten to boycott the wedding, to press legal action, and often leave your office in tears.

You do acknowledge that the couple will be facing enormous challenges, and you wonder how well they will be able to cope. They fluctuate between a genuine (and quite charming) naïveté, and extreme frustration when things do not go well. Finances are a particular challenge, and the issue of having children has not yet been dealt with. You ask them what kind of wedding they want. "Pretty!" is their unison response. And they want it to be "all about love" and to "say thank you to God" for bringing them together. As the day of the wedding approaches, you are uncertain about what kind of adaptations, if any, you wish to make to the service.

You are especially aware of the nature of the congregation that will gather for Peter and Jane's wedding. A number of residents of the facility will be there, as well as many members of the congregation who have watched the love between Jane and Peter blossom. Peter's parents and Jane's mother and siblings have decided, in the end, to attend the wedding. The social worker and representatives of the residential complex (who have been quite bruised and exhausted by the threats and abuse of the couple's parents) are intending to come as well.

## Questions for Reflection and Discussion:

1. What are the various participants feeling and thinking?
   - Jane and Peter?
   - Margaret and Geoffrey and Jane's mother?
   - members of the congregation? the extended family?
   - the health-care and social work professionals?
2. What do the various participants want from this rite? What do they need from this rite?
3. What Scripture lessons will you choose? Where is the good news for this family and for the community?
4. What issues does this situation raise in your mind about
   - divine providence?
   - blessing (and the power of the Holy Spirit)?
   - disability and weakness?
   - "intelligent participation" in a worship service?
   - freedom?
   - success and failure?
   - marriage as a Christian vocation?
5. Write a prayer of blessing for this couple.
6. What hymns would you choose for this service?

## CASE STUDY 9: MAGGIE'S FUNERAL (CHAPTER 5)

You are the pastor of Hoglett Memorial Church in Jericho, a large county-seat town. It is your first pastoral charge, and in the eighteen months that you have been there you have come to know and love the place and its people. During this time, your own ministry has developed over a wide range of activities. Since you were a nurse in a pediatric ward before you trained for the ministry, you have especially enjoyed working with the chaplaincy at the local hospital, although (much to your surprise) you have found the youth group work an interesting challenge as well.

Soon after you arrived you became concerned about one family whom you knew from both the chaplaincy and the youth group. Steve and Patricia Gardener have two teenage boys (Robin and Joseph, ages 13 and 14) and when you first met them Patricia was pregnant again. Robin and Joseph were both active in the youth group, and Robin turned up with some frequency at the emergency room of the hospital with minor injuries. His parents jokingly described him as "accident prone."

Although it was an unexpected (and quite difficult) pregnancy, Steve and Patricia began to be pleased with the prospect of being parents again in their early forties. When their baby daughter, Maggie, was delivered, they met her arrival with real joy. The older son, Joseph, was equally pleased at the prospect of being a "big brother," but Robin had more difficulty, and as the months went on, he became increasingly uncontrollable. You noticed his disruptive behavior in the youth group and one or two times he was involved in fights with other group members. You also noticed that he was not in church on the day when his baby sister was welcomed and dedicated.*

During the months after Maggie's birth, her parents grew increasingly concerned about the changes in Robin and the resulting strains on the family, and Steve and Patricia came to you for pastoral counseling on several occasions. You asked to see the family as a group. Steve, Patricia, Joseph, and baby Maggie made three visits on their own before they could convince Robin to come with them. When he did, he was silent and withdrawn, and hostile to your attempts to get him to express his feelings. Joseph expressed considerable anger at his brother's behavior and was visibly protective of his baby sister.

One rainy afternoon, Patricia received a telephone call from her sister Annie who had accidentally locked herself out of her house. She sounded desperate, and asked Patricia if she could come right away with an extra set of

*Or, if you come from a denomination that baptizes babies, on the day she was baptized.

keys. Since Patricia's sister lived only a short distance away, and since the weather was so bad, Patricia asked Robin if he would look after Maggie, then an active one–year-old, while she sorted out the problem with the keys. Robin grudgingly agreed, and Patricia left the two children. She was gone no more than 25 minutes.

During Patricia's absence there was an accident, and when she returned she found an ambulance at the house, lights flashing. Baby Maggie had fallen down the steep cellar steps and was being attended to by paramedical personnel. Robin said that he had seen her heading for the stairs, but was unable to prevent her fall. He had called 911 and the emergency crew had responded immediately. On the way to the hospital, Maggie stopped breathing twice and had to be resuscitated. She was found to have a broken neck and severe head injuries, and emergency surgery was performed. Steve telephoned you and you arrived at the hospital as soon as you could. Joseph and Robin were also present, and Robin was clearly in real distress, seemingly guilt-stricken over the accident. You prayed with the family and talked to them about what had happened.

After several hours, the surgeon and pediatrician asked to see the parents and you went with them to hear the news. The prognosis was grim. Maggie has survived surgery, but her heart stopped as they were finishing and she is in a deep coma. There was no brain-wave activity, and she had been placed on life-support machines to keep her heart and respiration working. The doctors were frank with Patricia and Steve: there was only a slim hope of any recovery.

It is now five months after the accident. Robin has been questioned twice by the sheriff of Jericho about the accident, and he is being seen by a professional therapist. Four days ago, after much agonizing deliberation with doctors, counselors, and attorneys, and you as their pastor, Steve and Patricia have agreed to remove the life support from baby Maggie. Since the accident, Maggie has not regained consciousness, and three months ago she was classified as being in a persistent vegetative state and that the chances of recovery were practically (and statistically) zero. Patricia and Steve have worked toward accepting that their daughter will never come back to them, and they know that there is little choice open to them but to terminate her care. You are present for the procedure, and you say some appropriate prayers with the parents. It has been a long journey toward Maggie's death, and they are thoroughly exhausted.

It is now time to plan the funeral, and Steve and Patricia have come to your office to think with you about it. There will be a large congregation. The nurses and doctors from the hospital have grown especially fond of the family,

the congregation of Hogett Memorial has constantly prayed for and minis-
tered to them, and Maggie's cousins, grandparents, aunts, and uncles will all
be present. Robin has been in serious distress since the accident, and seems to
blame himself for Maggie's death. His elder brother Joseph has told him that
he will "never forgive him" for what happened.

### Questions for Reflection and Discussion:

1. What are the participants in this case likely to be feeling? Patricia and
   Steve? Robin? Joseph? the congregation? the nursing staff? you as the pastor and counselor of this family? What is each needing to hear or to say at
   the funeral?
2. Can all of this be managed within a single service? What, if anything, may
   need to be put to one side until a more appropriate occasion?
3. What are the likely thoughts and feelings of the various participants about:
   • answers to prayer?
   • divine providence?
   • sin and evil?
   • God's justice and God's punishment?
   • forgiveness, both human and divine?
   • death and the afterlife?
   • guilt and innocence?
4. For whom is this funeral? What is the good news for this family and this
   congregation?
5. Are there any visual symbols, gestures, or rituals which will help to communicate what words may not be able to say?
6. Is the funeral rite in current use in your denomination (or the standard
   funeral practice of your church) appropriate for this occasion? In what ways
   might it need to be adapted or augmented? What hymns would you choose
   for this service?
7. What are your specific anxieties for the future of this family, and how
   (specifically) might the funeral address them?
8. Compose a pastoral prayer for this occasion.
9. Does it make a difference to the content of this service if baby Maggie has
   been baptized? In what way, specifically?
10. The sheriff of Jericho has phoned you to say that he and a forensic psychol-
    ogist from the state police would like to attend the funeral to assess Robin's
    reactions. What do you say?

## CASE STUDY 10: HOSPITALITY (CHAPTER 6)

You are the pastor of First Community Church in Smallville, which has an
average attendance of 50 at worship on a Sunday. Two doors down from your
church is the Christian Caring Rehabilitation Center, a residential facility for

those with various developmental disabilities. Since you began your work at First Church seven months ago, you have been going to CCRC once a week to hold a service there and have become close with a number of the residents. The services are fairly raucous affairs, with sounds made at inappropriate times and people wandering about, but it seems increasingly clear to you that the "kingdom of God is made of such as these," and it is usually the high point of your week, the time when you learn more about who Christ is than at any other time.

Last week when you finished the service, James T. Kirk, the CCRC director, called you into his office, saying that he wanted to have a conversation with you about the work you were doing there and the kinds of results he was seeing in the residents because of your contact with them. You were surprised when you walked in to find that Kirk was not alone in the office. Wilbur Post was also there. Wilbur is a 43-year-old resident, who had been placed in the facility as a young child because his parents could no longer care for him. Although his speech is very difficult to understand and he has all of the difficulties with body control typical of those with severe cerebral palsy, Wilbur's intelligence is only slightly below average, and it is thought that this deficit is largely due to lack of mental stimulation in his formative years. The director asks you to sit down and says that Wilbur has a question for you and that he will be happy to translate if you need it. After a number of false starts and many odd and disturbing vocal noises, Wilbur begins to get the words out, and although you do have some trouble figuring out what he is saying, after a bit you realize that he is asking if he can come to church on Sundays. "He is not only asking for himself," the director says, "he wants to know if all those residents who are able and wish to be there can come too."

Although you have seen how much the services you conduct at the facility mean to many of the residents, you are a bit startled by this request. Kirk says that he would like you to think about the request carefully and to talk to the members of the congregation about it, since for many of the residents a bad experience at the church would be worse than none. You agree to get back to him next week.

You have several immediate concerns. The order of worship in your congregation is quite formally structured, and many members of the congregation have said that the "peace and quiet" of the sanctuary is particularly important to them. Disabled access is also a problem since you have never had the extra money to provide ramps or other facilities for the differently-abled. Your congregation is mainly made up of middle-aged and older people, who have in the past resisted change. At the same time, you recognize in yourself the widening of horizons that has come from being a part of the lives of the residents at CCRC, and you know that if the church were to take this step, that it would understand the gospel in a new way, and understand church in a new way that you think might bear fruit in abundance.

### Questions for Reflection and Discussion:

1. Are you ready to have a conversation with your congregation about the inclusion of the residents of CCRC in services of worship? If not, what will you need to have in place before the conversation occurs?
2. How do you go about initiating this conversation and with whom?
3. What changes (architectural, liturgical, social-structural) will you need to make to insure that the residents are successfully included in the worshiping community?
4. Who will make the final decisions on these matters? What will you do if the answer from a significant proportion of the congregation is "no" at any point? Would you agree to an "experiment" with the inclusion of the CCRC residents, or will you insist that it is "all or nothing"?
5. Presuming that the congregation agrees to invite the CCRC residents to join the community for worship, what changes, if any, will you have to make in the service to accommodate them?
6. The congregation is asking for a draft order of service for the first Sunday that the group from CCRC is present in church. What will the shape of the service be? How will you propose "inculturating" the service to the new community that is forming? If you do not use the lectionary, what lessons would you choose? What would the theme of the prayers be?
7. You have decided to include a ritual act that would serve to welcome the CCRC group. What kind of act will this be? What objects, gestures, and words would be used?

## CASE STUDY 11: BAD LANGUAGE (CHAPTER 6)

You are a member of the worship committee at Peace Memorial Church in Smallville, a suburb of the capital city, Metropolis. For the past five years, as the edges of the city have increasingly pressed toward Smallville, the congregation has been growing after a long period of stability. There is some pressure on space, and the church is beginning to form committees preparatory to a building project. Newcomers have sometimes found assimilation a challenge, since the chairs of committees have a great deal of power and have tended to be appointed from the more long-standing members of the congregation. The worship is quite traditional, with a mixture of "old standard" congregational hymns, dignified ritual, and formal prayers. Although laypeople read the lessons, the conduct of the service is largely in the hands of the minister. Communion is held every other Sunday.

The worship committee generally handles minor matters, such as the timing of special festivals and the upkeep and decoration of the interior of the church building. But at your regular business meeting in March, you have a more serious matter to discuss. At the last meeting of the worship committee, a letter signed by five newer members, all women, had been forwarded to the committee by the minister for final deliberation. The letter asked the minister to consider changing some of the language used in services of worship at Peace Memorial, and particularly the word "Father." In the discussion on this matter, which was very short, some members of the committee used words like "ludicrous" and "heresy." Although you thought the issue worthy of further time and attention, you were overruled, and the secretary was charged with writing a letter in response, in which the committee thanked the women for their concerns about language but said that they were unable to do anything more.

But the issue has not gone away, largely because the women who wrote the letter, having had no satisfaction from either the minister or the committee, have decided to take matters into their own hands. At every point at which the congregation is invited to say the word "Father" in worship, the women in unison shout out the word "Mother"; at every point at which the congregation is invited to say the word "Lord," they shout out "God." They also deliberately leave out the pronoun "he" for God, which often throws off the rhythm of unison speaking. Two of the women sing in the choir, and last Sunday the anthem itself was disturbed by two voices obviously changing the words. The minister has told you that this issue is much more appropriately solved by the worship committee and has asked you to sort it out at your next meeting. He says that he will abide by whatever decision you make.

Although you feel as if he has abdicated his responsibility, you are ready to press for a more serious discussion at the March meeting. Next Sunday is a Communion Sunday, and you suggest that the committee looks at the text of the service itself as a starting point for discussion. The chair, a member of Peace Memorial for fifty years, asks you to lead the discussion, and to propose a strategy for dealing with the disruption in the congregation and choir.

## Questions for Reflection and Discussion:

1. Whom will you involve in this meeting?
2. What are your feelings about the substitution of the word "Mother" for "Father" in these services? Are there some points at which it is more necessary than others? Which might these be? How about the use of the pronoun "he" for God?
3. Speak for the various participants in this matter. What would each of the following be thinking and feeling:

- the women who have made the request?
- the minister of the church?
- the chair of the worship committee and more long-term members of the congregation?
- the newer members of the congregation?

4. What is at stake here? What theological principles will you want to cover in the discussion?
5. What strategy for resolution to this problem will you suggest? What are the implications of the various outcomes?
6. One of the suggestions is that some of the hymns and songs sung might be "inclusivized." This coming Sunday you foresee the following problems:
   - the doxology sung at the offertory, in the words of Thomas Ken (see p. 29 for the text)
   - the hymn "My Soul Now Magnifies the Lord"

   > My soul now magnifies the Lord,
   > My spirit leaps for joy in him,
   > He keeps me in his kind regard,
   > And I am blessed for time to come.
   >
   > For he alone who shows such might
   > Has done amazing things to me.
   > His mercy flows, his name like light,
   > Remains in time perpetually.

   - the Great Prayer of Thanksgiving which ends with a doxology to be said by the congregation: "All this we ask Father of all, through your Son Jesus Christ, in the Holy Spirit in the Church."
   - the Lord's Prayer
   - The Nicene Creed which begins "We believe in one God, the Father Almighty, and in his Son Jesus Christ . . ."
   - the responses to the intercessory prayers which are "Lord, have mercy" and "Lord, hear our prayer."

   Can you recast the language of these in ways that would be sensitive to the concerns of the women? Are there some that you would not touch at all? On what grounds do you make these decisions: pastoral? theological? historical? other?
7. What are your hopes for an eventual resolution to this problem?

## CASE STUDY 12: THE FAITH OF ANNIE EDWARDS (CHAPTER 6)

You are the pastor of Faith Community Church, in a suburb of Big City. You have in your congregation a married couple, John and Frances Edwards, who have three children. The oldest, Andrew is married to Elaine. They are both teachers, one of mathematics and the other of French, but Elaine has recently quit her job and is preparing to go to seminary. John and Frances' youngest, Catherine is in college where she is an ardent member of the Campus Crusade for Christ. You know John and Frances, Andrew and Elaine, and Catherine pretty well, and you know too that their Christian faith means everything to each one of them. They have often spoken to you in their different ways of their reaction to the middle daughter of the family, Annie, who lives on her own in Big City and has joined the Divine Light Mission, a Hindu sect. John and Frances are fairly reconciled to this, but worry about whether Annie will go to heaven when she dies. They reproach themselves for failing in their Christian upbringing of their daughter and have asked you several times where they went wrong. Catherine is sure that Annie is "lost" since, as she says, "Jesus is the only Way" and "there is no other name by which we can be saved." She does, however, love her sister and because she believes implicitly in the power of prayer, has asked her college Bible Study group to pray for her. Andrew and Elaine have tried to mediate in this situation, and for the sake of family unity they hope that one day Annie will "see sense."

Just a few weeks ago Annie phoned her parents to say she wasn't feeling well, and asked if she could she come home for a few days. The family was shocked to see how thin and ill she looked and has been rallying around her. Suddenly, Annie went into a serious decline and was taken to the hospital by ambulance. She died the next day without regaining consciousness at just 22 years of age. The autopsy revealed an aggressive brain tumor.

John and Frances are devastated and now overwhelmed by guilt for whatever it was they did wrong as parents. Andrew and Elaine feel helpless to comfort them and wish Elaine had already been to seminary so that they had some theological answers. Catherine can't understand why God has not answered any of her prayers and has let her sister die without returning to the Christian faith so that she could go to heaven.

The family has asked you to preside over Annie's funeral. You are aware not only of the family's reactions but also that many members of the Divine Light Mission will be attending the funeral. Indeed the local leader, Ananda Das, has phoned you to ask if he could take part and read some passages from Hindu holy books that had meant so much to Annie. Taken aback by that request you haven't said either yes or no—you are still thinking about it. Perhaps you might get your head clear about that by starting to plan the funeral. What are you going to do?

## Questions for Reflection and Discussion:

1. What do you hope will happen in this service
   • for the various members of the grieving family?

- for the members of your own congregation, many of whom have known Annie since she was a child?
- for the members of the Divine Light Mission who will be present?

2. What things come into play as you think about whether to include Ananda Das as a participant in the service?

3. If you do decide to have him participate, what role will he play? Will you place any restrictions on his contribution? Will you alter the service in any way to accommodate Annie's faith commitment?

4. Write a Pastoral Prayer or series of individual prayers of confession, intercession and petition for this service. What hymns will you choose?

# Appendix 1

# Guidelines for Theological Analysis of Liturgical Texts

The worship of the Christian church has traditionally been seen as a "primary source" for Christian theological reflection, since worship is the most visible of all the church's acts of faith. Many theologians, from Augustine onward, have taken the texts and actions of common worship as the starting points for their understanding of what the church has believed at any given point in time. It is important for every student of Christian worship to learn to subject the worship they plan and participate in to quite rigorous theological analysis in order to discover what it is saying about the faith of the worshiping community.

Although worship is made up of much more than simply words and texts, the theological analysis of liturgical words and texts is one way of getting at what is happening theologically in Christian worship. Hymns, prayers, affirmations of faith, exhortations, and other elements of worship can all be investigated in this way. This sort of investigation will not only uncover what the texts say in themselves, but also will unmask any theological inconsistencies between and among them. For example, it can be the case that the words of a particular hymn will be making one theological claim, and the words of the prayer that follows it will contradict this claim entirely.

The following set of questions is designed to guide the student of worship in analyzing the words of particular liturgical texts. These questions do not exhaust the possibilities for the interrogation of the texts of our worship, but will give a sense of the kinds of issues that are at stake in this process. By the same token, not all of the questions below will apply to every text, and some will be more pertinent than others.

## Questions

1. What does this text say about God, and about God's attributes and actions? From which sources are the images of God taken?
2. What does the text say about Jesus Christ? What is the relationship between the risen Christ and the historical Jesus of Nazareth? From which sources are these images taken?
3. What is the nature and action of the Holy Spirit?
4. What does this text say about the Trinity and about inter-trinitarian relations?
5. What does this text say about human beings or about communities of human beings?
6. What does this text say about the nature of salvation? From what are we saved? By whom? When, under what conditions, and how? Is it an event or a process? What images are used to describe this event or process?
7. What is the nature of sin and judgment? How do these relate to redemption?
8. What does it say about the final destiny of things; the second coming; heaven and hell; the Christian hope?
9. How does the text talk about goodness, power, suffering, and self-sacrifice?
10. What does this text say about the church, about its nature and mission? What images are used to describe the church and from where do they come?
11. What is the nature of belief and faith? Are they essentially corporate or individual?
12. How is the Bible treated in this text? What biblical images are used and how? Do the biblical images come from one particular portion or book of the Bible?
13. How are certain key elements of Christian doctrine expressed and interpreted (such as, incarnation, resurrection, crucifixion, atonement)?
14. What does this text say about the Christian sacraments? About their institution and purpose?
15. Who is speaking in this text (for example, is it the voice "righteous redeemed" or the "penitent sinner"; the "seeker"; the "church triumphant")?
16. Can anything be discerned about the historical or doctrinal context of this text simply by reading it?
17. Are there any serious theological difficulties or inconsistencies in this text?
18. What would be an appropriate liturgical use for this text?

## Suggested Texts for Analysis

Hymns:

    (*a*) "Ah, Holy Jesus, how hast thou offended?"
    (*b*) "All Hail the Power of Jesus' Name"
    (*c*) "Wash, O God, Your Sons and Daughters"
    (*d*) "The Church's One Foundation"
    (*e*) "It Came upon a Midnight Clear"

Prayer texts:

(*a*) The prayer over the water in your tradition's baptismal rite.

(*b*) The eucharistic prayer of Communion meditation from your tradition or another.

(*c*) The central prayer of blessing over the couple in a service of Christian marriage.

(*d*) The prayers from the funeral rite of your tradition or another.

(*e*) Compare two or more forms of confession and assurance of pardon.

(*f*) The central prayer for the candidates for the ordained ministry in a service of ordination.

# Appendix 2

# Helpsheet for Worship Observation

Learning to analyze how worship works within a congregational setting is an important skill for those engaged in the formal study of Christian worship. Many of those reading this book will already be involved in worship planning; others will be doing so at some time in the future; everyone will at some time have been at least a participant in a service of public worship. A worship service sends many kinds of messages to those who participate in it. Although sometimes these messages are intentional and explicit, more often they are unintentional and implicit, conveyed by such things as the roles people play, the interactions which take place between and among members of the congregation, the relationship between sound and silence, light and darkness, and the shape of the worship space. These sorts of things can often be more important to the overall experience of worship than the verbal content of the prayers, hymns, sermon, and exhortations. Often, however, it is difficult for those with responsibility for worship to detach themselves sufficiently from the experience to identify and evaluate the theological, social, and ecclesiological messages it is sending to participants.

All students of Christian worship should observe at least one service of Christian worship and report the results of that observation in writing. There are several possible techniques for observing worship, and several kinds of questions that one should have in mind when making such an observation. Some students make an effort to detach themselves by pretending not to understand the language of the service; thus they can attend to the nonverbal aspects of worship. Others focus on one significant aspect, such as body language or role differentiation, others attend to the patterns of sound, color, or

206

light. Still others intentionally observe a service which is culturally and theologically "foreign" to them—for example, a Greek Orthodox liturgy if you are a Baptist, or a Pentecostal praise service if you are a Presbyterian. Most good observers simply ask the questions: If I had never been to a worship service before, what would I think was going on? What would I know about the purpose of this gathering, of this community, and about the God to be met here from being present in this service of Christian worship?

Some other hints for acute observation include:

- For at least a part of the service, try to "suspend belief" and experience the service as if Christianity is totally foreign. Can an "outsider" make any sense of it at all?
- For at least part of the service, attend to the messages the building itself is sending. Are there "sacred spaces"? How do you know? If there are sacred spaces, who occupies them and when?
- For at least part of the service, attend to the ways in which the community functions. What are the boundaries to participation and how does a newcomer negotiate them? For example, do you need to be sighted; well dressed; mobile; extroverted; intelligent; in order to feel comfortable here?
- For at least part of the service attend to the model of Christian ministry (ordained and lay) that is being communicated by the service. Most often these messages are unintentional, carried by such things as the assignment of roles, variations in dress, and in the spaces people occupy, so read and interpret these nonverbal elements carefully.
- For at least part of the service focus your attention on "Who is the God to be met in this place?" For example, is it the transcendent "God of mystery dwelling in inaccessible light"? Or is it the near God who befriends us and suffers alongside us? What is the operative theology expressed in this service, and how (by what media) is it expressed?
- For at least part of the service, try to determine which of the models of worship discussed in chapter 1 are at play. How are these communicated?

Students planning to do worship observations should also study Appendix 3, which is a questionnaire for examining religious ritual.

# Appendix 3

# Religious Ritual: A Questionnaire

The following instrument for the observation of various types of religious ritual may be helpful to those planning for and observing Christian worship services.

## A. EXAMINING THE RITUAL SPACE

1. Is the space designed and constructed for this purpose, or for some other purpose? How is this indicated?
2. Does the space focus the attention of the worshipers on the action of the service; the decorative elements of the church building; other worshipers; the presiders; something else?
3. What actions does the space encourage?
4. What action does the space discourage?
5. What impressions do light and color give in this space? Is light or color focused in one particular area of the space?
6. Are there more or less "sacred" parts of the space? How is this indicated?
7. What signals are used to mark the boundaries between sacred and less sacred spaces?
8. Where can people best: see; hear; be near others; be alone; be near the action; be seen and heard? Where is the "center" of this space? Who occupies the "center"?

## B. EXAMINING THE RITUAL OBJECTS

1. What objects does this ritual employ: furniture; vessels or containers; consumable items; other things?
2. Are certain objects regarded as precious? How is this indicated?

3. Is power identified with these objects?
4. Who can handle these objects? Who cannot handle them?
5. Is the object precious only when it is being used? Does its preciousness persist after the ritual is finished? How is this indicated?

## C. EXAMINING RITUAL TIME

1. What time of day does the ritual occur? Is the time of day significant?
2. How is it related to the times of other scheduled events or activities?
3. Does the time of year matter to this ritual? Does the day of the week matter?
4. How long does the ritual take? Does it seem carefully timed?
5. What signals its beginning and its ending?
6. How often is it repeated?
7. Do events in this ritual happen in a linear way, with one action following another, or do things overlap one another? Do some things happen simultaneously with others?

## D. EXAMINING RITUAL SOUNDS

1. Does the ritual use non-linguistic sounds, or only speech?
2. Is music used? How, when, and by whom?
3. Is silence a part of the ritual? How is the beginning and end of the period of silence indicated? (Who has control over the silence?)
4. Does the ritual presuppose that participants can read?
5. What kind of language is used? Is it ordinary language or a special form of ritual speech?
6. What other kinds of sounds are heard during the ritual? Is there extraneous "noise"? From where does it come? What is its effect?

## E. EXAMINING RITUAL IDENTITY

1. What roles do people play in this ritual?
2. How are those who play the various roles distinguished from one another and from non-participants?
3. Who controls the action? Are there changes in the locus of control during the ritual?
4. Do the various participants occupy particular spaces? Under what conditions can participants move from one space to another?
5. How and under what circumstances do participants interact with one another? Who controls this interaction?
6. How are people dressed? Are those with leadership roles in the action dressed differently from other participants?

# F. EXAMINING RITUAL ACTIONS

1. What actions are essential to this ritual?
2. What actions seem to be optional?
3. Do the participants touch one another? Under what circumstances?
4. Are some actions reserved to particular people?
5. How much of the body is used by participants? Is it only the hands and arms, or is more of the body involved?
6. Are there occasions when the action is accompanied by music?
7. Does the ritual presume that participants are able-bodied; that they can see; that they can hear?
8. Are any smells or tastes a part of this ritual? Are they essential or peripheral to the action? Are there smells present which are not a part of the ritual action? What is the impact of these smells?

# Appendix 4

# Helpsheet for Worship Planning

On Sundays and special occasions the Christian community gathers for public worship. Planning that worship is the task of clergy and worship committees, lay preachers, lay readers, and others who have been entrusted with and trained for the task. For students of Christian worship, these occasions are not only experiences of praise and adoration of God and mutual reconciliation with our neighbors. They are also experiences of learning and reflection upon the activity of Christian common prayer and its meaning. Because it is important that this learning and reflection be intentional rather than haphazard and accidental, the planning of, preparation for, and evaluation of actual services of worship should be a part of the course of study.

Ideally, this exercise should be a collaborative one. One of the besetting sins of the church in the modern period is that of individualism, and teamwork is its natural antidote. Cooperation, the sharing of ideas, resources, and talents, and the ability to "let go" of the service are all important skills for the worship planner to master. The following are guidelines for worship planning and preparation in general.

1. Learn the names for locations and objects (see the glossary). Knowing the words for things speeds up the process considerably and helps you to convey the impression of being a person knowledgeable in the area of Christian worship. Because different people and groups will have different words and designations for the various objects, furnishings, and spaces (for example, "lectern," "ambo," and "reading desk" all refer to the same piece of liturgical furnishing) try to become familiar with them all.
2. Prepare the space carefully. Insure that lights, candles, sound system, linens, books, and other things needed for the conduct of the service are in place and ready to use. Double-check these just before the service. See that the

211

space itself is clean and free of clutter. Keep maintenance work current so that emergencies are less likely to occur.

3. Be particularly aware of copyright restrictions on worship materials. Violation of these could involve you in costly legal action. When in doubt about the copyright status of a particular item, err on the side of caution.

4. Insure that readers and other worship leaders are briefed and ready to fulfill their roles. Have a list of reliable replacements on hand in case a participant is absent. If readers are anxious, mark the beginning and end of texts to be read with removable adhesive labels. Allow readers sufficient time to acquaint themselves with the furnishings and pathways.

5. Make certain that all robes or vestments (if worn) are clean, pressed, and in good repair. Ask participants to dress neatly.

6. The service sheet is an important theological text. Make certain that it has sufficient information to guide the congregation (including first-time visitors) through the service. Design the service sheet in such a way that everyone will know what words they are expected to say and actions they are to make, so that they can worship without anxiety.

7. Particularly if a certain number of the congregation is elderly, it is a good idea to have copies enlarged (many photocopiers are equipped with an enlarging capacity) for easier reading. In all cases proofread the service sheet very carefully for accuracy, and make a sufficient number of copies for everyone in the congregation.

8. See that all musicians have a marked copy of the service sheet, with cues for music clearly indicated at the appropriate points.

9. Insure that special materials are on hand and ready. For example, if it is a service of the Lord's Supper, is there sufficient bread and wine? Are there plates for the offering? If it is a baptism, is the water for baptism warm enough? Is the paschal candle in place?

10. Guest participants or preachers should be briefed about where they should sit, and the various "customs" of the congregation that might not be indicated elsewhere.

11. Make certain that sightlines (and "soundlines") are clear and that all parts of the liturgical action can be seen and heard without difficulty by everyone. See that any visual elements of the service are large enough (and placed high enough) so that they are visible to all.

12. Be especially sensitive to issues of inclusiveness, both in language and in the choice of leadership for the service. Offense is likely to be caused in a mixed community if worship is always led by or directed towards one particular age group, gender, or race. Find ways of including people with handicapping conditions.

## QUESTIONS TO ASK WHEN PLANNING A PARTICULAR SERVICE OF CHRISTIAN WORSHIP

1. What is the organizing principle of this service? Will the decisions made about the content of the service be determined by (choose as many as

apply): the lectionary readings; the preacher's chosen text; the time of year; something happening in the community, the nation, or the world; the text of the choir anthem; something else (be specific)?

2. How will the intention of the service be conveyed? What thematic weight will be carried by: the prayers; the hymns; the choir anthem; other music; visual, symbolic, or ritual material; the sermon; other service elements?

3. Are there logistical or organizational problems with the service that will need to be overcome?

4. How many leaders (including readers, intercessors, singers, and so forth) will be required for the service to run smoothly? Do any of these people need special preparation or training?

5. Are there particular issues on which negotiation will be necessary? With whom must this negotiation be done? At what stage will it be done? If this is a "special" service (a wedding or funeral, for example), can the persons most directly affected be involved in the planning and execution of the service? What will happen if they disagree with you about the direction the service should take?

6. What is the general feeling or attitude you are hoping to invoke among members of the congregation during this service? (For example, attentiveness; commitment; joy; peace; reverence; penitence; awe; admiration; something else?)

7. After the service do you want people to feel: happy; rededicated; relieved; wiser; refreshed; remorseful; sociable; reflective; something else? (Choose as many as apply.) How will this be encouraged?

8. What are the focal points of this service? What is its climax? Which elements do you hope will be particularly meaningful to participants?

9. Are there patterns of repetition that may help to carry the theme of the service? Can silence be used to good effect (without making people anxious)?

10. Can the worship space be used creatively? Must the congregation and leadership always be in a "confrontational" or "audience/performer" position?

11. What corporate rituals, movements, or gestures might help the congregation to move into closer communion with God and with other worshipers?

12. Who has overall presidency over this service? Can this person relinquish total control so that others can participate creatively?

13. If this is an ordinary Sunday service, how does it relate to the service which went before it and the one which follows it? Is there a sense of progression and momentum, or is each one an isolated event?

14. How long will this service last? How important is accurate timing in this case? What plans are made if the service looks as if it will run longer than is allowable? Are there elements of the service that can be cut out in this instance? How will such changes (or others) be communicated?

15. Using the analogy of a good novel, what is the "plot" of this service? Does one element lead naturally and logically into the next? Is there a climax of the service? At what point does it occur? Has the congregation been drawn forward through the service so that it leaves worship in a different place (emotionally, theologically, spiritually, doctrinally) than where it began?

# A Glossary of Liturgical Terms

This glossary is intended to provide a quick reference to key terms and concepts in the study of Christian worship. For more detailed or exhaustive explanations of the words below, see either the *Oxford Dictionary of the Christian Church* or Westminster John Knox Press's *New Westminster Dictionary of Liturgy and Worship*.

**Absolution** (also called the "Assurance of Pardon"). A statement by the president of the service (or other leader) of God's love and willingness to forgive the sins of the penitent, most often following the confession. (In some traditions, the statement of absolution is reserved to ordained ministers.) See also *comfortable words*.

**A cappella.** Choral music sung without instrumental accompaniment.

**Advent.** From the Latin word for "coming," Advent is the period four weeks before Christmas (ending on Christmas Eve) during which the Christian community prepares for the celebration of the Incarnation. "Coming" not only refers to the birth of Jesus, but also to the second coming of Christ in the end times.

**Advent wreath.** A circle of green branches (usually evergreen) with four colored candles, one to be lit on each of the four Sundays before Christmas. Often a fifth candle, placed in the center of the wreath, is lighted on Christmas Day as a sign of the coming of Christ who is the Light of the World.

**Affirmation of Faith.** A statement of Christian belief made by the congregation (sometimes in a responsive form). Although generally this is the also definition of a creed, when the term affirmation of faith is used it indicates that the words employed are not the words of one of the historic ecumenical creeds of the church (i.e., the Apostles', Nicene, or Athanasian Creeds).

**Agape** (also called the "Love Feast"). The fellowship meal of the earliest Christian communities referred to in 1 Corinthians 11. During this meal, some of the bread and wine were specially set apart for the Lord's Supper. Quite soon the meal was separated from the bread and cup ritual, and disappeared altogether. Revived among Moravians and the early Methodists, and more recently advocated by those planning ecumenical services.

**Alb.** A long white tunic used as the "undergarment" for other vestments worn by participants (both clergy and lay) in a service of public worship. Sometimes it is belted with a rope or "cincture."

**Altar-table.** The piece of liturgical furniture on which the bread and wine for the Lord's Supper are placed. The presider at the service stands behind the table facing the congregation. Sometimes called simply the "altar" or the "Communion table."

**Ambo.** See *pulpit.*

**Amen.** The congregation's response to prayers said on their behalf by a worship leader. It derives from the Hebrew word meaning "trust."

**Anamnesis.** From the Greek root meaning "to remember" or "to re-present," the *anamnesis* is a portion of the Great Thanksgiving, usually following the words of institution, in which the community declares that it is committed to remembering God's action in its behalf.

**Anointing.** The application of oil, usually to a person's head, to signify healing, commitment to serve, or initiation. See also *unctio in extremis.*

**Anthem.** A piece of music sung by the choir, usually a setting of a biblical or liturgical text.

**Antiphon.** A verse from Scripture which is repeated as a response to a psalm, a canticle, or a prayer.

**Apostles' Creed.** An affirmation of faith which originated in the third century as the first profession of adherence to Christ for those being baptized.

**Apse.** The semicircular niche at the east (altar) end of a church building. Originally the apse was the place where the presiders' chairs were located.

**Ash Wednesday.** The first day of the season of Lent. Traditionally, Ash Wednesday has been a day of corporate penitence and fasting, signified by the making of a cross-shaped mark with ashes on the forehead of worshipers.

**Athanasian Creed.** The third of the so-called "ecumenical creeds," devised to combat certain doctrinal errors at the turn of the fifth century. In past times, the Athanasian Creed was required to be said on Trinity Sunday and on certain other holy days, but its use is becoming obsolete (see *creed*).

**Baptism.** The washing with water of a person as a part of the process of Christian initiation.

**Benediction.** See *blessing*.

**Bidding.** An exhortation in which the congregation is asked (or "bidden") to pray. Often this simply consists of the words "Let us pray." Also called the "Call to Prayer." A bidding can occur many times in a service.

**Blessing** (also called the "Benediction"). A declaration, usually by the presider and in the subjunctive mood ("may such-and-such be the case") which calls for God's blessing on the congregation before they are dismissed (see *dismissal*). Also used for other prayers said over people or objects, such as the water at a baptism or a newly-married couple at their wedding.

**Calendar.** An arrangement of days within the church year in order to commemorate certain events in the life of Jesus, the apostles, or the history of Christianity.

**Call to Worship.** An exhortation to the congregation stating that the purpose of the gathering is to worship God and the response of the congregation that it is ready and willing to do so. Can also include a statement of God's worthiness to be worshiped. (In other words, it is not a prayer to God.)

**Canon.** Can refer variously to (1) the authoritative list of the books of the Bible, developed in the middle of the 3rd century; (2) the central prayer of the Eucharist (see also Great Thanksgiving); (3) canon law, which is the body of legislation by which a church is governed; (4) persons who live by the rules of the organization which supports them, especially applied today to refer to the canons of particular cathedrals.

**Canticle.** One of the various short hymns or songs either from the Old or New Testament or from the early centuries of the church. Examples are the Magnificat (Luke 1:46–55), the Benedictus (or "Song of Zechariah," Luke 1:68–79), the Nunc Dimitis (or "Song of Simeon," Luke 2:29–32), and the Song of Moses (Exod. 15:1–18).

**Cassock.** A floor-length tunic, usually black, sometimes worn by the participants (both clergy and laity) in a service of public worship. A common vestment for a member of a choir.

**Catechesis.** From the Greek word meaning "instruction," catechesis is instruction in the Christian faith, especially the instruction of new converts.

**Celebrant.** See *presider*.

**Chalice.** The cup that holds the Communion wine at a celebration of the Lord's Supper. See also *paten*.

**Chasuble.** A large sleeveless garment with a center opening for the wearer's head. The chasuble is traditionally worn only by the presider at the Lord's Supper.

**Choir.** The group of singers who take part in a service of Christian worship. Also, the section of the church building in which these singers sit.

**Christmas.** The day in the church year which celebrates the birth of Jesus. Also called the "Feast of the Incarnation."

**Church Year.** The church year (or Christian year) is composed of festivals and commemorations which highlight the various aspects of the gospel and the Christian life.

**Churching of Women.** See *Thanksgiving for the Birth or Adoption of a Child*.

**Collect.** Sometimes called the "Prayer of the Day," although the collect follows a particular structure, and the "Prayer of the Day" can be freer in its form. The collect is the prayer which highlights some aspect of the lessons for the day, or the time in the church year. It begins with an ascription (God or some aspect of the working of God is addressed), followed by an attribution (a statement of what God has done in the past), then a petition (asking God to act again as God has acted in the past), a purpose clause (a reason why the action of God is needed), and a doxology (usually Trinitarian in shape, this is a declaration that the prayer is made to the Father through the Son in the power of the Holy Spirit).

**Colors** (liturgical). Traditionally, the different seasons and days of the church year are distinguished by particular colors for the vestments and other elements of liturgical furnishing. Usually these are purple (or more commonly now unbleached rough cloth) for penitential seasons and days (e.g. Ash Wednesday, Lent, Advent, Good Friday), red for seasons and days associated with the Holy Spirit (Pentecost, ordination, and commemorations of the saints and martyrs), white for festival celebrations of Jesus Christ (Christmas and Easter) and green for ordinary Sundays, especially the summer Sundays after Pentecost.

**Comfortable words.** The passages of Scripture (Matt. 11:28, John 3:16, 1 Tim. 1:15, and 1 John 2:1–2) which are used as words of assurance of pardon in the absolution. See also *absolution*.

**Committal.** The service at the graveside in the burial of the dead in which we commit the body of the departed to the mercies of God.

**Communion.** Used as a synonym for Lord's Supper or the Eucharist, the term Communion technically refers to the receiving and consumption of the eucharistic bread and wine.

**Communion Table.** See *Altar-table*.

**Confession** (*of sin*). A prayer to God which acknowledges that we have failed to be the people God wants us to be, that, in the language of one of the oldest prayers in English, "we have erred and strayed from your ways like lost sheep," have "followed too much the devices and desires of our own hearts," and "have sinned exceedingly in thought, word, and deed." The prayer goes on to ask for God's forgiveness (see also *absolution*). Note: "Confession" is also used in the phrase "Confession of Faith" which is an alternative term for a creed or affirmation of faith.

**Confirmation.** Originally an integral part of the rite of Christian initiation, now the first public reaffirmation of baptismal vows for those who were baptized as infants.

**Covenant Service.** Commended by John Wesley for the Methodist societies, the covenant service became an annual service of solemn rededication and commitment.

**Credo.** See *creed*.

**Creed.** A corporate affirmation of faith used in a service of Christian worship. The two historic creeds used in worship are the Apostles' Creed and the Nicene Creed. The word derives from the Latin word *credo* meaning "I believe."

**Daily Office.** Traditionally, the daily services of morning and evening prayer, but also includes noontime prayer and night prayers (called "compline"). The word "office" comes from the Latin word for "duty" or "service."

**Deacon.** The form of ordained ministry which represents the Christian vocation to service.

**Dies irae.** The hymn which was a part of the medieval rite for the burial of the dead and which describes the "Day of Wrath" or final judgment.

**Doxology.** A hymn of praise, usually to the Trinity, which is used to conclude a prayer, psalm, or hymn.

**East** (liturgical). Since ancient times, many church buildings were situated so that when the congregation faced the altar-table it was facing geographical east, acknowledging Christ, who is the Sun of Righteousness. Today liturgical east is the end of the church in which the altar table is placed, regardless of the actual geographical direction.

**Easter Day.** The Sunday which celebrates the resurrection. The date of Easter is calculated as the first Sunday after the first full moon that falls on or after the Spring equinox (March 21).

**Easter Vigil** (also called "The Great Vigil of Easter"). The first service of Easter which is celebrated sometime between sunset on Saturday and sunrise on Sunday morning. It usually consists of the lighting of the paschal candle, a series of readings (from two to nine) which take the congregation through the events of salvation history, Christian initiation or a renewal of baptismal vows, and a celebration of the Lord's Supper.

**Elder.** See *presbyter*.

**Elements.** Another term for the bread and wine used at the Lord's Supper.

**Epiclesis.** From the Greek word meaning "invocation," the *epiclesis* is a calling down of the Holy Spirit upon an object or action in Christian worship. In the Lord's Supper it specifically refers to the section of the Great Thanksgiving that asks for the Holy Spirit to come upon the celebration of Communion to infuse it with power and fruitfulness.

**Epiphany.** The celebration of the church year which commemorates the various forms by which Jesus of Nazareth was manifested as the Christ. This manifestation includes both the visit of the magi and the first miracles of Jesus.

**Epistle.** The reading in a service of Christian worship from the New Testament letters, the book of Acts, or the book of Revelation.

**Eucharist.** From the Greek word for "thanksgiving," the Eucharist refers to the combined service of Word and Table which makes up the celebration of the Lord's Supper.

**Eucharistic prayer.** See *Great Thanksgiving*.

**Excommunication.** The barring from communion of those who have committed serious sin. Refers not only to a prohibition from partaking of the Lord's Supper, but also from continued fellowship (communion) with the community of believers more generally.

**Exhortation.** An address to the congregation to declare the purpose for gathering or to encourage the action or devotion of the congregation.

**Extempore prayer.** Spontaneous, unwritten prayer, composed for a particular occasion by the one who prays it.

**Font.** The container in which the water for baptism is held. Depending on the mode of baptism (sprinkling, dipping, or full submersion), it can be anything from a small basin to a large tank or pool.

**Footwashing.** A liturgical rite commemorating Jesus' action at the Last Supper when he washed the feet of his disciples as a sign of his servant ministry. Usually takes place as a counterpart of the Lord's Supper held on Maundy Thursday.

**Fraction.** The breaking of the bread for distribution at the Lord's Supper.

**Frontal.** A cloth or tapestry which covers the altar for a celebration of the Lord's Supper. Usually the altar frontal is in the liturgical color of the day or season.

**Gloria in Excelsis.** Also called the "Great Doxology" and extended hymn of praise to the Trinity. Beginning with the words "Glory to God in the Highest and peace to God's people on earth" (or in the older form: "Glory be to God on High and in earth, peace, good will to men"), the Gloria is said or sung as the congregation's hymn of praise before the proclamation of the Word.

**Gloria Patri.** A Trinitarian doxology: "Glory be to the Father and to the Son and to the Holy Spirit; As it was in the beginning, is now, and shall be forever, world without end, Amen." Traditionally said after the recitation of a psalm or a canticle.

**Godparents.** The sponsors of candidates for baptism.

**Good Friday.** The service which commemorates the crucifixion of Jesus on the Friday before Easter. Usually consists of the reading of the passion narrative in the presence of a replica of the cross.

**Gospel.** The reading in a service of Christian worship of a portion of the four Gospels.

**Gradual.** Any piece of music (usually a congregational hymn or psalm) sung just before the Gospel lesson. From the Latin word *gradus* meaning "step," this was sung as the procession with the Gospel book was coming down the steps from the chancel to the main body of the church where the Gospel was traditionally read.

**Great Fifty Days.** The fifty days from Easter Day to Pentecost.

**Great Thanksgiving.** (Also called the "Eucharistic Prayer," the "Canon," or the "Anaphora"; and sometimes, erroneously, the "Prayer of Consecration.") The central prayer of the Lord's Supper. Not to be confused with a "Communion Meditation," or with the "Words of Institution" (or "Warrant") which are usually an integral part of the Great Thanksgiving.

**Great Vigil of Easter.** See *Easter Vigil.*

**Greeting.** This is a formal expression of mutual recognition, in the name of Jesus Christ, between congregation and presider, such as: Presider: "The Lord be with you!" Congregation: "And also with you." (In other words, "Good Morning!" is not a liturgical greeting.)

**Holy Saturday.** The day before Easter Day. The Easter Vigil can be held anytime from sundown on Holy Saturday to sunrise on Easter Day.

**Holy Week.** The week from Palm Sunday to Easter Day which is the final week of Lent.

**Homily.** See *Sermon.*

**Host.** The wafers of unleavened bread used in some celebrations of the Lord's Supper. The word "host" comes from the Latin word for "sacrificial victim," highlighting the identification of the Communion bread with the sacrifice of Christ.

**Hymn.** A piece of religious poetry, usually set to music for singing in a service of religious worship.

**Intercessory prayers.** Liturgical prayers for the needs of the church and the world. Also called the "Prayers of the People." These are often in the form of a dialogue between a leader and the congregation (see also *Litany*).

**Initiation, Christian.** The composite process of the making of a Christian, including water baptism, the laying-on-of-hands with a prayer for the gifts of the Holy Spirit, and the celebration of Communion. See also *Baptism, Confirmation.*

**Institution Narrative.** The section of the Great Thanksgiving which recalls the events of the Last Supper. It is usually composed of various elements from the accounts in the Synoptic Gospels and 1 Corinthians.

**Intinction.** The practice of dipping eucharistic bread into the chalice of wine so that both elements of the Communion can be received at once.

**Invitation.** An exhortation to respond to the proclamation of the Word with renewed dedication or a commitment to discipleship.

**Kiss of Peace.** See *Peace.*

**Kyrie eleison.** From the Greek words "Lord Have Mercy," the *Kyrie eleison* is a repeated response which forms part of the prayers or litany of confession or intercession.

**Laying-on-of-hands.** The placing of the hands on a persons head as a sign of spiritual power. Used in services of healing, initiation, reconciliation, and ordination.

**Lectern.** The piece of liturgical furniture from which the Scriptures are read in public worship. Increasingly seen as redundant in the presence of a pulpit.

**Lection(s).** The portions of Scripture read in the service. Traditionally the lessons set the theme for the service as a whole and come as close to the sermon as possible so that the reading and preaching of the Word is seen to be a unity. See also *sermon.*

**Lectio continua.** A mode of liturgical Scripture reading in which parts of the Bible are read in course during successive Sundays, rather than the reading of selected pericopes. Often a particular book of the Bible is read from beginning to end, chapter by chapter on each Sunday.

**Lectionary.** The arrangement of readings for the various Sundays and other occasions of Christian worship.

**Lent.** The forty days (excluding Sundays) before Easter. Originally a time of preparation for baptism and the reconciliation of penitents, later a time of fasting and penitence for all Christians in anticipation of the Easter feast.

**Litany.** A responsive reading (or singing) between a congregation and leader. Often used as the form for an intercessory prayer, but can be used for other prayers and readings as a method for the congregation to participate and "own" the prayer or reading. The leader begins with the versicle, which is followed by the congregation's response. Sometimes the response is invariable (e.g. "Lord, have mercy" or "Hear our prayer") and the leader elicits the response with an invariable "cue."

**Liturgical east.** See *East* (liturgical).

**Liturgy.** From the Greek words meaning "a public work," the term liturgy refers to a pattern for Christian public prayer.

**Lord's Prayer.** The prayer which Jesus taught his disciples as recorded in Matthew 6:9–13 and Luke 11:2–4.

**Love Feast.** See *agape.*

**Lugubria.** The red or black garments worn by mourners in ancient Rome.

**Magnificat** or "Song of Mary." A canticle, taken from Luke 1:46–55, traditionally used at Evening Prayer.

**Maundy Thursday.** The Thursday of Holy Week which commemorates the Last Supper and the inauguration of the Eucharist. The word "maundy" comes from the Latin word for "commandment" which refers to Jesus' command in John 13:34 that we should "love one another."

**Metrical psalms.** Versified versions of the psalms, arranged in regular lines for setting to music. For example, the opening verse of this metrical version of Psalm 23:

> The Lord's my Shepherd, I'll not want
> > he makes me down to lie
> in pastures green; he leadeth
> > me the quiet waters by.

**Mitre.** The traditional headgear worn by a bishop in the Western Christian church.

**Mystagogical catechesis.** A series of instructional sermons given by the bishop to new converts to the faith in the fourth and fifth centuries.

**Narthex.** The entry or vestibule of a church building.

**Nave.** The main body of a church building, the gathering space for the congregation.

**Nicene Creed.** Also called the Niceno-Constantinopolitan Creed. The profession of faith creed devised by the Ecumenical Councils of Nicaea and Constantinople (325 and 381 respectively) and used in public worship on Sundays and other festivals of the church year.

**Nunc Dimittis.** Also called the "Song of Simeon," a canticle from Luke 2:29–32 which is traditionally used at services of Evening Prayer.

**Nuptial blessing.** The central prayer of blessing over the couple in a marriage service.

**Offertory.** Those prayers and actions by which the congregation symbolizes its self-offering to God. Usually the combination of a collection of money and a prayer along with (in services of Holy Communion) the offering of bread and wine for use in the Lord's Supper. Also used to describe the hymn or anthem sung during the offertory.

**Office.** See *Daily Office.*

**Opening Sentence.** A sentence from Scripture at the very beginning of the service. Usually the Opening Sentence is from one of the lessons used as readings for the service, and serves to set the theme for the service. Can be recited as a verse and congregational response.

**Ordinary.** The invariable parts of a service of Christian worship, such as the Lord's Prayer and the Creed.

**Ordination.** The setting apart of those who will serve as public professional ministers for the church by a service of prayer and the laying on of hands.

**Pall.** A cloth covering for a coffin, often decorated with Christian symbols.

**Palm Sunday** (also called Palm/Passion Sunday). The Sunday before Easter which commemorates both the triumphal entry of Jesus into Jerusalem before his crucifixion and the passion of Jesus on the cross.

**Paschal.** Pertaining to Easter, from the Greek word *pascha*, which was a reworking of the Hebrew word for the Passover.

**Paschal candle.** The large candle that is lit on Easter Day (or during the Great Vigil of Easter) as a symbol of the light of Christ. Traditionally, it burns at each Sunday gathering until the Day of Pentecost, and thereafter stands by the font and is lit for baptisms.

**Pastoral Prayer.** A prayer (usually) by the presider, which functions to gather the prayers of the congregation. Usually comprised of elements of thanksgiving, confession, petition, and intercession.

**Paten.** The plate on which the bread to be used in the Lord's Supper is placed.

**Peace** or **Kiss of Peace** (sometimes also called the "Pax," or the "Passing of the Peace"). A gesture of reconciliation shared among members of the congregation. As a liturgical greeting, it probably began as a true kiss (it is widely agreed that the exhortations in many of the Epistles to "greet one another with a holy kiss" refer to this liturgical practice—see e.g. 1 Peter 5:14 and 2 Corinthians 13:12), but most often today a handshake or embrace has replaced the kiss. This is not an expression of sociability or friendship, but a symbolic enactment of the Lord's command in Matthew 5:23ff. The Peace is usually exchanged just before the Lord's Supper, signifying reconciliation and unity in Christ.

**Penance.** See *reconciliation*.

**Pentecost.** The festival which takes place fifty days after Easter Day and commemorates the disciples' experience of receiving the Holy Spirit recorded in the book of Acts.

**Pericope.** A section of Scripture read in public worship from the Greek word meaning "to cut around."

**Petition.** A form of prayer which asks God to act in a particular situation.

**Pew.** A type of congregational seating, usually in the form of a long bench with arms and a solid back. Pews were not introduced into churches until the late thirteenth century.

**Prayer of Illumination.** A prayer which asks for the grace to hear and respond to the Word of God in the service.

**Prayers of the People.** See *intercessory prayers*.

**Preaching gown.** A vestment sometimes worn by the person leading a service of public worship, and especially by those who expound the Word of God.

**Prelude** and **Postlude.** Pieces of music (either choral or instrumental) which precede and follow the main body of the service.

**Presbyter.** A form of ordained ministry, sometimes translated "elder," "priest," or "minister."

**Presider.** The person who oversees the proceedings in a service of public worship. (From the Latin word meaning "to sit in front of.")

**Propers.** The variable parts of a service of Christian worship, such as the lessons of the day and the collect (see also *ordinary*).

**Psalter.** The collection of psalms which are appointed to be read in services of Christian worship.

**Pulpit.** The piece of liturgical furniture from which the Scriptures are read and the sermon preached. Occasionally other parts of the service are led from the pulpit as well. In ancient churches the place of proclamation of the Word was called the "ambo," and this term has gained currency among students of Christian worship.

**Reconciliation.** A type of worship service which is focused on the public restoration of a penitent person to full fellowship with the Christian community. Also called "penance."

**Rubrics.** The directions for the conduct of public worship. The term rubric comes from the Latin word for "red," since the ceremonial directions were always printed in red ink to distinguish them from the texts of prayers and other spoken parts of the service.

**Sabbath.** The seventh day of the week (Saturday), appointed as a day of rest in the Ten Commandments.

**Sanctoral cycle.** The calendar of the commemorations of the saints, heroes, and martyrs of the faith. Traditionally the festival of a particular person was celebrated on the day of his or her death.

**Sanctus** and **Benedictus.** The hymn which combines acclamations found in Isaiah 6:3 and Luke 1:68–79. Traditionally a part of the Great Thanksgiving said by the whole congregation.

**Sermon** (also sometimes called the "Homily" or "Message"). The proclamation of the Word of God in the context of Christian public worship.

**Song of Mary.** See *Magnificat*.

**Song of Simeon.** See *Nunc Dimittis*.

**Stole.** A badge of office for ordained ministers consisting of a narrow strip of cloth, usually corresponding in color to the liturgical color of the day or season. For the presbyter the stole hangs across the back of the neck with the two ends down the front; for the deacon it is worn diagonally over the left shoulder and under the right arm.

**Thanksgiving for the Birth or Adoption of a Child.** The contemporary rite which often replaces the old service of the Churching of Women, or gives liturgical expression to thanksgiving for a child when a baptism is inappropriate or delayed.

**Trinity Sunday.** Traditionally, the Sunday after Pentecost, when the theology of the Trinity is given special attention in the propers. Traditionally, the *Athanasian Creed* was appointed to be said on this day, but this practice is largely obsolete.

**Unctio in extremis.** Anointing with oil at the time of death.

**Vernacular.** The ordinary language spoken in a particular place.

**Versicle** and **Response.** The parts of a liturgical dialogue, usually between the presider (who says the versicle) and the congregation (which makes the response).

**Vestments.** Special garments worn by the various participants in a service of Christian worship. The most usual of these are the alb, the cassock, the stole, the chasuble, and the preaching gown.

**Viaticum.** Meaning "that which goes with you on your way," the final reception of Communion for a person before death.

**Vigil.** A service which is held during the night before a feast day.

**Voluntary.** Another term for the organ prelude and postlude.

**Watchnight Service.** A type of vigil held monthly at the full moon by the early Methodists. Later it came to be the service for New Year's Eve.

**Whitsunday.** See *Pentecost*.

**Words of Institution.** See *Institution Narrative*.

# Notes

## Chapter 1: The Foundations of the Study of Christian Worship

1. He argued his case from texts in the book of Romans, and particularly from such passages as Rom. 3:28ff., "For we hold that we are justified by faith, apart from works of law."

2. John Wesley translated this from the hymn of Gottleib Spangenburg (1704–1792). It can be found in *Hymns and Psalms* at number 807 as "What Shall We Offer Our Good Lord?"

3. These include those in the Greek and Russian Orthodox churches, and in those churches which follow Syrian, Armenian, and Coptic traditions of worship.

4. This hymn was written by James Montgomery in 1819. Unfortunately it is not found in any contemporary American hymnals, but it can be found in the British Methodist Church's *Hymns and Psalms* at number 512 and in the Church of England hymnal, *Hymns Ancient and Modern* (New Standard), at number 190.

5. It also refers more specifically to the sharing in bread and wine in the Lord's Supper: "The cup of blessing that we bless, is it not a sharing (*koinonia*) in the blood of Christ? The bread that we break, is it not a sharing (*koinonia*) in the body of Christ?" (1 Cor. 10:16).

6. "I Came with Joy," by Brian A. Wren (1936–), can be found in the *Chalice Hymnal* at number 420, in the *Hymnal 1982* at number 304, and in the *United Methodist Hymnal* at number 617.

7. This hymn is found in the *Lutheran Book of Worship* at number 228, in the Presbyterian Church (U.S.A.) *Hymnal* at number 260, and in the *United Methodist Hymnal* at number 110.

8. *Gates of Prayer: The New Union Prayer Book* (New York: Central Conference of American Rabbis, 1975), 441.

9. See Marva J. Dawn, *Reaching out without Dumbing Down* (Grand Rapids: Wm. B. Eerdmans, 1996).

10. This hymn was originally written by Isaac Watts (1674–1748) and reworked by John Wesley. It was number 316 in *A Collection of Hymns for the Use of the People Called Methodists* (1780).

226

11. This hymn can be found in *Hymns and Psalms* at number 283, in *The Lutheran Book of Worship* at number 472, and in the *United Methodist Hymnal* at number 603.

12. "Speaking in tongues" is also called *glossolalia*, and there is a long discussion of this form of worship in 1 Corinthians 14.

13. Walter Brueggemann, *The Bible and Postmodern Imagination* (Fortress Press, 1993), 23.

14. This hymn, "And Can It Be that I Should Gain an Interest in the Saviour's Blood," was written by Charles Wesley in 1738 and appeared at number 201 in *A Collection of Hymns for the Use of the People Called Methodists* (1780).

15. For a history of the development of unfermented Communion wine, see Susan J. White, *Christian Worship and Technological Change* (Abingdon Press, 1994), 81–86.

16. See for an example of the use of this kind of first-person material S. J. White, *A History of Women in Christian Worship* (Cleveland: Pilgrim Press, 2004).

## Chapter 2: The Components of Christian Worship

1. Two hymns by Thomas Ken end with this verse. They can be found in the Presbyterian Church (U.S.A.) *Hymnal* at number 592, in the *United Methodist Hymnal* at number 95, and in the *Lutheran Book of Worship* at number 564.

2. See above, p. 4.

3. This hymn can be found in the *United Methodist Hymnal* at number 102, in the *Chalice Hymnal* at number 715, in the *Lutheran Book of Worship* at number 533, and in the Presbyterian Church (U.S.A.) *Hymnal* at number 396. It is worth noting here that although we usually think of a hymn as a piece of music, it is really a piece of religious poetry, or indeed a prayer in the form of a poem, which can (but not necessarily) be later set to music.

4. The Faith and Order Committee of the Methodist Church, "An Order for Ash Wednesday," proposed, 1995.

5. The Faith and Order Committee of the Methodist Church, "A Service of Baptism," proposed, 1995.

6. Clement of Alexandria (ca. 150–ca. 215) says, "When a man occupies his time with flutes, stringed instruments, choirs, dancing, Egyptian krotala and other improper frivolities, he will find that indecency and rudeness are the consequences. . . . Leave the syrinx to the shepherds and the flutes to superstitious devotees who rush to serve their idols. We completely forbid the use of these instruments in our temperate banquet" (J. Quasten, *Music in Pagan and Jewish Antiquity*, National Association of Pastoral Musicians, 1983).

7. The five sections end respectively at the Psalms numbered 41, 72, 89, 105, and 149, with Psalm 150 providing the doxology for the whole collection.

8. "Old Hundredth" is the hymn tune usually used for the doxology written by Thomas Ken. See note 1 above.

9. In every age, Christians have wrestled with the question of how to deal with the "cursing psalms" (such as Psalm 137). Often they were simply reinterpreted to accommodate Christian sensibilities. (Augustine, for example, said that the "little ones" in Psalm 137 were sins, which were to be "dashed upon the Rock that is Christ.") Others, such as Martin Luther, excised offending verses. John Wesley, in the psalter which was appended to his *Sunday Service*, excised thirty-four psalms altogether as "highly improper for the mouths of a Christian congregation." Portions of fifty-eight other psalms were also removed.

10. "When in Our Music God Is Glorified" is found in the *United Methodist Hymnal* at number 68, in the *Chalice Hymnal* at number 7, and in the Episcopal

Church (U.S.A.) *Hymnal 1982* at number 420. Some versions of this hymn in other hymnals have different words in the third line: "As music moves us to a more profound Alleluia!"

11. This hymn "Come let us anew, our journey pursue" was originally number 47 in *A Collection of Hymns for the Use of the People Called Methodists*.

12. See, for example, James Barr, *Biblical Words for Time* (SCM Press, 1962), 127f.

13. December 25 is the date of the winter solstice in the Julian calendar. St. Chrysostom wrote of the feast: "They call the day the day of Invictus. Indeed, who is as unconquerable as our Lord, who has victoriously subjected death? And if they call it the birthday of the sun, now he himself is the sun of righteousness of which the prophet Malachi (4:24) has spoken."

14. In the Eastern churches, the Epiphany is principally the celebration of the baptism of Jesus by John.

15. *1 Apology*, 67.

16. *Revised Common Lectionary* (1992).

## Chapter 3: The Nourishment of the Christian Life I

1. Those peoples who did not practice circumcision found the practice revolting, and Jews who wished to be absorbed into Hellenistic culture did various things to "remove the marks of their circumcision" (1 Cor. 7:18).

2. See also Titus 3:5: "He saved us, not because of any works of righteousness that we had done, but according to his mercy, through the water of rebirth and renewal by the Holy Spirit."

3. See also Phil. 2:11.

4. *Didache* is the same word that is used in Acts: "they continued in the apostles *teaching*, the breaking of bread, and in the prayers."

5. Chapters 61 to 65.

6. From his treatise *On the Resurrection of the Body*.

7. There are many questions about both the authorship and the geographical origins of this document, and about the degree to which it represents early Christian practice. See Paul F. Bradshaw, *The Search for the Origins of Christian Worship*, rev. ed. (Oxford University Press, 2002).

8. These included charioteers, soldiers, actors, pimps, some teachers, and sculptors. Many of these were barred because they would have been involved in swearing oaths of allegiance by sacrificing to the gods, creating images of the gods, dramatizing the pagan myths, or teaching religion in a set curriculum.

9. See above, pp. 63–64.

10. "On the Holy and Blessed Sacrament of Baptism," in *Luther's Works* 35, ed. Hans Hillerbrand (Fortress Press, 1970).

11. The practice of believer's baptism among segments of the Christian population led all later reformers to insert the words from Mark 10:14 into the baptismal rite as a part of anti-Anabaptist polemic: "Let the little children come to me; do not stop them; for it is to such as these that the Kingdom belongs."

12. See above, pp. 79–80.

13. *Responses to BEM*, six volumes (Geneva: WCC, 1985–1989).

14. See, for example, Mark 7:1, Matt. 14:13–19 and 9:11, Luke 5:30, 6:2, 15:1, and 19:1–10.

15. See above, pp. 63, 79.

16. The word "Mass" comes from the final words of the Latin service, "Ite, missa est," which, although generally acknowledged to be very difficult to translate, means roughly: "Go, you are sent out."

17. Fourth Lateran Council had required the laity to receive Communion at least once a year.
18. See below, p. 122.
19. See above, p. 86.
20. Similar influences led to a wave of religious awakening in America; the breakdown of stable patterns of society on the Western frontier fueled the fires of revival.
21. Many North American Christians have deemed the use of the word Father to be offensively sexist in the context of corporate worship (see pp. 167–69), and have attempted to eliminate it from their eucharistic praying. Here we have retained it since it remains the wording in the official texts of most mainline denominations, and since it highlights the Trinitarian structure of the eucharistic prayer.
22. One exception to this amalgamated form of the Institution Narrative is found in the churches of the Reformed tradition, which tend to take the narrative directly from 1 Corinthians.

### Chapter 4: The Nourishment of the Christian Life 2

1. See above, chap. 2.
2. See above, p. 107.
3. See above, pp. 59–60.
4. The term "office" is derived from the Latin term *officium* meaning "service" or "duty."
5. Women, children, and slaves were not under this obligation, largely because their time was not seen to be under their own control.
6. There is still a great deal of debate about the extent to which the earliest forms of Christian daily prayer were influenced by the patterns of Jewish daily prayer in the first century.
7. See above, pp. 34–36.
8. See John Wesley "A Roman Catechism . . . with a reply thereto," section III, questions 75–80.
9. For other New Testament examples of the setting apart of various people for specific ministries by prayer and the laying-on-of-hands, see Acts 6:3–6 and 13:1–3; 1 Tim. 4:14; 2 Tim. 2:6.
10. See above p. 12, chap. 1, note 11.
11. This is the traditional list taken from Isa. 11:2.
12. WCC Faith and Order Paper 111.
13. Paragraph 27:1.

### Chapter 5: Christian Worship through the Life Cycle

1. This is the same number necessary for a valid synagogue service.
2. This prayer is from the 10th century "Pontifical of Egbert."
3. *The Apostolic Tradition of Hippolytus*, ed. G. Cuming, *Grove Liturgical Study 8* (Bramcote, Notts, 1978), section 5, 11.
4. Sermon XCVIII: "On Visiting the Sick."
5. Some rabbis suggested that the soul of the dead person cleansed itself in water immediately after leaving the body, others that the angel of death cleansed his sword once the victim was dispatched.
6. John Wesley, *Journal*, August 8, 1738.
7. *Constitution on the Sacred Liturgy*, III, 81.

## Chapter 6: Contemporary Challenges to Christian Worship

1. See above, p. 15.
2. In the Byzantine family are the Eastern Orthodox churches, including the Greek and Russian Orthodox churches; in the Syrian family are the Malabar Church in India and the Lebanese Maronite churches; in the Alexandrian family are the Coptic and Ethiopian rites in North Africa.
3. The best brief treatment of the issues involved in multi-faith services of worship is still *Can We Pray Together?: Guidelines on Worship in a Multi-faith Society*, a 1983 publication of the British Council of Churches. See also Kenneth Cracknell, *In Good and Generous Faith* (Cleveland: Pilgrim Press, 2006).
4. *The Constitution on the Sacred Liturgy*, III, 36.2.
5. See the 1984 General Conference (United Methodist Church in the USA) report titled *Words that Hurt; Words that Heal: Language about God and People*.
6. You will, for example, find no pronominal references to God have been made in the text you are reading, and that "Godself" has been employed as the reflexive.
7. There are several lines of argument against the abandonment of "Lord," many of them resting on the normative nature of biblical language. The first is that Lord is part of the earliest form of Christian confession we have, "Jesus is Lord" (in Acts 2, for example) and it has a rich and continuous tradition in Christian prayer-language since the first century. It is also argued that "Lord" is not actually a gender-specific word, but that it simply denotes a relationship of faithful obedience.
8. See above, pp. 159–61.
9. 1 Peter 2:13, 16.

# Select Bibliography

## General Resources

Bradshaw, Paul, ed. *The New Westminster Dictionary of Liturgy and Worship*, Westminster John Knox Press, 2002.

Bradshaw, Paul F., and Lawrence A. Hoffman. *The Making of Jewish and Christian Worship*. Notre Dame: University of Notre Dame Press, 1991.

Costen, Melva Wilson. *African American Christian Worship*. Nashville: Abingdon Press, 1993.

Cross, F. L., and E. A. Livingstone, ed. *The Oxford Dictionary of the Christian Church*. 3rd ed. New York: Oxford University Press, 2005.

Gonzalez, Justo, ed. *¡Alabadle! Hispanic Christian Worship*. Nashville: Abingdon Press, 1996.

Pak, Su Yon, Unzu Lee, Jung Ha Kim and Myung Ji Cho. *Singing the Lord's Song in a New Land: Korean-American Practices of Faith*. Louisville, KY: Westminster John Knox Press, 2005.

Senn, Frank C. *New Creation: A Liturgical Worldview*. Minneapolis: Augsburg Fortress, 2000.

Webber, Robert E., ed. *The Complete Library of Christian Worship*. 7 vols. Nashville: Star Song, 1993.

White, Susan J. *A History of Women in Christian Worship*. Cleveland: Pilgrim Press, 2004.

## Chapter 1

*Theology*

Dulles, Avery. *Models of the Church*. Rev. ed. New York: Image, 1991.

Lathrop, Gordon. *Holy Things: A Liturgical Theology*. Minneapolis: Fortress Press, 1993.

Lathrop, Gordon. *Holy People: A Liturgical Ecclesiology*. Minneapolis: Fortress Press, 1999.

Lathrop, Gordon W. *Holy Ground: A Liturgical Cosmology*. Minneapolis: Fortress Press, 2003.

Saliers, Don E. *Worship as Theology: Foretaste of Glory Divine*. Nashville: Abingdon Press, 1994.

*Bible*

Brueggemann, Walter. *Israel's Praise: Doxology against Idolatry and Ideology*. Minneapolis: Fortress Press, 1988.
Martin, Ralph. *Worship in the Early Church*. Grand Rapids: Wm. B. Eerdmans, 1975.

*History*

Adams, Doug. *Meeting House to Camp Meeting: Toward a History of American Free Church Worship from 1620–1835*. Saratoga: Modern Liturgy Resource Publications, 1981.
Bradshaw, Paul F. *The Search for the Origins of Christian Worship: Sources and Methods for the Study of Early Liturgy*. 2nd ed. New York: Oxford University Press, 2002.
Fenwick, John R. K. and Bryan D. Spinks. *Worship In Transition: The Liturgical Movement In the Twentieth Century*. New York: Continuum Publishing Group, 1995.
White, James F. *Documents of Christian Worship: Descriptive and Interpretive Sources*. Louisville, KY: Westminster/John Knox Press, 1992.

*Human Sciences*

Douglas, Mary. *Natural Symbols*. New York: Pantheon, 1982.
Driver, Tom. *The Magic of Ritual*. San Francisco: Harper and Row, 1991.
Turner, Victor. *The Ritual Process*. New York: Cornell University Press, 1987.
Van Gennep, Arnold. *Rites of Passage*. Chicago: University of Chicago Press, 1960.

## Chapter 2

*Prayer*

Bradshaw, Paul. *Two Ways of Praying*. Nashville: Abingdon Press, 1995.
Stookey, Lawrence Hull. *Let the Whole Church Say Amen!: A Guide for Those Who Pray In Public*. Nashville: Abingdon Press, 2001.
Wainwright, Geoffrey. *Doxology*. New York: Oxford University Press, 1980.
White, Susan J. *The Spirit of Worship: The Liturgical Tradition*. Maryknoll, NY: Orbis, 1999.

*Music*

Begbie, Jeremy. *Theology, Music and Time*. Cambridge: Cambridge University Press, 2000.
Foley, Edward, ed. *Worship Music: A Concise Dictionary*. Collegeville: Michael Glazier/Liturgical Press, 2000.
Hawn, Michael C. *Praying Locally, Singing Globally*. Grand Rapids: Wm. B. Eerdmans, 2003.
Wren, Brain. *Praying Twice: The Music and Words of Congregational Song*. Louisville, KY: Westminster John Knox Press, 2000.

*Time*

Bass, Dorothy. *Receiving the Day: Christian Practices for Opening the Gift of Time*. San Francisco: Jossey-Bass, 2000.
Stookey, Laurence Hull. *Calendar: Christ's Time for the Church*. Nashville: Abingdon Press, 1996.

Talley, Thomas J. *The Origins of the Liturgical Year*. Collegeville, MN: Liturgical Press, 1986.

### Environment for Worship

Jensen, Robin M. *The Substance of Things Seen: Art, Faith, and the Christian Community*. Grand Rapids: Wm. B. Eerdmans, 2004.

Visser, Margaret. *The Geometry of Love: Space, Time, Mystery and Meaning in an Ordinary Church*. New York: North Point, 2000.

White, James F. and Susan J. White. *Church Architecture: Building and Renovating for Christian Worship*. Rev. ed. Cleveland: OSL Press, 1996.

## Chapter 3

### Christian Initiation

Kavanagh, Aidan. *The Shape of Baptism: The Rite of Christian Initiation*. New York: Pueblo, 1978.

Stookey, Laurence Hull. *Baptism: Christ's Act in the Church*. Nashville: Abingdon Press, 1982.

Whitaker, E.C., and Maxwell E. Johnson, eds. *Documents of the Baptismal Liturgy*. Rev. and expanded ed. Collegeville, MN: The Liturgical Press, 2003.

### Eucharist

Macy, Gary. *The Banquet's Wisdom: A Short History of the Theologies of the Lord's Supper*. New York: Paulist Press, 1992.

Senn, Frank. *Stewardship of the Mysteries*. New York: Paulist Press, 1999.

Stookey, Laurence Hull. *Eucharist: Christ's Feast with the Church*. Nashville: Abingdon Press, 1993.

World Council of Churches. *Baptism, Eucharist, and Ministry* (Faith and Order, Paper No. 111). Geneva, Switzerland: World Council of Churches, 1982.

## Chapter 4

### The Sunday Service

Schmit, Clayton J. *Too Deep for Words: A Theology of Liturgical Expression*. Louisville, KY: Westminster John Knox Press, 2002.

Troeger, Thomas. *Preaching and Worship*. St. Louis: Chalice Press, 2003.

### Daily Prayer

Bradshaw, Paul. *Daily Prayer in the Early Church*. London: Alcuin Club/SPCK, 1981.

Guiver, George. *Company of Voices: Daily Prayer and the People of God*. New York: Pueblo, 1988.

### Ordination

Bradshaw, Paul. *Ordination Rites of the Early Churches, East and West*. New York: Pueblo, 1990.

Sprinkle, Steven V. *Ordination: Celebrating the Gift of Ministry*. St. Louis: Chalice Press, 2004.

### Reconciliation

Browning, Robert L., and Roy A. Reed. *Forgiveness, Reconciliation, and Moral Courage*. Grand Rapids: Wm. B. Eerdmans, 2004.

## Chapter 5

*General*

Bradshaw, Paul F., and Lawrence A. Hoffman, eds. *Life Cycles in Jewish and Christian Worship*. Notre Dame: University of Notre Dame Press, 1996.

Driver, Tom F. *Liberating Rites: Understanding the Transformative Power of Ritual*. Boulder, CO: Westview Press, 1998.

Ramshaw, Elaine. *Ritual and Pastoral Care*. Minneapolis: Fortress Press, 1987.

Westerhoff, III, John H., and William H. Willimon. *Liturgy and Learning through the Life Cycle*. Rev. ed. Akron, OH: OSL Publications, 1994.

*Marriage*

Searle, Mark, and Kenneth W. Stevenson. *Documents of the Marriage Liturgy*. Collegeville, MN: Pueblo/The Liturgical Press, 1992.

Stevenson, Kenneth. *Nuptial Blessing: A Study of Christian Marriage Rites*. New York: Oxford University Press, 1983.

*Healing*

Empereur, James L. *Prophetic Anointing: God's Call to the Sick, the Elderly, and the Dying*. Wilmington, DE: Michael Glazier, 1982.

Gusmer, Charles. *And You Visited Me: Sacramental Ministry to the Sick and Dying*. Rev. ed. Wilmington, DE: Michael Glazier, 1989.

*Burial*

Rush, Alfred Clement. *Death and Burial in Christian Antiquity*. Washington, DC: Catholic University of America, 1941.

Rowell, Geoffrey. *The Liturgy of Christian Burial*. London: Alcuin Club, 1977.

## Chapter 6

Blount, Brian K. and Leonora Tubbs Tisdale, eds. *Making Room at the Table: An Invitation to Multicultural Worship*. Louisville, KY: Westminster John Knox Press, 2001.

Gaillardetz, Richard R. *Transforming Our Days: Spirituality, Community, and Liturgy in a Technological Culture*. New York: Crossroad, 2000.

Hawn, C. Michael. *One Bread, One Body: Exploring Cultural Diversity in Worship*. Bethesda MD: The Alban Institute, 2003.

Pecklers, Keith, ed. *Liturgy in a Postmodern World*. New York: Continuum Publishing, 2003.

Ramshaw, Gail. *Reviving Sacred Speech: The Meaning of Liturgical Language*. Cleveland: OSL Publications, 2000.

Redman, Robb. *The Great Worship Awakening: Singing a New Song in the Postmodern Church*. San Francisco: Jossey-Bass, 2002.

Webber, Robert E. *Blended Worship: Achieving Substance and Relevance in Worship*. Peabody, MA: Hendrickson Publishers, 1996.

White, Susan J. *Christian Worship and Technological Change*. Nashville: Abingdon Press, 1994.

Wren, Brian. *What Language Shall I Borrow?* New York: Crossroad, 1989.

# Index of Biblical References

# General Index